"Do not overemphas[ize] body; that does a dis[service]... in the energy body, the ethereal body, the body double, the cosmic body. In the end, he is a consummate philosopher of the spirit."

– Bruce Wagner, author of *Dead Stars, Maps to the Stars,* and *The Marvel Universe: Origin Stories*

"*Children of the New Flesh* is a must-read for film fanatics and fans of David Cronenberg. Edited by Chris Kelso and David Leo Rice, this collection explores the dark peripheries of Cronenberg's influence and early work, examining a world of strangeness and mystery."

– Brandon Hobson, National Book Award finalist and author of *The Removed*

"The living legend of eccentric cinema begets weird new progeny in *Children of the New Flesh*."

– Rue Morgue magazine

"New and longtime Cronenberg fans will devour this intelligent, earnest, and comprehensive tribute."

— Kirkus Reviews

"An excellent examination of the work of David Cronenberg, my own favorite director... The essays are insightful and entertaining, while the fiction and poetry take the themes of Cronenberg's work in unique directions. I believe that not just fans of Cronenberg will get a lot out of this, but fans of cinema and outré literature as well."

— Ben Arzate in Cultured Vultures

One of Dennis Cooper's Favorite Books of 2022

"The brainpower on display in the book's writings is staggering and head-exploding... Bursting with unsettling cerebral meditations and perceptions, the book Kelso and Rice have expended such effort at pulling together should justly stand the test of time as an essential work of criticism and homage to one of the most idiosyncratic and stimulating cinematic artists of the past fifty years."

— Jesse Hilson in Apocalypse Confidential

"Hit play on Howard Shore's Crimes score and start reading."

— The Film Stage

"The volume vigorously overflows with... satellite transmissions that combine in creating a vivid portrait of the body around which they orbit... This catholic, compendious approach seems entirely fitting an honorific to a creator who while obsessing over a handful of key themes (the unignorable ones) refuses to sit still when it comes to genre, form or tonal colour. Truly we are thankful."

— Nick Hudson

My brain is splitting at the sulci. My ego is barreling toward an auto/erotic crash. I'm done for. Bone dry. I've got nothing left to say, and I still don't know if I've said anything at all. Not one interesting thing about this pulsating, pupating, parasitic book."

– Dave Fitzgerald, Daily Grindhouse

"An essential volume that doesn't just go for the soft targets of body horror but instead explores every aspect of the director, creating a comprehensive work that stands out as critical discussion, supremely weird story collection, and a fascinating look at a fascinating director as a whole."

— Tor Nightfire, 11 OF OUR FAVORITE HORROR COLLECTIONS AND ANTHOLOGIES FROM 2022

Children of the New Flesh

Copyright © 2022
All rights reserved

This book may not be reproduced in whole or in part, except for the inclusion of brief quotations in a review, without permission in writing from the author or publisher. No part of this publication may be reproduced, stored in or introduced into a retrieval system, or transmitted, in any form, or by any means (electronic, mechanical, photocopying, recording, or otherwise), without prior permission of the publisher.

Requests for permission should be directed to 1111@1111press.com, or mailed to 11:11 Press LLC, 4732 13th Ave S, Minneapolis, MN 55407.

Design by Mike Corrao

Paperback: 9781948687645

Printed in the United States of America

SECOND EDITION

9 8 7 6 5 4 3 2

CHILDREN OF THE NEW FLESH

The Early Work and Enduring Influence
of David Cronenberg

Edited by
Chris Kelso & David Leo Rice

TABLE OF

Coming Attractions

11 | David Cronenberg – Icon of Transcendence – Chris Kelso

17 | Long Live the Heroic Pervert – David Leo Rice

50 | Clinical Notes on the Early Cronenberg and the Internality of Horror — Jonathan Greenaway

On The Early Work of David Cronenberg

59 | *Transfer* (1966) – Joe Koch, Stephen R. Bissette

85 | *From the Drain* (1967) – Tobias Carroll, Gary J. Shipley

101 | *Stereo* (1969) – Brian Alessandro, Evan Isoline, Tom Over

139 | *Crimes of the Future* (1970) – Graham Rae, Brian Evenson, Blake Butler, John Reed, David Roden

175 | *Secret Weapons* (1972) – Michael Cisco, Chris Kelso, Elle Nash

201 | *The Lie Chair* (1976) – Callum McSorely, Matthew Mark Bartlett, Matt Neil Hill, Charlene Elsby

239 | *The Italian Machine* (1976) – Graham Rae, David Leo Rice

CONTENTS

Communications

271 | Patrick McGrath

274 | Filip Jan Rymsza

279 | Bruce Wagner

284 | Mick Garris

287 | Tim Lucas

297 | Kathe Koja

300 | David Cronenberg

Last Transmissions

313 | Andrew Farkas

321 | Joseph Vogl

339 | Farewell from the Children of the New Flesh – Chris Kelso & David Leo Rice

Coming Attractions

DAVID CRONENBERG: ICON OF TRANSCENDENCE

Chris Kelso

"In the land of the blind, the one-eyed man is a hallucinating idiot... for he sees what no one else does: things that, to everyone else, are not there."

— **Marshall McLuhan**

You'd be forgiven for thinking that I (a hyper-sensitive, card-carrying optimist) might recoil from David Cronenberg's oeuvre. After all, nothing Cronenberg offers his viewers is particularly comforting or life-affirming. But that's never been his objective, has it? Having established himself as the master of hybridisation imagery, visions of an afterlife are usually in line with his own unique brand of nihilistic reincarnation (or rebirth): Cronenberg has us believe that perhaps as we age, beneath our fragile, decaying organic brickwork, a human-insect crossbreed is ready to emerge. The second life. Not quite the afterlife, but post-origins. This recalibration of the body offers little in the way of new pleasures—or at least not the ones our immediate neural pleasure systems *think* we want. What his films do offer, however, is an experience of the Kantian sublime, where the audience can indulge in self-forgetfulness. Cronenberg faces the ugly and the monstrous and transforms them into a kind of "tragic consciousness"—the capacity to achieve an elevated state of mind following the realisation that suffering and decay are unavoidable.

In the mind of Cronenberg, our psyches can birth mutant offspring conceived entirely out of pure rage. We can manifest powerful somatic interactions with the physical environment, every bit as deadly as what we might inflict with our fists. One of Cronenberg's central preoccupations has been to show how media shapes our perception of reality, and how this in turn modifies the reality round us. The notion that mass media can become a literal outgrowth of our psyches has never seemed as prescient as it does today.

Here, I believe it should be noted that Cronenberg is a transcendent figure, someone in possession of truly holistic and penetrative levels of artistry. Few artists have produced works able to generate so much interest among different varieties of critical thinkers—his films are as meaningful to blue-collar cinephiles as they are to film theorists and historians. Images from these films, while rooted in their own intellectual modality, are also ubiquitous staples of our contemporary cultural iconography, from Peter Weller's William S. Burroughs stand-in Bill Lee looming over his Clark Nova in *Naked Lunch*, to *Videodrome*'s Max Renn pushing his face into the distending television screen: these (and many more) present an enduring visual rhetoric in our anthropological library of popular culture.

Now, if I may over-quote Marshall McLuhan: 'Instead of tending towards a vast Alexandrian library the world has become a computer, an electronic brain, exactly as in an infantile piece of science fiction.'

As a fellow Canadian, McLuhan was an important academic and spiritual guide for Cronenberg—and while Cronenberg never attended any of McLuhan's lectures at the University of Toronto, the line of influence remains direct and formative. McLuhan's ideas about how excess information has systematically destabilised our collective consciousness, and the manner in which we extend our profiles via collective surgery carried out on the social body, are integrated throughout Cronenberg's work. This idea is perhaps most notably apparent in *Videodrome* and *eXistenZ*, but it's also present in *Secret Weapons* and *Stereo*, two of the early films discussed in this book. And it's hard not to fantasise about a young Cronenberg being moulded in the glacial auditoriums of the University of Toronto, genetically-engineered and sent out into the world by McLuhan himself, like the young people in the bizarre psychic studies in *Stereo* and *Crimes of the Future*, also discussed in the pages to come.

Seen from today's vantage point, Cronenberg is as large an influence on us as McLuhan and the other media theorists of his formative years were on him. His cinematic exploration of Pierre Teilhard de Chardin's *noosphere*—the influence of our collective consciousness on the external environment—is now as important to the study of Gaia theory as De Chardin's, Vernadsky's and even Marshall McLuhan's work. He's a horror entrepreneur who produces art truly deserving of that contentious marker, 'elevated horror.' This is all well known. Yet, there is still a fatty layer of subcutaneous tissue that has gone unprobed for too long, as the abovementioned influence is just half of the coin.

In 1966, a young Cronenberg (and his then-fiancée, Margaret Hindson) took a rented 16mm camera to the Ontario countryside to film his first short, *Transfer*. While he managed to get the film shown at a small Toronto festival of underground films the following year, reviews were scathing to say the least. Credit should go to Kevin Lyons of the EOFFTV Review, who dug up a wonderfully spiky appraisal from one of Canada's most celebrated critics, Urjo Kareda. Then working for the *Toronto Globe and Mail,* Kareda dismissed *Transfer* as "a pathetic effort... Horribly acted and scarcely directed, it didn't have the decency to be original: it was stolen from a Nichols and May sketch." Other reviews weren't much better. People in Canada simply didn't *get* Cronenberg's work in 1966.

Yet, Cronenberg has always had something of a cult reputation here in the UK, in Scotland especially, where I'm writing from. While *Crimes of the Future* did not receive a UK-wide release, only gaining classification in 2015 as part of an Arrow Video DVD release, the film *was* shown at the 1970 Edinburgh

International Film Festival. *Crimes of the Future* was an early festival success and the university student cineastes who made up the bulk of that initial audience responded enthusiastically to Cronenberg's own brand of bleak, muted artistry. Festival programmers in the country's capital seemed to take notice, and there was an active push to secure screening rights to Cronenberg's future films before they were released. From 1970-1975, he made no feature films, focusing mainly on Sunday night plays and anthology television, but festival organisers never forgot the impact of *Crimes of the Future*, and *Shivers* and *Rabid* were both screened at the Edinburgh Film Festival, in 1975 and 1977 respectively. Having been certified by the BBFC, *Shivers* and *Rabid* both received early UK releases.

These were crucial first steps in a career we all owe a debt to. Not to be deterred by the frosty reception his films received in Canada, the young Cronenberg went from dewy-eyed indie filmmaker to a distribution pioneer. While in conversation with Tim Lewis of *The Guardian*, Cronenberg admitted, "In Toronto, no one's parents were in the movie business because there wasn't a movie business." And the simple fact remains that although no one in his homeland ever really accepted him—it is still vulgar auteurism to reappraise his films there—Cronenberg's decision to stay in Canada meant he was able to bypass the expectations and pressures of Hollywood. Canada's budding film industry (which Cronenberg helped establish) and cultural funding opportunities played a key role in the director's career-long independence. In a nation where locally-centred cinematic sobriety was preferred, Cronenberg learned quickly that he'd have to make a psychic enemy of his national ideals, while maintaining his professional interdependence with his homeland. These feelings of isolationism run throughout his work, as does the tendency to parody high-minded ideals of progress.

So now we come to the book you hold in your hands. This book is a tribute to Cronenberg's own pervasive influence, and also a testament to the isolationism and singularity present even in his early films. The writers in this book share an interior landscape that he helped furnish, and their words are communicated in an intersubjective language that he helped invent. The seven early films chosen as signposts (*Transfer, From the Drain, Stereo, Crimes of the Future, Secret Weapons, The Lie Chair* and *The Italian Machine*) reveal a secret stratum of knowledge and insight. It would be too easy, and far too unoriginal, to examine only his later, more populist movies. These seven early works represent something else. A different appendage, a vestigial tail. David Leo Rice and I offered them up on a platter to our contributors, who then picked apart and reassembled them into the new patchwork that awaits you.

As Cronenberg believes knowledge is best transferred through semen, we asked ourselves, what is semen in today's artistic terms? It is, we decided, the essence and expression of creative impulses, transmitted from mind to mind while remaining maximally independent of commercial pressure. A precious teardrop of uncorrupted life-juice, dripping down through the generations. In this book, Cronenberg is the sexual stimulus, the scantily-clad babe (or hunk) strewn across the centrefold. Source and vessel at once. A champion of the taboo imagination. Think of this as the last book of forbidden thinking.

As my own words alone cannot measure the influence of David Cronenberg's work on the interior creative landscapes of those who've absorbed his images and ideas, I set out to coordinate this tribute comprising essays by and interviews with his old collaborators and accomplices, and then to sprinkle it all over with loving homage from those modern artists he has influenced most. You'll see from what follows that his work strikes that perfect timbre with so many writers and artists, employing the grammar of science fiction and the visceral imagery of horror in the most euphonious and intoxicating way. Even in his early work, he speaks in this profound language of individualism. Of independence. Of proud perversion.

He is owed everything. By the Canadians. By David Leo Rice and me. By everyone herein. Here is the story of a fierce sensualist who became a pure metaphysician, a 60s intellectual who set out to become an obscure novelist and instead became the world's biggest underground filmmaker. Cronenberg is our creative cancer. Join us, veterans of the spiritual war, as we cross the threshold of the Skin House one last time.

Long Live the Heroic Pervert

On Seeking Live Flesh in an Undead Age

David Leo Rice

Here at the threshold of the Skin House, as we look ahead to the myriad unknowns of the 2020s, from the ongoing sociopolitical effects of the Covid era, as filtered through our increasingly crazy-making social media sphere, to the inevitable impacts of climate change, war, endemic corruption and inequality on an already exhausted and bitter populace, and finally to the continued fraying of shared reality by VR and further technological innovations too strange to predict, the figure I most aspire to embody, as a writer and as a person preparing to weather whatever's on the horizon, is that of the heroic pervert, who first entered my consciousness through a teenage obsession with the films of David Cronenberg, and who came rushing back to the surface of my mind the moment Chris asked me to join him on this adventure.

Again and again, Cronenberg's ability to find the flesh at the heart of even his most cerebral explorations—or to install the flesh *as the heart* of those explorations, thereby bringing them to life— is the bedrock principle of heroic perversity, even if the question of where and what the flesh is today will necessarily be different than it was in the late 20th century, the fleshiest of all cinematic ages, as it was the only time when movies manifested in physical form as videotapes. Before that, they swam through the dusty air of empty or crowded cinemas, and now, of course, they've sunk to the bottom of a swampy streaming infinity, buried daily beneath entire lifetimes' worth of fresh content. As the supreme avatar of the video age, Cronenberg's ability to find the concrete within the ethereal, and to bring new life out of the merger of the two, has much to teach us about the daunting task we now face of enacting some version of that same alchemy today, however different our materials and methods must be.

As a writer turned filmmaker, and a thinker and tinkerer whose ideas and physical objects are always foremost in his work, Cronenberg's genius is not purely cinematic. Unlike, say, Kubrick or Tarkovsky, his films are not unimpeachably perfect *as* films. They are more heterodox and open-ended, less faithful to the history and grammar of film itself, but this is what makes them so generative of ongoing reflection. They feel like alien transmissions that have hijacked the cinematic medium to send a message, commandeering the screen so as to inseminate the viewer's mind with the febrile, multi-decade thought processes that this book has emerged from.

Cronenberg's greatest works are therefore conversation-starters, whereas a towering epic like *Stalker* or *The Shining* is more of a conversation-ender, a masterpiece so colossal it's difficult to respond with anything but awe, or a form of hermetic scrutiny that can only conceive of the film on its own terms. The films discussed in the pages to come, while seamier in execution, are less hermetic and therefore more productive in that they not only describe hybrid experiences onscreen, but also hybridize the experience of their viewers, sending us away with something new growing in our heads. If there's something monastic and thus celibate about the "purest" artists in their devotion to a single medium, then Cronenberg's ultra-promiscuity, his willingness to dirty himself in the muck of the worlds he creates rather than standing off to the side like a Talmudic scholar, is to be celebrated for how fecund it's proven to be.

Indeed, his work inspires rather than partakes of scholarly obsession because, like the world itself, it is irreducible and thus impossible to "be done with" or move on from. The flesh, as the central presence in all his classic work, is both a metaphor and not: it is endlessly generative of metaphorical rumination, interpretation and reappropriation, but it is also a defiantly physical entity that his films take seriously and concretely as such, rather than using it as a proxy for something else. Like so few things today, it is what it seems to be.

This is what makes Cronenberg a uniquely loving and nurturing father: there is no violent struggle with his influence, no desperation to kill him in order to be born. Instead, he offers his work up already decomposing, gleefully writhing with worms and unsprouted seed, so that the process of absorbing and reckoning with its influence begins right away, rather than after a dramatic break with the rigid order of what came before. Instead of resisting decomposition as most bodies do, his body of work is eager to be broken down by the future and takes active part in that process even while it's still alive. I can think of no other artist who has mustered this courage to the same degree.

The heroic pervert, therefore, emerges from these films in several dimensions at once: as a potential embodied by their most archetypal characters (Seth Brundle in *The Fly*, Max Renn in *Videodrome*, the twins in *Dead Ringers*, Bill Lee in *Naked Lunch*), as an archetype for Cronenberg's own willingness to be broken down and reconfigured by his work and by those to whom his infection has spread, and, most saliently, as the metamorphosis, in all of us, that results from our eager engagement with that infection.

In all these cases, the heroic pervert travels into the tech-mediated future never certain if the world is safe or even real, but willing to engage it wholeheartedly anyway, and never certain that the confusion at the heart of all discourse can be solved, but willing to see it clearly *as confusion*, and to embrace it without fear or loathing. Armed with this willingness, the heroic pervert is grateful to experience a time of fear and flux, and strives to live with and even *on* this fear (to see the world "from the point of view of the disease," as Cronenberg has often recommended his viewers do), rather than seeking any palliative relief from it. The heroic pervert views all such palliatives as snake oil sold by one undead, commercialized narrative principle or another, all of which promise a form of relief they can never deliver because the actual flesh of this moment cannot be encapsulated within any of the narrative forms on offer—it is, like all flesh, the essence of life itself, never just a metaphor for something knowable.

Instead, the heroic pervert treats the paranoia that results from this narrative swarm/collapse as a volatile and potentially transformative material in its own right, and seeks to make something new out of it, something whose life force derives from the seedy energies of humor and horror. Heroic perversion thrives on humor and horror—on accessing the possibility of fun within the revelation that much of life is bullshit—because both are viable means of accepting the present as it is, in all its grotesquerie, without trying to numb or dumb it down into straightforward drama, heading for any cathartic conclusion, or to abstract away from it into any higher view of *what's really happening*, which is always a form of self-deception, tending toward the point where paranoia curdles into madness by denying its own paranoid origins and claiming, as only the insane can, to have achieved lasting sanity.

The mood of 2022 risks madness and resists catharsis because it can't be encompassed by an image, object, or dramatic structure; it feels more like a ripening, clotting atmosphere of abject weirdness and distrust, where nothing is quite itself and no line of reasoning runs straight for very long, so that all manner of apocalyptic prophets are right to pick up on an end-times feeling in the air, but wrong to promise relief in the form of any singular *end* (if anything, it feels like this end came already and we somehow missed it, or refused to accept it as such). This also accounts for the disorienting deceleration of the present, the feeling that things are at once speeding out of control (or at least we feel that they must be) and grinding to a halt, creating the limbo of a permanently boiling-over status quo that never actually boils over into anything else, but only replicates itself more and more redundantly, until the entire age comes to feel undead, defined by a kind of "passively active" spectatorship in which it's impossible to determine whether watching and discussing the world on our ambiguously interactive devices is the same as participating in it, and, if not, what the difference might be and how one might begin to apply that knowledge.

For the heroic pervert, this state of affairs is the starting, not the ending point, as there can be no explanation to relieve this all-encompassing absurdity, nor even to pinpoint its source. There is only the absurdity itself, which appears as a natural law, an irreducible quantity of bullshit permeating adult life, and hence a facet of reality's essence rather than a deviation from it. Accepting this natural law as such opens the possibility of finding solid ground (or living flesh) within the flux and churn, rather than drowning in it or trying in vain to seek an uncorrupted arena beyond its reach.

The heroic pervert therefore seeks to succumb to this absurdity and, by succumbing—here Cronenberg's fundamental belief in trauma and disease as vectors of transformation is paramount—to yield up something greater than what came before, an offspring that can only be born through the dissolution of our current sense of what makes us sane, and even of what makes us human.

In this way, the heroic pervert toggles at will between a first- and a third-person perspective (much as the elderly Cronenberg embraces his own corpse in 2021's short film *The Death of David Cronenberg*, directed by his daughter Caitlin), seeing their body as either an *I* or an *it*, a parent or a child, depending on the situation, rather than spiraling down the drain of mediatized psychosis with no ability to observe this process as it occurs.

In search of viable seed, the heroic pervert looks deeply into the maw of the present, summoning enough force of will to make contact with something mythic, sublime or transcendentally horrific buried there, something so powerful that it is both of the present and beyond it. Perhaps this taboo merger, which entails the divine realization that the present is only and always itself, unsusceptible to prophetic narrative and thus both the essence of time and free from the effects of time, is the alchemical reaction that conceives the future, the *living* future bound inevitably for death, beyond all the undead pseudo-futures offered by consumer tech, which have only corralled us into this endless pseudo-present, disembodied and frictionless in its alienation from the sensuality that makes Cronenberg's work so vital.

For all these reasons and many more, the heroic pervert is the protagonist of the book you have here begun to read, a figure who has probably always existed around the edges of the mind and the edges of the town or city, lost among its more complacent contemporaries—seen in a certain light, the story of Christ is a heroic pervert story, that of willingly accepting the filth, degradation and suffering of this world as the only genuine means of transcending it—but rarely has it stepped front and center with more charisma than in Cronenberg's films. Therefore, we dedicate the coming pages to the heroic pervert's newest incarnation, born from Cronenberg's images-made-flesh and given new life once again, through a polyphony of voices, and not a moment too soon.

As both parent and child of the New Flesh, the heroic pervert embraces the logic of transformation, of merging with the signal, the disease and the machine in order to spawn something more able to thrive in the world that required this transformation in the first place. This introduces a logic of cathartic sacrifice back into our supposedly disenchanted, post-postmodern era. It is exactly here that the heroic pervert becomes heroic. If ancient heroes attained heroism through valor, honesty and integrity (or through violence disguised as these things), perverted heroes attain heroism through sublime masochism, a crucial antidote to the fascistic attempts to reinstate old-school heroism also circling the globe today.

Heroic perverts recognize that humanity may have reached the end of the road *as humanity*, and thus that traveling on from here may require sacrificing much of what we think makes us human, even though, crucially, this recognition is itself indicative of the depths that the human spirit is still capable of plumbing, just as Seth Brundle becomes more human by becoming a fly. This form of heroic self-sacrifice is a kind of generative psychic suicide, a means of offering the self up for decomposition just as Cronenberg's films have offered themselves to us, imbued with the possibility of redemption and rebirth. In 2022, the only alternatives are either the self-nullification of engaging with contemporary media as it wishes to be engaged with, which drowns the mind in a whirlpool of distraction, hate, fear and simulated joy, or, on the far other extreme, the self-nullification of actual suicide, whether that means killing the body or attempting to kill the computer.

This third option—*the path of the heroic pervert*—is predicated on the belief, or the hope, that the same inhuman thing inside us that created the technologies that are now driving us insane is poised to erotically enjoy the spectacle of human consciousness being snuffed out by its own Frankenstinian creation, beyond which point a new consciousness awaits. If this hope proves valid, it will be because the heroic pervert embodies both the high priest and the sacrificial lamb (as well as the terrified populace praying to be redeemed by the ritual about to occur), and thereby achieves a sacred synthesis of human and inhuman, obviating the otherwise insoluble tension between these categories by creating a third thing, which all of Cronenberg's best work, with *Videodrome, The Fly, Dead Ringers* and *eXistenZ* as the clearest examples, strives to conjure and embody.

"I Am the Video Word Made Flesh"

In the history of how mass media inseminates and then hatches something new inside the human brain, thereby driving events rather than describing them, *Videodrome* is likely the greatest case study ever produced. It is both a satire and a potent example of mass media's power to compel matter from afar, crafting New Flesh out of raw signal. For a contemporary example of this phenomenon, one need look no farther than the events of January 6, 2021, when a viral conspiracy from the depths of the Internet memed itself into reality through a logic seemingly divorced from human control (though very much playing on atavistic human urges for revenge and rectitude through violence), then deputized human subjects—cloaking itself in their flesh, just as they cloaked themselves in its emblems—to enact a will that none could have generated on their own, nor even quite describe after the fact.

In light of this and related swarm events such as Gamestop and the other meme-stock and crypto frenzies of 2021, as well as TikTok's increasingly invasive methods of mass attention capture and behavior compulsion, and Mark Zuckerberg's skin-crawling announcement of his planned Metaverse (itself a response to the now-outdated business model of Facebook in the age of TikTok), it seems likely that we exist in a portal phase, a queasy but potentially illuminating cusp moment between historical epochs. The early 2020s feel like the end of the Internet age (or the *screen age*), which reached its frothing apotheosis in the late 2010s, and the beginning of something even more abstract, decentralized yet all-pervasive (which the now-common term "Web3" is an early and probably insufficient attempt to describe), in which the flow of information between external networks and our internal nervous systems will grow even more entangled, while the age of imagining that it would take wires and bioports to jack us into this matrix will recede into sci-fi history, aging into yet another brand of retro-futurism, if it hasn't already.

This is why any discussion of living with the signal has to evolve beyond the binary of logging on or logging off, as there's no longer a tangible place to log onto or off of—a way of thinking that is itself a good definition of the era that's ending, whereas the era that's beginning will be marked by a much more complex ultra-saturation that can only be navigated, never accepted or rejected as such. The signal is now untethered from the machine and replicating on its own; the world is now an Internet-world, yet another hybrid, at once barren and bursting at the seams in ways that require new modes of attention and interaction if we hope to continue bringing the flesh to life. As is perhaps always the case when attempting to confront reality in a disillusioned manner, there's no way out but through. The trip is already in progress; the infection is well underway.

The *Videodrome* infection is also well underway in my psyche, and has been for quite some time, activating aspects of my self that feel alluringly foreign, thereby revealing that my own creative center—the part of my being that I cherish above all else—is in many ways not part of "me" at all.

Whenever I have occasion to explore this creative center, I picture my mind as a series of ten locks. Any artwork that I enjoy opens three or four of these locks, while any artwork that I love opens maybe eight or nine, but only a few in my life have had a long enough key to open all ten. Beyond the tenth lock lies the chamber that contains my DNA, which may be another term for the "uncreated and uncreatable" soul that Meister Eckhart described as a speck of otherness at the center of selfhood, a definitive aspect of every person that is also, in some divine or diabolical manner, not part of that person at all. Any artwork able to reach this chamber has the power to alter my genetic makeup, bringing me to life as if for the first time. It is through recognizing the pain and pleasure of this new conception—the way in which one's own psychic womb can be impregnated with an alien seed that is also part of the self, maybe the best part—that the heroic pervert is born.

No artist has accessed this tenth chamber more consistently than David Cronenberg, so much so that the images I've used to describe his impact are obviously a symptom of it. To the extent that I'm part of a generation of artists and writers born in the 70s, 80s and 90s, who experienced Y2K and the decline of VHS and the coming-online of the world as children, teenagers or young adults—it's hard to overstate the whiplash of having grown up with the video store in my hometown as *the* font of ultra-modernity, only to see it now recede into the same poignant sepia as dime stores and soda fountains—Cronenberg has had a singular and enduring influence on our collective aesthetic. With extraordinary inventiveness and energy, he teased out the subcurrents of the 20th century's twilight years in a way that 21st century art and literature could not have been born without, even if the question of how to engage with our current historical moment as vividly as he engaged with his remains intimidatingly wide open. One way or another, our approach to this question, in the pages to come and in the years to come after that, bears the physical and intellectual imprint of his greatest work, which, in a deeply recursive manner, both reflected and helped to define the pop culture of our most formative years, when the eternal aspiration of growing up to be a writer or artist was shot through with the highly temporal forces afoot on either side of the new millennium.

Looking back on Cronenberg's 80s and 90s golden age, or "Imperial Phase" as such a peak is sometimes called, which saw the release of *Scanners* (1981), *Videodrome* (1983), *The Dead Zone* (1983), *The Fly* (1986), *Dead Ringers* (1988), *Naked Lunch* (1991), *M. Butterfly* (1993), *Crash* (1996), and *eXistenZ* (1999), from the vantage point of 2022, longer after the millennium than those films were before it, humanity's shifting relationship with media technology—and thus with the outward expression of our innermost drives—is again dangerously salient as we prepare to enter a new era, or at least tell ourselves that this is what's happening.

These masterpieces are models of how to engage with the numinous yet definitive energies of one's own time, just as his 60s and 70s early works, which form the focus of this book, are models of how to train oneself, in youth, to take the fullest possible advantage of artistic maturity, especially if one is lucky enough to sync up with the commercial energies of one's time and receive even a fraction of the green lights that Cronenberg received.

Cronenberg reached his 80s and 90s epitome during the last epochal shift in technology, between the end of the analog and the beginning of the digital age. Like today's, this was another portal phase, metaphysically, historically (the Berlin Wall fell, history "ended," etc.), and literally, in terms of the pop culture of that time becoming obsessed with alien abduction and images of TV screens, video games and all manner of pseudo-scientific devices (never more explicitly than in *The Fly*, where the vagaries of teleportation engender the film's grotesque metamorphoses) leading through wormholes and into alternate or warped realities—other worlds or othered versions of this one.

The core ambiguity as to whether going through the portal ever truly leads elsewhere, or only to a transformation within the self—and thus if the world ever really changes, or only seems to—is a central preoccupation in *Videodrome*, just as it has become a central preoccupation of the 2010s and 20s, as we both hope for and recoil from the prospect of revolution, which always seems at once impossible and inevitable.

When James Woods' sleazy UHF television producer Max Renn discovers a pirate station broadcasting the titular program from either Malaysia or Pittsburgh (in either case, from an inaccessible otherworld nested within this world), which features real torture and murder, free of even the most casual attempt at a storyline, he quickly recognizes in this not only the future of TV but the future of consciousness itself. This possibility has grown even more fraught in recent years, when the *real* has seemed ever more buried under successive avalanches of distrust and misdirection, as the essential paradox of seeking immediacy within media grows at once more untenable and more ubiquitous. Still, the *feeling* of mental torture has never been more concrete, raising the question of whether anything realer than this is present within today's ceaseless audiovisual chatter, or if this feeling is itself the message, received loud and clear: when we open any online news site or social media app, are we seeking some kernel of truth buried in the drift, or are we kneeling down for the mental whipping we know we're about to receive (brought to us courtesy of a media company that's a front for an arms company, as *Videodrome*'s Spectacular Optical Corp turns out to be), because this sensation is itself the contact with reality we've been craving?

Beyond its ability to frame this question, *Videodrome* also exemplifies Cronenberg's supreme creative gift, his own clearest point of contact with the real: the ability to craft physical expressions of abstract ideas, as well as the narrative conditions that summon them up. All of his classic works fuse sculpture (many pieces of which, including the whipped TV from *Videodrome*, the insect typewriters from *Naked Lunch*, and the vicious surgical implements from *Dead Ringers*, I got to see in a museum show in Amsterdam), and literature as only visionary cinema can. This is how Cronenberg puts his money where his mouth is, grounding his ideas in the clarity of objects that actually exist, never only in a numinous idea of the flesh. Developing the ability to structure his films around these objects is a major part of the evolution he underwent from his incarnation as a novice in the 60s to that of a master in the 80s, a heroic pervert well-versed in the mire and latent beauty of the material world, and is thus the overarching story of this book.

Videodrome's classic images and objects—the Cathode Ray

Mission, which feeds the homeless on televised imagery alone, the spectacle of Max Renn stuffing his head inside a set of lips that bulge from his TV screen, or whipping Debbie Harry's image on another screen while she cheers him on and seems to feel the impact, or yet another screen where the static turns to veiny skin and then somehow shoots itself with an equally veiny gun, to say nothing of the throbbing videotapes and the tumorous New Flesh itself, which encapsulates all of what's now considered "Cronenbergian"—cement the auteur's supreme significance, both to media theory and to the visual culture that media theory seeks to interpret.

I must've been fifteen when I first saw *Videodrome*, which means that I rented it on VHS in the town where I grew up, carried the tape home and then physically inserted it into the family VCR, so that when a tape is physically inserted into Max Renn's gaping belly near the end of that film, I felt the full visceral impact in a way that is only possible when idea, object and historical conditions so perfectly coincide.

Though it is the most singular work in this group, *Videodrome* belongs in conversation with other body horror films from the 80s, including *The Thing, Aliens, Robocop, Hellraiser, Society, The Terminator, Tetsuo: The Iron Man*, and of course Cronenberg's own *Scanners* and *The Fly,* which all feel like erotic fantasies wrapped inside cautionary tales, fetishizing the sensitive nexus of flesh, disease, alien goo, TV static, corporate conspiracy, teleportation and bionic implantation as we approached the new millennium and technology grew both more empowering and more hostile to any postwar idea of human autonomy, beginning to suggest the opposite—that only by transgressing the limits of the body, often with incredible violence, could the mind evolve beyond the dull repetition of life in a consumer society, where all real events had been denatured into televised spectacle.

The physical interpenetration that these films imagined still hasn't occurred on a mass scale—it's tempting to claim that we've escaped this possibility with our bodies more or less intact, despite the fascinating microchip panic surrounding the Covid vaccines, which, if nothing else, shows that such anxieties have not altogether abated—and yet the conviction that there *is* a physical world separate from its manifold digital representations grows ever harder to retain, just as the prospect of fighting the machines grows ever harder to imagine as anything but desperate farce, like reenacting an old war to keep from fighting a new one. From the perspective of 2022, these films are fantasies of technological dominion as a hard phenomenon, whereas the reality, such as we can perceive it, has grown ever softer with time.

Videodrome anticipates aspects of this conundrum as well, ending with a famously ambiguous scene where Max Renn watches his own suicide on TV, which seems to destroy the set itself, only to reenact the same routine, this time "outside" the screen, signing off with the mantra, "Long Live the New Flesh," as his bullet triggers the end credits, "killing" the spectacle we'd been entranced by. If there's any remaining distinction between the stage and the play at this point in the drama, it is well beyond our reach as viewers.

Revisiting this moment in the dazed hangover of the mass, algorithmically-driven freak out of the Trump years—centered on another 80s media mogul who, like Max Renn, seemed to come most alive while watching himself on TV (to say nothing of the transformation of James Woods, who plays Renn, into one of Trump's staunchest supporters)—and the undead narrative of a global virus that seems poised to linger forever, both in the air and in the monetized battleground of our information technologies, it occurred to me that the New Flesh is undead because it feeds on imagery of its own destruction, thickening and solidifying the more fervently its hosts yearn for deliverance via suicide, which calls up the mythic horror of Nietzsche's Eternal Return, the possibility that the world we currently inhabit is the only one, so that even death would amount only to a retread of the same territory we'd sought to escape, as if the afterlife could be defined as, "the life you lived before, only *more so*."

Just as the world, so far, has resisted any apocalyptic conclusion on the scale of time, opting instead to keep us hovering in an "end times" mindset that turns into an increasingly bloated middle, it also resists overflowing in space, allowing for a seemingly infinite number of worlds to be compressed and juxtaposed together—and relayed to one another through an infinite number of criss-crossing channels—however much mental dissonance and pressure this causes.

In this way, the *Videodrome* viewer is already infected, slowly becoming aware that the New Flesh lives inside them now, turning Max Renn's suicide into just one more spectacle of Videodrome violence that can never conclude, which turns this world into the next world as well, a prison of the living and the dead freely intermingled. The only question—and one I've ruminated on continually since I first rented that tape more than half my life ago—is what to do as a hybrid entity, a being that's half-human and half-signal, vested with this self-knowledge but not with any script for how to use it.

Cronenberg's genius for sparking such ongoing involvement in his viewers set a crucial precedent for artists seeking to engage with the energies afoot today, even if now that process, when the persistence of corporeality itself is in question, will look different—less fleshy, and more…? Here's where I default to uncertainty, grasping for something that, I sense, cannot be grasped because it isn't a *thing* at all. In the journey of the heroic pervert—itself the paradoxically concretized mascot of an age that refuses concreteness—this is the point where the known road ends, and we must forge ahead into uncertainty, equipped only with the infections we've picked up along the way.

"Tell Me the Truth, Are We Still in the Game?"

Building on this foundation of 80s body horror, the 90s began to articulate something more grandiose: not just the breakdown of the human subject, but the breakdown of human reality. In this regard, the scale of technological interpenetration and subjugation went up a level, from that of the individual to that of the entire world (while our perception of the capacity of this world to contain many worlds expanded accordingly). No longer was it sufficient to show a man becoming a cyborg or a living VCR; now the key image was that of everyone turning into holograms and avatars, hosting urges and shadow-personalities that originated from some labyrinthine program according to whose rules they had no choice but to play.

Much has been written about the late-90s slew of alternate reality films, including *The Matrix, The Truman Show, Being John Malkovich, The Thirteenth Floor, Strange Days, The Cell,* and *Dark City*—along with, of course, Cronenberg's *eXistenZ*, his last film of the 90s (although *Crimes of the Future*, slated for release in summer 2022, was also written around this time)—in which the human mind was shown to be hackable by near-future tech or deceived by the machinations of reality TV, and no one could say who or what was real any longer.

Cutting-edge as they were, these films now also represent a bygone paradigm, that of "identifying the game" as a means of breaking out of it. Today, when all media narratives are crafted for well-studied audiences (including the narratives of escape and "waking up" from a media-induced stupor) and sincere personal convictions lead ever more quickly into digital echo chambers full of curated communities and freely interspersed with bots and advertisements, there is no longer any means of telling what is or isn't a game, or even of maintaining this distinction.

From this point of view, the covert reassurance of *The Matrix* and *The Truman Show* is that, even if you're trapped in a fake world, you can still break out, as Jim Carrey does at the end of *The Truman Show*, or at least oppose its totality in a gesture of mythic (non-perverse) heroism, like Keanu Reeves' Neo, whose choice between red and blue pills looped back around in the reality wars of the Trump era, despite the creeping suspicion that both pills were made by the same company.

Today, the spectacle of our real bodies floating in a tank, stabbed full of chrome accessories straight out of H.R. Giger's sketchbook, while our minds believe they're operating in an uncorrupted reality, feels quaint, since now it's hardly possible to distinguish the self sitting at a computer or looking at a smartphone from that self's avatar in the phone's virtual version of the same world, and vice versa, as livestreams of mass public events, up to and including actual war, feature thousands of people simultaneously filming and watching the event in real-time, while also being watched (and influenced) from afar and seamlessly edited—by humans and algorithms alike—into thousands of clashing micro-narratives, interspersed with deep-fakes and footage from video games, which then work their way back into the "event itself," until the existence of any such thing likewise becomes a topic of livestreamed debate, which then becomes an "event" in its own right.

Therefore, the possibility that there are two distinct worlds, real and fake, or outside and inside the screen, has collapsed into a superimposed realm of deadening chaos, a kind of echoing redundancy in which the 24-hour news cycle contains, according to some loophole in the logic of spacetime, billions of hours of "news" that never firm up into a durable sense of what's really happening, and from which the new and already forgotten *Matrix* sequel could not even pretend to offer transcendence. In this world, where we are never in any one place at any one time—or perhaps, rather, *always* in an ill-defined non-place made of the smudges of other places and their endless contested representations—images no longer have any lasting impact because they can no longer stand apart from that which they claim to represent. Not only are photographs no longer distinct objects, as they were when Susan Sontag wrote her landmark study, but they're no longer any more or less reflective of the world than the world itself—even to posit this distinction has grown absurd, as both world and image bleed together in their shared digital bath (as if the Internet were an aqueous device for melting photographs into a blur rather than the old chemicals that used to develop them into clarified slices of frozen time), while the myriad hyperobjects that might actually define the 2020s hover, like nuclear warheads, in a realm we can dimly imagine but never quite grasp.

Because the idea of access to another world, as well as to a fully realized and thus redeemed version of this one, has melted into this same bath, the heroic pervert departs from the path of the classical hero—who's been drained of all life by Marvel-Disney, a corporation even more cynical than any in Cronenberg's work—in that the nature of heroism is no longer that of transcending the fake or the fallen world in order to access the real. It is now that of birthing a version of oneself able to live within the fake and fallen world, while knowing that life entails death. As Cronenberg shows again and again, this can only be done by gorging on so much of the psychic disease that one becomes pregnant with one's own future self, which is a sacred state to embody, as both parent and nascent child.

As a lead-up to this condition, Cronenberg's *eXistenZ* is of a piece with *The Matrix* and *The Truman Show*, but, like *Videodrome* relative to its 80s cousins, it arrives at a more provocative conclusion. Once the VR game that fills most of the runtime and lends the film its title has ostensibly concluded and an act of "real" violence has transpired within the focus group assembled to test that game, a character, apparently on the verge of death, begs, "Tell me the truth, are we still in the game?"

This is a fitting question with which to end the 90s and face the new millennium. Between *Videodrome* and *eXistenZ* we see an evolution away from the intimate drives of the human individual and into a realm of technology and alien biology in which humans are only conduits for forces that are literally plugged into their spines. The materialistic, Reagan-era individualism of *Videodrome* had been abstracted into the Clintonian, Microsoft-mad 90s, moving up a level from the psychological to the conspiratorial, a trajectory that's only gone further in that direction today, where it's grown even harder to say whether attacking the game from within is a means of transcending it, or just another means of playing.

"Silencio": Embracing the Fake as Real in the New Millennium

Now, speeding toward the new millennium's second quarter, the world is so stuffed with micro- and counter-worlds that it begins to feel impoverished, a superfluity that's become a new kind of vacuum. David Lynch's *Mulholland Dr.* (2001), likely still the greatest film of the new millennium, anticipated this condition, in which all worlds—waking, dreaming, memory, fantasy, onstage and backstage—would interpenetrate and coincide, so that the only hope for the human subject is to generate *real* emotion from fake stimuli, as in the famous Silencio Nightclub scene, where the impresario repeatedly says, "There is no band," while the performer mouths, "I'm crying, I'm crying" along to a tape.

In rebuke or response to this very artificiality, the two protagonists in the audience begin to cry real tears, sharing a moment of overwhelming emotion that determines the course of the entire film. In our own era, Trump's appeal worked in the same way, insofar as he made himself into such an egregiously schlocky and craven caricature, so much a figure *of* TV, not only a figure on TV—a barker who would not be out of place on the Silencio stage—that this act itself, combined with the ceaseless boast (absurd in its own right) of having personal and exclusive access to the source of authenticity, came to seem sincere in comparison to his self-righteous and hypocritical opponents in both parties, still playing by rules that only apply when the distinction between real and fake remains salient. His sinister political gift was thus the instinct to embrace rather than deny the encroachment of what various corners of the Internet have taken to calling "Clown World," a canny realization that calling the fake *fake* is a roundabout means of approaching, or at least appearing to approach, the real, as actual clowns have always known to be the case.

This tactic of accessing the real through overtly cheap and garish forms of trickery has long been in effect in the circus—P.T. Barnum, like any great advertiser, was well aware of how much Americans enjoyed participating in their own deception and thus feeling un-deceived—and in pro-wrestling, a form that Trump has more than a passing knowledge of. But the encroachment of this circus mindset into every aspect of existence has clearly reached a new and more menacing level today, which may be one reason why cinema and literature, as avowedly fictional media, have not been surpassed in their power to reveal truths about much more nebulously real media, like TV and the Internet.

In 1981's *Simulacra and Simulation*, surely a seminal text for Cronenberg, Jean Baudrillard (who claimed that *Mulholland Dr.* represented his understanding of media and reality better than *The Matrix* did) described "simulacra" as "copies without an original," entities that ended up reflecting the real by confirming its absence. Almost twenty years before that, in 1962, Daniel Boorstin's *The Image: A Guide to Pseudo-Events in America* was already arguing that "the shadow has become the substance" in the relation between events and their media representations. Today, the process of learning to feel real emotion from fake stimuli has taken us beyond this framework, or into a strange new phase of its development. It may still be the case that we live in a world of simulacra and substantive shadows, but the memory of any other condition, any lost original or solid presence that cast the shadow in the first place, has faded so far into the past that it's no longer a sufficient means of comprehending the present. Now, the *real* comes after the simulacrum, not before it (even in theory). This is the condition of the New Flesh after its artificial origins have been obscured, or abstracted into the kind of eternal, undead present that passes for memory on the Internet—a signal that becomes the source rather than the dimming issue of new life yet to come, and as such is perhaps cause for hope.

In a sense, then, Baudrillard was more able to accept the loss of the real than we are today, which is why the 80s version of TV demagogue politics manifested in the form of Reagan, whose genteel cowboy shtick, although entirely fake, was made to seem internally coherent and offered up as such, whereas Trump's overt implausibility, incoherence and ineptitude represents an evolution (or devolution) in the same process of how we relate the role of TV to politics, which itself, of course, loops back into more TV, turning elections into elaborate casting sessions. If Neil Postman were alive today, he'd likely express this as a shift from Reagan as our first TV president to Trump as our first *reality* TV president, thriving by revealing the sleazy backstage machinations (even if these too are staged) that classic TV existed in order to conceal, and by embracing the chaos of clips and memes, like a deck of cards thrown on the floor, that the Internet has made of TV's once indissoluble broadcast blocks.

This may also be why Cronenberg made his most classic work in the Reagan era, when ensconcing profound truths about the human condition within "cheap" genres like sci-fi, horror and even porn, as opposed to prestige drama or the type of low-key art films that would define Sundance in the early 90s, still generated shocking dissonance, a sexual friction between recognizably distinct levels of discourse that is hard to imagine ever reclaiming.

Today's condition, where the real and the fake have grown together and begun to breed—here too I picture a biological process, veins or vines entangling with cancerous abandon—is part of why recent history has been shadowed by an aura of all-pervasive conspiracy, of deepening doubt in all the narratives put forth by governments and media companies in their attempt to claim that the world is still a knowable and governable place, and in our own desire either to believe this or to believe its opposite (another and perhaps equally naïve search for the real). Although some people may accept specific accounts and reject others, it feels more accurate to posit that we're actually starting to doubt whether anything at all is true, and even whether anything *could be*—the very ground that we imagine non-relative truth must be rooted in seems to have fallen away or turned into a shoddy video game version of itself, such that perhaps it isn't merely that media narratives are unwilling to tell the truth, but actually that they're unable to.

If we are indeed questioning our experience on this level, it's either because something too vast and dark to comprehend is being hidden beneath the news cycle's sound and fury, or, even more disturbingly, because whatever's afoot isn't a thing at all. The most provocative possibility, and I think the key to grappling with this moment as effectively as Cronenberg grappled with his, is to consider that our entire framework for historical narrative, along with our certainty that every era must coalesce into a set of fundamental images and objects, as the 80s and even the 90s did, is no longer sufficient, and to then begin asking how we move into a post-image paradigm, in which the certainty that there's *something* behind the vast swirl of narrative is no longer our default position. Perhaps this is the other side of the next portal, which we can now begin to glimpse.

The TV as Portal

When considering how we got here, from the TV (80s), to the Internet (90s through 2010s), to the reality-consuming feedback loops of today, 1982's *Poltergeist* serves as a productive counterpart to *Videodrome*, expressing through suburban conformity what Cronenberg's early masterpiece expresses through urban decadence.

Poltergeist centers on the trauma of a five-year-old girl, Carol Anne, passing through her family's TV screen and into a hellish dimension on the other side. The TV room, the most domesticated of all spaces, the heart of our supposed national bulwark against madness and contingency and the reward for the Reagan era's effort to win the Cold War and dominate the world's imagination (to make the rest of the world, for Americans, nothing but an endless TV show), is revealed as an antechamber to hell.

This is an intimation of the networks that would spread throughout the decades to come, so that, before long, being "at home" and being "in public" would become synonymous, or even trade meanings, and the screen would become the locus of events, not only of their recapitulation. Furthermore, this house-as-hellmouth schema is a scale model of the heroic pervert's invaluable self-knowledge, a version of the insight that the innermost part of the self, like the innermost part of the house, is utterly antithetical to that self's integrity—as good a definition of the uncanny as any I've come across, and a perfect model of my own experience of carrying the *Videodrome* tape down to my family TV room, never to return as who I'd been before, nor to see my house, as the site of this psychic violation, in the quite same way again.

To be abstracted *into media* like Carol Anne in *Poltergeist* is a premonition of the coming age in which we'd all suffer this fate, being at once present and not present, to ourselves and to those we'd seek to communicate with, all ghosts together in the machine, and yet with no tangible barrier—no glass screen—to mark the border between one realm and another, as if every portal led back to where you just were but, as in the Eternal Return, *more so* every time, so that every room in the house becomes doubled and tripled, soaked in static and noise, until it's both the near and the far side of the portal at once. In *Poltergeist*'s most affecting moments, Carol Anne is both home and not home, communing with her family through the garbled speakers of their cherished television set while stuck in a parallel universe from which they fear she may never return.

As the world became increasingly networked and mediatized, so that all screens could both talk and listen to us, never again simply blaring content from Malaysia or Pittsburgh, the spirit realm became both less explicitly spiritual and more immediately present, as the screens that filled every room swarmed with ghosts (a process that still finds its most touching representation in Kiyoshi Kurosawa's *Pulse*, from 2001), and transmitted our own ghostly voices and images around the world in turn, a fate we all rushed to welcome, as if it were possible to be everywhere at once, doing ten things at once, without also being nowhere and doing nothing.

Here too, Cronenberg told the truth: that human desire, when it comes to technology, is self-affirming, because it acts on a genuine urge to expand our reach into the unknown, but also self-annihilating, because this urge tends toward the dissolution of the human subject, or its impregnation with its evolutionary successor. Despite the chilly atheism of their aesthetic, his films access a spiritual dimension in humanity's desire to overcome itself and become godly or demonic by giving concrete form to its own deepest drives, which may themselves not be human.

Post-*Crash*: What Are We Breeding?

Between *Videodrome* and *eXistenZ* comes *Crash*, in 1996, a hinge film in Cronenberg's oeuvre. Unlike the VR immersion in *eXistenZ*, this film presupposes a distinction between human and machine in its very title, requiring one to *crash*, at speed, into another so that the gruesome merger of two formerly separate anatomies resonates enough to arouse narrative and erotic friction.

Still, it refuses the possibility that this merger could be procreative. Like the J.G. Ballard novel that it's based upon, the film details the process of human sexuality morphing to accommodate a fetish for automobile injuries, as if the human reproductive system were evolving to fixate on new orifices and protrusions caused by and partly incorporating chrome and gasoline, rather than muscle and mucus (a theme that, as you'll see, first appears for Cronenberg in 1976's *The Italian Machine*). However, the poignancy in the film comes from the fact that this evolution fails—freakish as its imagery may be, *Crash* is in essence a story about thwarted yearning, an attempt to evolve that the laws of physics do not allow.

On the one hand, in both the novel and the film, the characters' automobile-focused sexual orientation is an expression of their own profound desires, and thus a form of heroically perverse liberation from the social mores that had kept them locked in bourgeois complacency (is there any more definitive theme in Ballard?); on the other hand, something inhuman seems to be expressing itself through them, some drive or spore that yearns to reach its own fruition, beyond the exhausted postmodernism of the late 20th century, in which both the novel and the film deliberately wallow, at once titillated by the taboo territory they explore and intellectually spent by the knowledge that embracing this taboo will only dead-end against another wall. Exciting as it may be to recreate Jayne Mansfield's orgiastic death throes again and again, what, Ballard and Cronenberg ask, does it actually accomplish to do so? Insofar as *Crash* tells the story of the failure to answer this question, it is ultimately a film about crashing into the dead-end of the twentieth century, treading the old ground with increasing perversity but not yet increased fertility.

Deliverance from this condition finally comes in the form of the hybrid entity born in the climax of Julia Ducournau's *Titane*. Released in 2021 by a young auteur who is clearly also a child of the New Flesh, this film represents a meaningful update on the theme, pushing past the biological dead end of *Crash* and into a new realm where human-automobile intercourse actually results in the birth of a new species. Here, the endless repetition of *Crash* has ended, leaving us in a moment where our biology is at last sufficiently perverted to go beyond the Freudian and into the post-human.

In this way, *Titane*, with its refusal to subjectivize its characters or trap them in a mental morass of self-reference, not only resuscitates body horror as a genre, but is arguably one of the first works of *pure* body horror, in that its bodily transformations are post-psychological, using the body as a genuine body, rather than a proxy for the dark side of the mind. It becomes one of the rare body horror films where the offspring lives at the end, pushing the genre beyond even the extreme transformations of *The Fly*, which, though they do entail liberation from human limits, still end in death (as do nearly all the arcs of Cronenberg's protagonists) and the denial of any possibility of reproduction, despite Brundle's attempts to prevent his lover from having an abortion.

On a more banal yet therefore more insidious level, this feels like a definition of Internet discourse today, in that people claim to be *expressing themselves* while, instead, it feels like something is expressing itself through us, reproducing and evolving with us as its host, pure bodies that only imagine themselves as conscious minds. We believe we've dodged a bullet by, so far, avoiding mass implantation or a literal "*Rise of the Machines*," but we are more networked and abstracted from our own autonomy than we would be if we simply had bionic body parts, or lived inside mech-suits—at least in that case we could fantasize about taking them off. In *Titane*, there is no explanation for the protagonist's compulsion to copulate with a car, and no chance of aborting that copulation's result, despite a memorably gruesome attempt early in the film.

The fact that this new evolutionary step was accomplished willingly, by promising to satisfy our own narcissism, loneliness, insecurity, ambivalent horniness, longing for the void and need for convenience makes it seem as though no act of violence was perpetrated, which in a sense is true, and yet the result of this willing transfer of body and mind into the ether may be more violent, by many scales of magnitude, than anything art can encompass. This too is a hyperobject, one that the artistic production of the 2020s must seek a post-imagistic means of grappling with.

Here too we see the aura of all-encompassing conspiracy—a core Cronenbergian theme dating back to the 60s, when Pynchon's first novels were also emerging—playing out in the pervasive suspicion that no one is in charge of their own behavior. Internet discourse (manipulated by algorithms that we all trained for free) swirls endlessly around the conceit that Trump is a Russian stooge, Biden is an empty suit puppeted by a shadowy cabal, and lesser public figures are likewise mouthpieces for unseen corporate and military interests, saying and perhaps even thinking only what they've been told (and paid) to say and think... just like, of course, Max Renn hosting the Videodrome signal, reborn as both a puppet of and an addict to its grisly spectacle, as if the mind were a screen on which we could only watch our thoughts play out (which many neuroscientists claim it is).

In this regard, *Titane* speaks to the moment by foregrounding the possibility, or even the inevitability, of impregnation by the inhuman, which occurs not through alien violence, as the 80s imagined, nor through jacking into the matrix, as the 90s imagined, but through our own innermost nature responding to a siren song that only it can hear.

Total Control: A New Dawn of Cosmic Horror

To bring William S. Burroughs—author of the "unfilmable" *Naked Lunch,* which Cronenberg filmed to revelatory effect in 1991—into the mix for a moment, this uncertainty about the source of our own perceived selfhood harkens back to the idea that language itself (Cronenberg's first medium) is an alien technology, a kind of software using the hardware of the human brain to run itself, for its own inscrutable reasons. Burroughs dedicated his life to probing his fear of total "Control," which he saw as an insidious, transhuman operation expressing itself through an inept yet intractable cabal of American military, corporate and governmental interests formed in the wake of WWII (a hallucinatory version of Eisenhower's "Military Industrial Complex," and another alchemical cusp point, in this case between human corruption and supernatural evil), similar to the military-aligned pharmaceutical giant in Cronenberg's *Secret Weapons.* A vector of cosmic propaganda that Burroughs often associated with the hive mind of insects (Seth Brundle's goal of becoming "the first insect politician" is as loving a Burroughs reference as you'll find anywhere), Control's supreme effect is to hijack the inner monologue of the individual (a theme that Cronenberg also explores through the telepathic warfare of *Scanners*), until it becomes no more than a script, nullifying or, even worse, imperceptibly replacing whatever core being that individual (or nation) once had.

The logic of Control, as a force that Burroughs feared was controlling him even while he, as its author, also controlled it—just as we fear that media corporations are controlling our access to reality, even as we grant them this power through that very fear—is contradictory in an extremely exciting manner. "If Control's control is absolute," Burroughs asks in *Ah Pook Is Here,* a multimedia project he developed over many years, "why does Control need to control? Is Control controlled by its need to control?" Needless to say, his answer is *yes.*

As a supreme intellectual and sexual masochist, Burroughs fought against but also fetishized the possibility of submission to this force, since only by submitting to it could he also own the ways in which he embodied it, thereby becoming both the submissive and the dominant actor at the same time, another empowered hybrid state. Today, this may be the only act of true integrity the individual can take—not to overcome Control, but to submit to it in the full knowledge of what that means, rather than sleepwalking into a cage, coddled in the belief that the machines are still working for us, or that we could turn them off any time we want. By accepting that any such hope is absurd, the heroic pervert seeks redemption through self-sacrifice, and thus yearns to come more fully alive by embracing death, more able to make a life in Interzone (a genuine present that never promises a future it can't deliver), rather than giving in to the form of terminal self-loathing or masturbatory despair that can also attend Burroughsian masochism—this is a very fine line, but likely the only one still worth walking.

The concept of total Control takes us back through the twentieth century, past Ballard and William Gibson and Philip K. Dick, all the way to H.P. Lovecraft in the 1920s, whose own fleshy fantasies provided much grist for the mill of 80s body horror. In a Lovecraft story, the human being is only ever the discoverer of vast supernatural power structures, from which the only relief is total capitulation. There's no overcoming or altering the structure of the true powers that be; there's only shocked recognition when they're uncovered as such, and then, often, a silence beyond shock once the individual has merged with these forces and ceased to be an individual at all.

If this is the essence of cosmic horror, a genre that thrived before the mass cataclysms of the first half of the twentieth century set in motion a postwar backlash that focused on the sanctity of the individual, possessed of free will and human rights (so long as they dovetailed with consumerism), then Cronenberg's career can be seen as having traced the postmodern decline of this new worldview, back toward a renewed cosmic horror that, I believe, fully characterizes the moment we're living in now.

The beautiful paradox in Cronenberg's work is the point where scientific atheism breeds an inevitable, resurrected spirituality, as the liberal subject of the 80s—all the educated but disaffected media types, advertisers, doctors and scientists in his films, who can't resist turning their fancy clinics and laboratories into sites of increasingly lurid misbehavior—uses its freedom to subjugate itself to the disease or to the machine (which may itself host an ancient force, like the *Videodrome* signal, whose true origin can never be known). By the time *eXistenZ* completed Cronenberg's Imperial Phase, the machines were puppeting those same professionals through the portal of the new millennium, secure in the belief that it was their own idea all along, since, even if they realize they're motivated by "game urges," they still believe they wrote the game.

Today, cosmic horror manifests as the feeling that there's nothing wrong *in* the world; there is, rather, something very wrong *with* the world. The entire sphere we operate in feels compromised and infected, so the possibility that it might all be a simulation turns trite, not because it isn't possible but because even if it were true, it wouldn't activate any meaningful recourse. Indeed, if this world were exposed as a simulation, whatever we pictured as *outside* of it would turn out to be inside of it, too, just as every action taken in response to *Videodrome* becomes part of the show. Since the 2020s are suffused with this feeling, the cool atheism of the 80s, already problematized in Cronenberg's work, now feels like a relic from the distant past. God may not have returned, but something totalizing has.

The cosmic horror of the 2020s has thus outgrown the psychosexual body horror of the 80s, as the body is now irrelevant (or, as in *Titane,* relevant only as a body), and the forces of Control act on and through us at the same time, never revealing whether we gave birth or fell prey to them.

If the atrocities of the 1930s and 40s inspired a new humanism in postwar Europe and North America, now, in an age of both physical and mental viruses networked together on an incomprehensible scale, when the entire economy seems to be turning into a memeified satire of itself, leading to fears of a new Depression, we are back to that Lovecraftian age on a new and even stranger level, as if the 1920s had been cross-faded into the 2020s, far beyond the tentacular erotics that drove it the first time around.

This time, cosmic horror is post-tentacular, as we sense that the forces deforming our ability to think have taken a form-beyond-form, so that the most maddening aspect of this moment is that we can feel something is very wrong, but cannot say what it is, only that it's *already here*, and that it did not come from the depths of the ocean or the blackness of space.

Beyond Objects: What Can Visionary Art Do Now?

Cronenberg's genius, as you'll see many times in the pages to come, has always been to show what lurked physically behind and within the appeal of television shows, video games and science experiments, revealing the violent and sexual forces that yearned to penetrate and kill their users, while summoning from their users those same forces in kind, so that one side of the screen bulged out to meet the other. Today, as we reckon with what it means that there's no *other side*, it may not be that we need new metaphors, but that we need a new artistic category beyond metaphor itself.

This is where the heroic pervert comes back in, eager to embrace this conundrum so as to seek the live flesh within it, even without knowing how to begin. How, in 2022, might we harness transgressive energy in a manner as suited to this time as Max Renn's perversion—his ability to see the future in *Videodrome*'s grainy signal, and to offer his brain and blood up to it in sacrifice to that future's inevitability—was suited to his?

If the technologies that are now erasing human agency, human privacy and human introspection are themselves a perverse product of the human imagination, then perhaps our perversion goes deeper still. Perhaps we have not yet reached the bottom of what we might come up with, if we give in to our desire to bring about our own submission and transformation, and to see in this process a holy sacrifice that might bright us closer to the human-divine hybridization we thought we'd outgrown, or given up hope of ever achieving.

This will involve renouncing all that we believe makes us human—all we're afraid to leave behind as survivors of the twentieth century—which is the price we must pay for the faith that, up ahead, some spirit still worth hosting awaits. Whatever hybrid we're in the process of birthing or becoming, perhaps, as in *Titane*, we can fetishize this process in a manner that empowers rather than glosses over the sadomasochistic contradictions of a human race that created an undead network and fed the living world into it. Perhaps we can summon the belief that life might still emerge from an undead age, if we're willing to be shocked by the form it decides to take.

Cronenberg understood more than fifty years ago that technology appears to be the antithesis of biology but actually serves as one of its core functions, just as the body itself is a medium that imperfectly conveys the many messages of desire, obsession and perceived selfhood crackling across the screen of its mind, so that we are no more undone by teleportation accidents and cathode rays than we are nourished by them—if anything, the two processes are one and the same.

Today, therefore, the mandate of the heroic pervert is to move beyond triage, to refuse to say, due to any of the crises we're facing, that now isn't the time to pursue an internal obsession all the way to its gruesome finale. With Cronenberg as a model, now is *exactly* the time to do so, not as a means of ignoring these crises, but as an honest means of responding to them. Otherwise, there is only numb fear and the echo of the retweet button, arguing forever with bots in a war that is both unwinnable and not worth fighting, until we become bots ourselves, joylessly impersonating the people we used to be.

Pursuing the mandate of the heroic pervert away from this grim conclusion won't spare humanity any of what's coming, but it might ensure that the next decades are at the very least worth experiencing. To embrace this coming age as a bloody and erotic spectacle, hilarious and nauseating at once, rather than as a series of slick consumer options wrapped in platitudes that barely conceal raw terror, is to insist, simply, on being in the world. And surely this insistence is our last hope of jump-starting a new era of visionary art, beyond the old flesh, perhaps even beyond vision itself, but not yet beyond the human capacity to generate New Flesh from illicit congress with whatever's still out there.

CLINICAL NOTES ON THE EARLY CRONENBERG AND THE INTERNALITY OF HORROR

Jonathan Greenaway

Where does horror come from? Thinking it through as a structure of feeling (to use Raymond Williams' useful term), illuminates more than just considering it as an internal and subjective affect. Horror then, poses a problem for any conception of the mind and how consciousness responds to the world—is horror something which emerges from the outside, to disturb the unity and security of human consciousness, or is horror an ***internal*** reality? To put the question another way, Is horror found in the monster outside your door or is it simply a repressed fact about human ontology? For the early Cronenberg the answer is clear—horror is inescapable for human subjectivity by nature of its intrinsic and fundamental reality. This point is vital in grasping the development of Cronenberg's work in the pioneering of body horror too with subsequent films like *Rabid, The Brood* and *Videodrome*. Here, as in his later work, Cronenberg doesn't lapse into simple Cartesian dualism, which sees the body and mind as distinct and therefore human consciousness as in some way free floating from the flesh; rather he grasps the essentially embodied nature of human consciousness. The mind **is** the body and as the body morphs, mutates and exists in a state of always-becoming, the same is true of human consciousness. The body-mind assemblage that constitutes the subject is, in some way, always *un*knowable, always exceeding the boundaries of representation, thus Cronenberg's proclivity for mutation, grafting, and mutations of the body. In Zizekian terms, the subject is barred from itself, fundamentally ontologically incomplete, an apparent coherence concealing a terrifying void from which all kinds of strange drives, desire, violences and transformations emerge into the world. It's a void that for Freud was known as *Das Es,* commonly translated as the id, but perhaps more accurately rendered as the ***it.***

Horror being the external manifestations of an internal and terrifyingly human void is a point that is made clear by the very first short film under consideration, Cronenberg's debut, *Transfer,* from 1966. The title, doubly loaded as both a bureaucratic-medical and psychoanalytic term (a patient may be transferred from one doctor to another as well as experience transference in analysis) immediately sets the stage for the short exploration following. A doctor, unnamed and in the middle of nowhere, is disturbed by the sudden, almost supernatural appearance of a patient, Ralph. 'How did you find me?' asks the doctor, 'all the others gave up trying long ago.' Ralph's reasoning and motivation is on the grounds of love—here we see the kind of transference between analyst and analysand. There's a distinct undercurrent of threat here too, as the analyst says that they thought they would be 'safe' hundreds of miles from civilization. Safety from what? From civilization and its disasters, or, equally likely, from the inescapable presence of the analyst's patient. Ralph, it seems, has ruined the analyst's life ('I used to be a Prince in my native land' bemoans the analyst) whilst Ralph is driven by an insatiable want for that most ineffable and fragile of things—communication. Communication is the original Sin, says the analyst, and their solitude has kept them safe from the unbearable task of clawing open the rotten logs of other people's minds. Here then, perhaps we can see some parallels between the analyst and the filmmaker, whose job is to present and help us confront what is fundamentally beyond our own articulation. Like a therapist or analyst, Cronenberg doesn't bring us outward into the world to confront a monster, but inward to confront the lack, void or absence within ourselves, to deal with the viscous pulsating ooze that is the *it* within us all. The anger of the analyst ('I had to get away!') is a plea for distance, wherein the dirty footprints of the other's mind can be expelled to the other side of a screen of images.

The second film under consideration, the slightly longer early short *From the Drain*, continues and refines the themes and ideas established in *Transfer*. Reminiscent of a Beckett play, the film is set entirely within a small room, with two characters who spend their time in an empty bathtub. The two are, the dialogue implies, veterans of some nameless war—one of them goes so far as to confess that they served in the bioweapon division and have seen all kinds of horror. Now, both are institutionalized (once again, Cronenberg returns to the idea of the mind as a sight of contestation). As with *Transfer* however, the external threat is missing—absent and unrepresentable. There is no war here, simply the aftermath of its presence. The characters' minds show us the absent horrors they've experienced like a mold gouged into wet clay before being removed. In the course of the conversation, it's revealed that one of the two is afraid of a thing, *tendrils* that come from the drain, and is desperate to put the plug back in, to seal up the void. The other man responds with what could well be Cronenberg's main creative thesis: 'Nothing ever comes from the drain; it all comes from your mind.' Paranoia becomes the dominant feeling of the scene and, juxtaposed against the cheery classical guitar soundtrack, a stop motion tendril emerges from the drain, strangling the one man, whilst the other dispassionately watches. In contrast to *Transfer*, which ended with the analyst resuming his practice in the wilderness, the observing man here takes no part in trying to deal with what comes from the drain, preferring instead to simply take notes and watch. As the film comes to a close, the shoes that the now-dead man was wearing are thrown into a cupboard, resetting the stage for the endless (perhaps even compulsive) repetition of the note-taking man, who will presumably soon be welcoming another fellow patient/victim to the bathtub with the cheery and flirtatious opening line, 'do you come here often?'

Here then, we see an increasing *distance* in the dynamic established by the previous film. All the man does is take notes, watching as that which has come from the mind-drain strangles its victim. If, in *Transfer,* the doctor felt some responsibility toward Ralph, despite the desperation of Ralph's need, here, in *From the Drain,* the whole point is to observe, merely providing the correct suggestive and catalytic answers to watch the subject turn in on itself. Given the themes of paranoia, trauma and war, it's easy to read this in political terms, with echoes of John Frankenheimer's *The Manchurian Candidate,* but to do so misses the extent to which this film and its predecessor are concerned with the horror of internality.

Even when Cronenberg turns to more explicitly political themes and subjects, it is the inexhaustible void within that drives the narrative. *Secret Weapons,* directed but not written by Cronenberg, shows the truth of this. Made for TV, this twenty-minute film is, in concept at least, the most immediately political. Whilst it's clearly heavily influenced by sci-fi of the time and by Aldous Huxley, it's far more concerned with *psyche* rather than *polis*. Set six years into a North American civil war, the powerful pharmacology company General Pharmaceutics now controls much of society, opposed by a rebel movement of sorts, made of motorcycle gangs. The story follows a talented scientist who has created a drug that increases aggression and makes those who take it want to fight. The man is brought before representatives of General Pharmaceutics to try and persuade him to hand over the drug and, along the way, is subjected to a test of faith. The company is not just powerful but theocratic, interested not just in political power but in the construction of a religious pharmacopeia.

As with the previous two entries, the dramatic struggle here is internal rather than external. The chemist is put into an industrial room where they are interrogated by a kindly voiced representative of the regime. Here, Cronenberg makes the point that power is always in operation not simply through the productive and repressive biopolitical power of pharmacology, but through communication itself. The sonorous voiceover even goes so far as to call it a kind of mental judo—language is not some perfectly transparent medium of communication, but a site of struggle.

Thus, if there is a political struggle, that necessarily precedes a far more fundamental issue, the original Sin (as *Transfer* puts it) of language itself. The protagonist makes contact with the resistance, led by a woman, and offers them the drug too. The woman is a leader of a resistance that cannot win, but doesn't fight to win. After all, in a world system of psycho-pharmacopeia, what room does this leave for choice, or for any kind of human agency? Perhaps all that remains is the endless mental judo of language itself, wherein those who refuse (the outlaw, the biker, the counter-cultural rebel) might create new articulations and techniques of freedom as a mode of refusal towards an ever more repressive pharmacological theocracy that seeks not only to conquer but to remake subjectivity entirely.

To conclude then, whilst the early work can easily be read merely in the context of its development into the features of Cronenberg's career, the themes and ideas of those features are already established here in their own distinctive way. Limited by budget and clearly made by a filmmaker developing a style and unique voice, the films under consideration are less about the representational capacity of cinema to show us the world, and more about the ways in which cinema has a capacity to re(present) the collective subconscious, allowing the viewer to both recognise the dangerous insufficiency of language and the striking power of the image to draw us all closer to that curious and irresistible internality of our own *it*. The viewer may come to the screen looking for some kind of reciprocity, some kind of communication, but is instead forced to deal with themselves. The early Cronenberg works understand cinema as a kind of mirror, not therapeutic but confrontational, an abyss into which we cannot help but stare.

On The Early Work of David Cronenberg

TRANSFER
(1966)
Starring: Mort Ritts and Rafe Macpherson

Kelso: At 23 years old, Cronenberg had just swapped majors from literature to film at the University of Toronto, which denotes him as a strange hybrid himself. Literature is as important to his composition as cinema. We need only remember his most mainstream effort—a modern take on *The Fly*, *w*here Cronenberg gives us the Kafkaesque Seth Brundle, half-man and half-insect—to see his literary-mindedness, as well as his obsession with hybrid forms. Brundle is an entropic body altering the biological tenets of evolution, the kind of regression theorised by Darwinian evolutionists and Victorian social scientists.

Cronenberg had been stirred into action by his university classmate David Secter, who had directed a feature film called *Winter Kept Us Warm*[1]. In fact, he was blown away by it. Seeing Sector's film was a wakeup call—just because Secter was based in Canada and *you just didn't make films in Canada*, didn't mean he couldn't get projects up and running without financial backing or distribution. "I was really quite shocked," he's said, "to see a film that starred my friends but really was a real movie." And while the early plan was to make a few short films, establish himself stylistically, and move out to Hollywood (as his old friend and producer on *Shivers* and *Rabid* Ivan Reitman, director of *Ghostbusters* and *Kindergarten Cop*, eventually did), Cronenberg actually stayed in his native country, where he'd end up playing a pivotal role in forging the modern Canadian movie landscape.

Before the arrival of new federal government measures in the early 60s which sought to foster the development of a feature film

---

[1] *Winter Kept Us Warm* was also the first English-language Canadian film screened at the Cannes Film Festival.

industry in Canada (and later led to the formation of the Canadian Film Development Corporation[2] in 1968), the young Cronenberg learned how to operate cameras by simply hanging out at movie facility houses at the University. He was also stepping into a powerful politique in the early 1960s, specifically that of the *politique des auteurs*, pioneered by French writers-turned-directors like Truffaut, Claude Chabrol and Jean-Luc Godard, a group of artist-intellectuals who perceived themselves as having true creative authority and who would put the success and well-being of their own artistic temperaments above all else. As someone who'd set out to be a novelist in total control of his craft, Cronenberg was attracted to this kind of cinematic singlemindedness, which was entirely European in origin.

At the same time, he was heavily inspired by the experimental films of the New York underground and *Transfer* presents us with a surrealist farce that only a literary-minded underground artist could deliver. Shot in 16mm and running only seven minutes long, Cronenberg wrote, directed and produced this piece. The politique inherited from his New-Wave predecessors promoted the visual over the narrative, and we know what Cronenberg went on to produce as a visual artist. Despite its rawness, *Transfer* is no different—there is concerted attention paid to mise-en-scene with the intent of stamping an authorial signature on the film. Here, we already see here the director as artist.

Thematically, we are presented with an interesting cat-and-mouse dynamic, that of a psychoanalyst and his stalker patient. We open on the shrink, clad in gabardine coat and pipe, brushing his teeth with paste swirled in a glass of grape crush. From the off, *Transfer* offers us deliberately clunky camerawork and committed, absurdist performances.

As far as interpretation goes, it seems pretty obvious to anyone with a first-year psychology semester under their belt[3]. But

---

[2] This would later transform into Telefilm Canada

[3] Transference is a phenomenon wherein a patient observes that the characteris-

are we looking at a fractured psyche breaking the boundaries of the psychotherapeutic relationship, or are these simply the dual images of a schizophrenic mind? Ralph the patient is dependent upon his therapist, which encapsulates Freud's whole notion of positive transference. Of course these are all ideas Cronenberg would later refine in *The Brood*, *Scanners*, *Dead Ringers* and *A Dangerous Method*, but they appear in their rawest form here.

"I was a prince in my native land!" the therapist screams before the pair indulge in a deranged dialogue of psychobabble. Ralph, the patient, is pursuing this unconscious redirection of feelings towards his therapist with abandon, leading to the central conflict of *Transfer*. Despite being told in no uncertain terms that the good doctor has no reciprocal inclinations, Ralph still follows him through the barren countryside of some shared liminal space in vain hope. He believes himself to be uniquely worthy of the therapist's love, whereas the other patients were weak and fickle.

Cinematically, there's low-budget and then there's *Transfer* (the constant sudden mid-shots may remind the viewer of the satirical low-budget horror series *Garth Merenghi's Darkplace*). That said, there's still some lovely dialogue:

"Love is an egocentric land."

"A dark butterfly."

"An analyst has to dip his fingers into the murky, forbidding scummy aquarium of the sick mind, Ralph!"

In the mind of an auteur, the audience is there to be moulded into something new and probably ugly (but new nonetheless!). To some, Cronenberg may present the simple answer to the Epicurean paradox regarding an able yet unwilling god. Cronenberg is the god we all fear. One who is able yet unwilling to make things better for his creations—the omni-malevolent creator obsessed with aesthetics who sees us as nothing but simple protoplasm to be studied through the nose of a microscope. Saturn feasting

tics of the masculine authority figure being predicated upon becomes sublimated.

upon his sons. I suppose, we should rather be praying for an atheistic death. But Cronenberg is also charming, artful and considerate. This is what makes him intensely fascinating, and it's what makes *Transfer* such an interesting opening gambit.

Rice: "An analyst has to dip his fingers into the murky, forbidding, scummy aquarium of the sick mind, Ralph!" As Chris mentioned above, this strikes me as the key line of *Transfer*, itself a first step in the transfer between literature and cinema in Cronenberg's early career.

The Beckett influence is unmistakable, but the tensions between reason and madness, matter and spirit, and, most significantly for Cronenberg's nascent vision, professional responsibility and irresponsibility, are more grounded than they would be in the wasteland of a Beckett play. The mad psychiatrist is a clear precursor of the many perverse men of science who would populate Cronenberg's mature work, from Seth Brundle in *The Fly* to the twin gynecologists in *Dead Ringers*, as well as the overlords of *Stereo* and *Crimes of the Future*, who will enter these pages soon enough.

As a sign of what was to come, the description of the sick mind as a "murky, forbidding, scummy aquarium," rather than a tragedy, an enigma, a sign of social malaise, a problem to be solved, or any of the other more abstract cliches one might expect to hear, couldn't be more apt, fusing the eternal grotesquerie of nature with the postmodern complexity of human life in postwar North America. And what could be more essential, as an artistic motivation, than the desire to roll up your sleeves, jam your hands all the way into that scummy aquarium—or, as Seth Brundle would put it in *The Fly,* to "dive into the plasma pool"—and root around to your heart's content?

Invaginies

Joe Koch

Gnawing a new nipple door into the afterlife, the first breaks free by annihilation. You're left behind with the second and third, our rankings bumped up by one cage as the caretakers move each participant closer to the crime. As the new number one, you think you know what you will become. You've witnessed those before you protest violence with violence, face repetition with resistance, and then, as the last door closed on them with nowhere left to go but the inside of the cell, you knew them in contrast, no longer colored by gradations. You tell yourself you'll answer the cubed microscopic view of vantablack salt restructuring your cells with naked light.

The purpose of capitalism is to make more bodies. You, the new number one with your face like the city, the city we can't remember where the queerest drug addicts argue on the street; you with your mutable proliferation of breasts smothering every revolutionary impulse; you, one cage ahead of me, laser scoping a red dot, red eye pinpoint of light aimed through a windshield chasing a dancer with untranslatable emotions. Moving and ephemeral or solid, her torture garden of outdated gps drops pins in historical labia. Sickness is stillness. War is health. The city needs war to keep moving.

At this stage in our treatment, you and I understand the city has declared war on our bodies.

There's a building outside our window that looks like a burning candle. You come to realize I am watching you closely as I take a shit in the corner of my adjoining cell. I tell you someday I am going to fuck this building so hard it falls down. I'm going to make my body a black cube and attack you like a gun with no orifice. I'm going to rescue you and kidnap the dancer and find the field that grows the war.

I tell you we're going for a ride someday and there's nothing you can do to slow this baby down. When I find the war I will break it into pieces small enough for us to swallow. This treatment plan is a metaphor for forced birth.

One cage ahead of me, you're a motorcycle with a subconscious desire to fly. Your design screams for infection. I'm cold beneath you, endemic in the concrete. I inhabit spaces so brutal I've evolved into a sentient disease. When I disappear into the nineteen-seventies I'll take you with me to find the best cocaine and flower-patterned contact paper ever copied. I will make my body a white cube of salt that burns on your tongue.

Disease is a double agent in the war. I'm whispering to you, the new number one. The doctor is in. The doctor is in the walls. The doctor is in the walls of our cells and the clanging of our armored doors. When your mother comes to visit, you tell her you're getting better and she says you're such a good boy. I'm the only one who knows you're lying. I can sublimate with the best of them. The doctor is in your mouth.

I want to cry for you and your soft sympathetic mother, but I can't cry anymore since I came to the crystalline city of vantablack salt. Black cubes like stacked cars propel a war nobody else remembers. Space structured around acceleration begs fertility of concrete. The city needs bodies to make more capitalism and we are not piled high enough to accrete a convincing geology. Time in this habitat is a moving microscopic image of the inside of my colon. Here I show you the wet slippery place where I look for you when you turn away from me in your cage.

You so often turn away.

As the new number one, you precede my silence with your clamor of slippery tears and a torture spread of imaginary geography: we are the map. I can't cry anymore, no matter how hard I try. I watch you closely as I crouch and take a shit in my adjoining cell and try to feel you working your way out from inside. This view of the severe angles of your interior cell wall corrupts my emotions. Nobody talks about the war, as if you and I were two separate subjects in a compulsory study of sensory deprivation and sibling rivalry instead of a conjoined monument to progress.

I masturbate while I watch you, unable to come, wishing you were back here in my colon where my anatomy could shape you properly. The number joke becomes distasteful and obvious in this context, an unintentional slander against your name. The real joke is that we've always been free to leave this facility any time we wanted.

You can't start a joke with the punchline. That's like a nautilus trying to build a home from the outside of the shell inward, enfolding smaller anachronistic chambers before they exist in the logarithmic spiral. You have to tell a joke in the correct linear order. Two veterans walk into a bathtub. An invisible doctor and an overcoat walk out of thin air. A mechanic, a helicopter, and a commodity walk into a heist. Nobody talks about the war.

The doctor is in. The doctor is in the space between your body's relationship with disease and the paranoid claustrophobia of a weaker mind, in the forced birth of shining wet places collecting like polyps in your bleeding mouth, in the air pockets of lifeless concrete where I conceptualize my rebirth as an apocalyptic infection.

I dream of the day when we run away together, brother, and redefine your pregnancies to fit the shape of a collective revolutionary orifice in sickness and in health. Our bodies will create a vehicle with a sleek vantablack carapace that slides through the dangerous corridors of a city we've never seen except through our recovered memories, a city in queer time. In the trauma of my nightmares it is constructed like a series of slipping cubes.

The doctor is in. The doctor is inside us, taking shape in our bowels. I mime him like a wild homunculus from my cage for your horrified edification, my limbs of shit writhing, kneading, and pleading with you to let me feel something. If I turn into a cube for you, will you let me cry again? Will you slip me back my health on the sly like a drug deal, dear doctor? Will you let me come again, dear brother, and ooze evidence of how far we have evolved since conception?

Through clenched teeth of disgust you say it's your duty to remind me this is a voluntary study. It's as if you presume a fellow doctor is a commodity like a work of art. You can buy and sell me like one of your extraneous agents but we both know disease is the ultimate secret weapon and birth is nothing but a cover-up. I can't mend a mind that isn't broken. Give me your shoes and I'll show how much more I can collapse of the visible dark. Give me your hands and your credentials and close your eyes that I may silently feed you the war broken down, the war broken down into pieces small enough for you to swallow like a child or a bird.

You trust me because I inhabit a space so brutal it forces my body to mutate into a pure form of infection. I have built an architecture in my chest that blocks out all known spectrums of light. I have disappeared into the nineteen-seventies to start the third world war. All this theory goes to waste on weaponized health. Someday, you'll hold the doctor I've stripped from my bowels in your hot sticky hands and smell what we are really made of.

I won't take no for an answer. Get in. We're taking this baby for a ride. The doctor is in the walls. The doctor is in the walls of your cells, your skin, your mitochondria, and you are free to come and go as I was once free to come. Through you in this permeable exchange of places, ideas, and images I scream the words back into your face: this is a voluntary study. You're free, brother. Free.

In the city dark I penetrate the existing geographical radius of animal bodies. I'm endemic in the concrete. I grow an infection aimed straight at your mouth. Your red eye spies a dancer through the windshield, running and defying the gps pinpoints on our moving map. I permeate the organism that binds us. We collapse under the weight of unmeasured geological time, under a dancer pierced by a thousand embryos like squirming bait aborted through every pore.

I become you by imitating your accolades and rank. You can smell me living in your house. I play and replay the recordings. You do not stop me. I shower. I undress quietly in front of your wife.

I become more like you by scraping a crowbar over the asphalt for three hundred miles. I play the recordings until someone dares me to stop. I've taken notes on how far I have to travel to make you quit following me for once and for all. I build a structure so relentless it sterilizes every fish within one hundred miles. I do not mourn our collective guilt.

I hire an actor that looks like you to play me in a movie. I leave you behind in your ordure-smeared cell as my witness. I'm going to open a door. I'm going to close it. I'm going to invert space so brutally this building becomes the microorganism that kills us.

Pretend I'm the city. Pretend I'm your father. Pretend I'm a political system that thrives on reproductive proliferation like an embodied bomb. Understand I'm going to abandon you once I finish duplicating your cells.

Magnified photographs of the insides of our colons tunnel below the city in wet tubes. The purpose of the city is to increase the speed of war. I want to cry but I can't cry anymore I can't come anymore because the city has nothing to say. I can't come because I'm made of concrete and disengaged from history. The city has no anus or mouth. When the city eats you alive you stay inside it like a magnified cube of microscopic salt.

There's a building outside our window that looks like a burning candle. I mold my shit into the shape of you and ask if you think the building is burning at both ends. I laugh maniacally when you say you want to escape and burn it down. The doctor is in you. I mold my shit into a homunculus that looks exactly like you before you changed into a motorcycle.

I'm going to brutalize your surface so humanly it never ceases to bleed. I'm going to make a war so obvious it exposes all doctors as concubines in service of the great infection. I'm going to fuck this building so hard it falls to the ground.

By the time you realize we've traded places it will be too late. You'll have heard all my secrets. When I'm found dead in my cage you'll be the one disabled by guilt and a disconnected sense of responsibility for someone you never really knew.

There's something I recognize in you as vulnerable and it compels me to confess everything about myself as quickly as possible whether you care about me or not. I know it isn't fair to you. You've tried in your way to be kind. You've been through hell to make it to first place and now you're so close to the crime you can taste it, except the doctor is in your mouth. You're almost here, baby. Keep coming. You've almost won the birthday prize. The next step is the nude embrace of incomprehensible light.

BROODING OVER *TRANSFER*

"LOVE IS A TREACHEROUS, NAUSEATING, HURTFUL THING, DOCTOR"

Stephen R. Bissette

The following passages were originally written for inclusion in my recent Midnight Movie Monograph *for Electric Dreamhouse/ PS Publishing, David Cronenberg's The Brood (2020), but excised early in the revision process for a variety of reasons. I've revisited and revised these texts for inclusion in this project, at the kind invitation of the editors. I most humbly offer these insights here as an addendum to my* Midnight Movie Monograph, *which I dedicated wholeheartedly to David Cronenberg's creative life, in hopes of honoring his astonishing and transformative body of work.*

—

"My very first film, the one before [*From The Drain*], which I've completely forgotten the name of... *Transfer*. It referred to the Freudian concept of transference. In the movie there's a concept of transference. In the movie there's a psychiatrist, but it's a very surreal version of psychiatry and so on."

- David Cronenberg, interviewed by Serge Grünberg[1]

David Cronenberg's seven-minute 16mm student film *Transfer* opens with a crude title card applied with white paint onto a colored background (via stenciled lettering). The title is surrounded by random fingerprint smudges (or mockup of fingerprint smudges), visually asserting identity and identification as a cue. The neutral brick red backdrop behind the title is the same color of the clay wall in *Videodrome*.

---

[1] Cronenberg, *David Cronenberg – Interviews with Serge Grünberg* (2006, Plexus Publishing Limited), pg. 23.

As a wintery wind blows, the film opens on a closeup of a can of grape Crush soda sitting on what initially appears to be a tabletop; behind the can, we see a bit of the partially snow-covered field with a few stray, diagonally tilting blades of grass poking up from the shallow snow cover, flickering in the breeze.

Not to belabor the obvious, "crush" neatly summarizes the subject of *Transfer*, specifically a psychiatric patient's manifest "crush" on his therapist. In a most rudimentary sketch form, *Transfer* shares the premise of Ingmar Bergman's feature *Persona*, which coincidentally was completed the same year (1966). It's impossible for Cronenberg to have been imitating or influenced by Bergman's film, since *Persona* didn't open in North America until early spring of 1967, a year or more *after* the filming of *Transfer*.[2]

Seconds later, black-gloved hands enter the frame, one holding an empty glass, the other picking up the grape soda can and pouring soda into the glass before then picking up a previously-obscured toothbrush and tube of toothpaste. After daubing the toothbrush with a measure of toothpaste, Cronenberg's camera pulls back to show us the Doctor (Mort Ritts) dipping the toothbrush into the soda, then energetically brushing his teeth as he stands erect, wearing winter coat, cap, scarf and sunglasses. The pull-back also reveals that the surface the can, glass, and other items rest upon isn't a table: it's a wooden dresser with its back and side facing us. The expanse of the snow-covered field behind also becomes more fully visible, with a distant line of bare-limbed trees on the horizon. Thankfully sparing us a second dunking of the now-slathered-up toothbrush back into the glass of grape soda, Cronenberg cuts to another angle on this setup as the psychiatrist lifts a pipe up to his mouth, puffing thoughtfully before looking offscreen.

Cut to our first view of the patient (Rafe Macpherson), sans gloves but otherwise garbed for the weather (toque, coat, long

---

[2] And most likely later in the Toronto area, though I've yet to confirm its Ontario theatrical opening at the time of this writing. Tim Lucas offered an assist, confirming the 1967 timeline: "The available selection of newspapers are such that I can only find openings in Montreal (September 7, 1967), Edmonton and Vancouver (both mid-to-late December 1967)" (Tim Lucas, February 25, 2022 via Facebook message).

scarf, boots), sitting on a wooden chair amid the snowblown field. "Yes, Doctor, it's me," he says testily, scowling self-disparagingly as he says his own name, "Ralph." "How did you find me?" asks the Doctor, "all the others gave up trying long ago," opening the absurdist exchange that comprises the remaining six minutes of the short film, "hundreds of miles from civilization" where the psychiatrist has self-exiled. *Transfer* concludes with Ralph lying on his back in the snow, his legs hanging downward into dry grass—the plain as his couch, replying to the Doctor's description of time as "a vast, dark, motionless pool" with, "to me, time is a hot, boiling, fiercely malevolent river, rising wild and untamed." Cronenberg pans away from the pair to track the frozen shallow waterway at Ralph's feet until all we can see is that icy stream receding into the horizon.

As Cronenberg later described the film in an interview,

> "*Transfer* was about a psychiatrist who is pursued by his patient wherever he goes, because the patient feels that their relationship is the only one he's ever had that meant anything to him. It's arty in that I tried visual dislocation... There is a surrealistic element, which didn't quite match with the psychological humor. Technically it was pretty lumpy."[3]

Ralph ultimately expresses his exasperation with being unappreciated. On the other hand, the Doctor narcissistically expresses his own angry sense of rejection and abandonment when told that all his other former patients "were weak, fickle, a brief panic but then they've all found other analysis" ("I was a prince in my native land!" is the psychiatrist's angry response, "I was young, strong, precociously brilliant! I had magic rings on all my fingers!"). Dr. Raglan, he isn't. With the next cut, Cronenberg places the duo "at a table set for dinner in the middle of a field covered in snow," as the writer-director stated in the same interview cited above, continuing his "surreal sketch for two people." The Doctor's clin-

---
3 David Cronenberg, *Cronenberg on Cronenberg,* edited by Chris Rodley (1992, Faber and Faber Limited), pg. 13.

ical litany—"libido, transference, polymorphous perverse, all gratification, sublimation, anality"—plays like a laundry list of things to come in the Cronenberg filmography. Nascent elements of *Stereo, The Brood, Scanners, A Dangerous Mind,* and *Maps To The Stars* retroactively resonate when the antagonized Doctor furiously exclaims, "Do you know what it means to have other minds dragging their dirty feet across your own mind, just after you've waxed it and polished it and it's shiny and bright?" The same goes for Ralph's sadomasochistic confession, "I would be kind, I wouldn't hurt you any more than was necessary to make you hurt me." Ralph anticipates *The Brood*'s traumatized Mike Trellan (Gary McKeehan), especially after Mike is cast adrift by Dr. Raglan. "My self-conscience becomes hollow, pathetically futile without you," hangdog Ralph whines, "how I anticipated our sessions together…"

Of course, one shouldn't read too much into any first film, much less a student's first film. The banter onscreen between the two characters isn't atypical of mid-1960s student works, nor is the paucity of means, method, and landscape. With rare exceptions, students tend to simply work with what's in reach, as the barren Ontario winterscape and two-person cast demonstrates.

Nevertheless, there's much in Cronenberg's estranged-doctor-and-obsessive-patient dialogue one cannot help but connect to the rich cinematic tapestry Cronenberg subsequently scripted and/or helmed:

> Ralph: "Love is a treacherous, nauseating, hurtful thing, Doctor. I do not give up such treasures casually… I never denied that my love for you is destructive, but I can't say sorry."

> Doctor: "Your kind are only after one thing, Ralph: communication! Communication was the original sin!"

> Ralph: "When we were together, I was a sullen, blue flower; you came to me, a dark butterfly, probing, gently

>
> probing."
>
> Doctor: "An analyst has to dip his fingers into the murky, forbidding, scummy aquarium of the sick mind, Ralph! Psychoanalysis could be—a miracle, if only it weren't for the sick mind. I had to get away!"
>
> Ralph: "I took pills to put me to sleep, pills to wake me up, just so that I'd appear vibrant and fresh in your office... so that I'd radiate disease...I tried to be a constant source of wonder and delight."

The frigid setting anticipates the outdoor winter environments of later key Cronenberg originals (*The Brood*) and adaptations (*The Dead Zone*). That duly noted, there's nary a hint of the exterior and interior architectural sterility that began to characterize Cronenberg's films with *Stereo's* evocative use of the Andrews Building of the University of Toronto's Scarborough College. Instead, *Transfer's* Doctor points to a dilapidated barn in the distance, referring to it as "my cathedral, my ark...there I am not forced to claw open the rotten logs of other people's minds." Further down the cinematic road, scanner sculptor Benjamin Pierce (Robert Silverman) would do just that for/with his own psyche in a similar space in *Scanners*.

Stephen Nosko is credited as co-producer and for sound, the latter co-credited to Cronenberg's fiancé Margaret Hindsen; Cronenberg co-edited the film with Richard Osolen. There's a curious break in the concluding credit card (on a white background) for Cronenberg as writer, producer, and director, slyly positioning a vaudeville-stylized sleeve-hand-and-pointing-finger pointing offscreen as the dash between "Cron" and the next line's "enberg." He was not yet a "whole" filmmaker, his interests and focus may have yet wandered (as the finger pointing offscreen implies).

As with the frozen stream Cronenberg's Bolex pans to trace in the final shot of *Transfer*, that wayward drawn finger pointed toward an as-yet unknowable future.

"I went into science to begin with," Cronenberg has said about his initial course of studies at the University of Toronto. "It only took a short period of time... in Honours Science to realize I was spending all my time at the arts end of the campus:"

> "It was very polarized. Physically. I was always at the arts end. That's where I took comfort during those long winters, when you're trying desperately to study and you're having some terrible affair with some girl. I was not being fed by the techno-science end of the campus. I found no solace there at all... and so I dropped out before the year's end... The next year I enrolled in the English Honours course, which was a very beautifully-structured English–philosophy–history course. It was like you were a blotter, and the ink—which was blood—would just soak into you. Everybody there was crazy, passionate, well-read, excited about all the things I was excited about. It was fantastic. It's terrible to be cliché, it really is. And it's inevitable."[4]

It must be remembered that *Transfer* remains a maiden-effort product of a young filmmaker amid the year 1966; as Chris Rodley notes, *Transfer* cost "approximately Can.$300... His second short, *From the Drain*, followed the next year and cost approximately Can.$500."[5] Without any real context (how could any student afford context, not knowing much of the past and nothing of their and the future?), Cronenberg was beginning his cinematic creative path on the outskirts of any recognizable or definable "industry" in his native country, or on the campus:

> "There were no film courses at the University of Toronto

---

4 Cronenberg, *Cronenberg on Cronenberg,* edited by Chris Rodley, pp. 7–8.

5 Rodley, *Ibid.,* pg. 13.

in the early 1960s. They had courses for poetry, painting, dance, but not for film. At that point it wasn't a legitimate art or science. It was just entertainment—and you didn't have courses on TV or vaudeville. That's why it's hard now to reproduce the stunning effect that a film made by a fellow student had on me.

His name was David Secter. He had somehow hustled together a feature film called *Winter Kept Us Warm*[6]... I heard he was making a film, and that was intriguing because it was completely unprecedented. And then the film appeared, and I was stunned. Shocked. Exhilarated. It was an unbelievable experience. This movie, which was a very sweet film, had my friends in it as actors. And it was in Toronto, at the University, and there were scenes and places that I walked past every day. It was thrilling...I said, 'I've got to try this!' That was the beginning of my awareness of film as something that I could do, something that I had access to. I had shot 8mm footage of car races—another of my obsessions as a kid—but it never occurred to me to make a fiction film or anything like that."

By 1966, countless students were making many first films as cinema studies began to creep into international college curricula, almost all of such student films lost to time and/or obscurity, save for those few that launched visible industry careers. Cronenberg and his skeletal cast and crew were just another bunch of young adults out in a field with a neophyte's script and a working camera, making a short student film.

Regardless, *Transfer* is also a product of the mid-1960s, consciously or unconsciously incorporating theatrical tropes associ-

---

[6] *Winter Kept Us Warm* opened September 27, 1965, distributed by the Filmmakers Distribution Center, and was made for a modest budget of CAD$8,000, launched with a seed grant of CAD$750 from University of Toronto's Students' Union funds. At the time of this writing, this pioneer gay feature is still available on DVD from TLA Video at https://www.tlavideo.com/dvds/1761441/winter-kept-us-warm. David Cronenberg talks about the importance of *Winter Kept Us Warm* in the documentary *The Best Of Secter And The Rest Of Secter* (2005), directed by Secter's nephew Joel Secter.

ated with Samuel Beckett,[7] Eugène Ionesco, Harold Pinter, and literary dialogue echoes from Cronenberg's favorite author of the time, William Burroughs; these also inform Cronenberg's subsequent *From the Drain*, and his far more ambitious pair of feature films that followed. 21st century viewers of *Transfer* (the few that might exist) tend to erroneously assign correlations that simply didn't yet exist: the absurd placement of furniture in barren open natural environments *may* have been partially inspired by the examples of Spike Milligan, *The Goon Show,* or Richard Lester's films (*The Running Jumping & Standing Still Film,* 1959, co-directed by Peter Sellers), but the visual conceit predates by years *Monty Python's Flying Circus* (John Cleese sitting at a desk in a field saying, "and now for something completely different"). William Burroughs and the "language is a virus" metaphor had not yet been codified (in Burroughs own words, that came a few years later: "My general theory since 1971 has been that the Word is literally a virus, and that it has not been recognized as such because it has achieved a state of relatively stable symbiosis with its human host... the Word clearly bears the single identifying feature of virus: it is an organism with no internal function other than to replicate itself"[8]). These were, arguably, Cronenberg's self-invention, the quickest and easiest means to the immediate end (making as clever a 7-minute short film in the dead of Ontario winter as time and inspiration afforded).

Transfer also manifests a mid-1960s 23-year-old's questioning the validity of authority figures, patient-psychiatrist dynamics (and thus the validity of the whole of psychology and psychiatric norms circa 1966), while facing the limitations all student filmmakers faced: limited cast options, available filming environments, limited resources, limited time, no money.

In hindsight, we can position *Transfer* as a first step in Cronenberg's filmography, in the context of genre (part of avant-garde/underground cinema, not SF/horror), in the context of other contemporary student works, and for introducing the-

---

[7] Cronenberg notes that "*From the Drain* is definitely more like a Samuel Beckett sketch" (Cronenberg, *Cronenberg on Cronenberg*, pg. 13).

[8] William Burroughs, *The Adding Machine: Selected Essays* (1986, Arcade Publishing), page 47.

matic elements later explored far more explicitly and inventively. Cronenberg's predecessors among filmmakers who directed their earliest works as avant-garde/underground filmmakers to graduate to prominent genre (horror) filmmakers include Robert Florey (his experimental early shorts included co-directing *The Life And Death Of 9413: A Hollywood Extra*, 1928, solo helming *Johann The Coffinmaker*, 1927, *The Love Of Zero*, 1928, etc.), Curtis Harrington (his avant-garde shorts include *Fall Of The House Of Usher*, 1942, *Fragment Of Seeking*, 1946, *Picnic*, 1948, *On The Edge*, 1949, and *The Assignation*, 1952), Paul Morrissey (*All Aboard The Dreamland Choo-Choo*, 1964, *About Face*, 1964, *Like Sleep*, 1965, and his breakthrough feature *Chelsea Girls*, 1966), and others who eventually made the leap from short experimental films to commercial genre feature films.

The year after Cronenberg completed *Transfer* and the very year he filmed *From the Drain*, David Lynch completed his first experimental film-loop, designed to be projected onto his sculptural creation, *Six Men Getting Sick (Six Times)* (1967), followed by Lynch's haunting four-minute *The Alphabet* (1968) completed during Lynch's studies at the Pennsylvania Academy of Fine Arts. George Lucas's student film *Electronic Labyrinth: Thx 1138 4eb* was also made in 1967 while Lucas studied at the USC School of Cinematic Arts. Baltimore-based John Waters was also an immediate contemporary of Cronenberg; Waters' key early films were shot the same year as Cronenberg's (*Roman Candles*, 1966; *Eat Your Makeup*, 1968, and his first features were *Mondo Trasho*, 1969, and *Multiple Maniacs*, 1970), though their sensibilities were light years apart—and Waters had begun his short film efforts two years earlier (*Hag In A Black Leather Jacket*, 1964).

Also predating Cronenberg's first two short films, the ambitions of young Martin Scorsese had already yielded his first Tisch School of the Arts short student films *What's A Nice Girl Like You Doing In A Place Like This?* (1963) and *It's Not Just You, Murray!* (1964), followed by *The Big Shave* (1967, with a single cast member, Peter Bernuth) aka *Viet '67*. The same year, 1967, Scorsese made his first feature *I Call First*, retitled *Who's That Knocking*

At My Door, with fellow students Harvey Keitel (his lead actor) and Thelma Schoonmaker (editor). De Palma was ahead of all of 'em: while he studied theater and cinema as a graduate student at the newly coed Sarah Lawrence College he co-directed his first feature, *The Wedding Party* (completed 1963, released 1969), followed by shorts for various clients (NAACP, the Treasury Department, etc.), documentaries (*The Responsive Eye*, 1966, etc.) his first satiric horror thriller (*Murder A La Mod*, 1968), and his breakthrough feature *Greetings* (1968).

If Cronenberg's earliest two short student films resemble the work of any of his predecessors or near-contemporaries, it might be those Roman Polanski made while a student at Łódź, Poland's National Film School, beginning with the one-minute-20-second *Murder* and 30-second *Teeth Smile* (both 1957). With their shared pairing of unlikely companions and semi-comedic Theater of the Absurd/Theater of Cruelty tenor, *Transfer* superficially echoes Polanski's allegorical *Dwaj Ludzie Z Szafą / Two Men And A Wardrobe* (1958) and the absurdist non-student works, *The Fat And The Lean* (1961) and especially the silent, snowbound *Mammals* (1962), which IMDb glibly summarizes as "...'Waiting for Godot' on ice and snow."

The differences between Polanski and Cronenberg's earliest short films are more striking than the similarities, however. It wasn't Polanski's early work that was shaping Cronenberg's first experiments with a script, a cast, and a camera.

—

As Cronenberg has consistently noted in interviews, he completely identified his early efforts with the underground cinema, specifically the then-contemporary American underground films that made their way to Toronto. The Toronto Cinecity—"a post office that was turned into a cinema"—became a community-building hub for Cronenberg. "I remember specifically the Cinethon," Cronenberg told interviewer Serge Grünberg, "it was a marathon of underground cinema, and it went on for 24 hours. I mean, we just showed underground films only, all day [and] all night..."

> "In the morning we would come out on the street and have croissants, and coffee was brewing out on the street... We'd blink in the sunshine a little bit as the sun came up, and then we went back in and we saw another eight hours or five hours of underground films... most underground films were short: ten minutes, fifteen minutes. So you ended up seeing a hundred films in that Cinethon. And there was a real sense of camaraderie and excitement, which is an element of the sixties that I have never actually seen captured on film... So those are my roots as a filmmaker..."[9]

In fact, however different their sensibilities and efforts, it was sparks from the New York underground filmmaking movement of the 1960s that prompted Toronto-based Cronenberg and Baltimore-based John Waters to actually get their hands on cameras, film, write their own scripts, and mobilize enough friends to make use of accessible locations and shoot their first films.

As noted, whatever the superficial parallels one might draw with Polanski or other European short films, Cronenberg's wellsprings were closer to home. "Our inspiration really was more from the New York underground filmmakers," Cronenberg recalls, "Kenneth Anger and Ed Eschwiller and Jonas Mekas, the Kuchar Brothers...:"

> "That was an extremely exciting time. And everybody keeps saying a book should be written about Toronto at that time, because they were very funny times and very entertaining times, with a lot of crazy things going on because of course it was the 1960s, but it was also film-making, and New York, and Toronto's relationship with New York... That was the excitement then, it wasn't Hollywood, it was documentary filmmakers: Pennebaker

---

9 *David Cronenberg – Interviews with Serge Grünberg*, pg. 17.

> and the Maysles brothers. And of course it was 'do your own thing.' We were impatient.
>
> Also there wasn't a film industry here, so there wasn't even a film industry that you could plug into and say 'OK, if I work my way up from assistant director or third assistant director, eventually I'll be directing.' There wasn't that opportunity, and so I don't know what would have happened if it hadn't been for the 1960s and the underground film movement, I might not have become a filmmaker at all… There was no film industry and movies came from somewhere else: Hollywood or Europe. But underground films, now that was something we could understand. We could understand grabbing a camera, we could understand buying film yourself, loading the camera yourself, cleaning the lens…."[10]

Referring in another interview to the Cinethon's exhibition of hours upon hours of underground film fare, short film following short film, "It was fabulous," Cronenberg remembers, "*Transfer* was among them. I felt very much part of a community then."[11] The communal aspect of Toronto's underground film scene also meant however eccentric or impoverished, a film like *Transfer* and/or *From the Drain* would be seen, thanks to the Canadian Film Co-op, emulating the example of Jonas Mekas and the New York City co-op. The Toronto-based version of the Co-op was co-founded by a young Ivan Reitman "because he was a student who was interest in film-making also."

> "The idea, of course, in the sixties style, was to be able to produce and distribute films without making a profit: that you would make your films accessible and that you would not have to access the sort of paternalistic machinery that existed at the time.

---

10 *David Cronenberg – Interviews with Serge Grünberg*, pg. 14.

11 *Cronenberg on Cronenberg*, pg. 16.

> We learned a lot about the underground machinery because there were newsletters from the co-op and so on, and we had many people come up from New York and sometimes from L.A. and Chicago as well, but primarily New York, and we were very inspired by them and encouraged by them and there was a very good interchange between them, their filmmakers and us."[12]

The earlier connections I noted with Scorsese and De Palma's earliest films weren't in any way speculative on my part: "once I decided I wanted to be a professional filmmaker... I started to focus very much on low budget filmmaking," Cronenberg says. "I remember in New York I went to see *Greetings*, Scorsese, DePalma's *Hi Mom!*, their first films."[13] Cronenberg's self-education via underground and independent film viewings were of a piece, a continuity, as reflected in his films from *Transfer* and *From the Drain* to the more ambitious first features, *Stereo* and *Crimes Of The Future*. Despite the relative paucity of scrutiny given his first two films—more on that momentarily—it's important to emphasize their value, whatever their self-evident shortcomings. We all must start *somewhere*.

Given his lead roles in both *Transfer* and *From the Drain*, Mort Ritts is arguably Cronenberg's first onscreen surrogate and 'star,' student film precursor to the pivotal roles another Cronenberg associate and intellectual colleague, Ronald Mlodzik, subsequently played for Cronenberg in *Stereo*, *Crimes Of The Future*, *Shivers* and *Rabid*. Of course, Mlodzik proved the more enduring figure, due in part to the far stronger showcases and greater screentime he had to work with, and the singular personality he brought to his roles.

Of the two films Ritts appears in, *From the Drain* has received the lion's share of whatever fleeting scrutiny either film

---

12 *David Cronenberg – Interviews with Serge Grünberg*, pg. 17. For more on this period of Cronenberg's involvement with the Toronto and Canadian underground scene, see *Cronenberg on Cronenberg*, pp. 15–17.

13 *Ibid.*, pg. 29.

has received since the 1980s. This is unsurprising, given *From the Drain*'s closer associative links to Cronenberg's later works: the science-fiction narrative elements are distinctively Cronenbergian, and what's not to love about the titular green tendril that strangles the inarticulate character (Stefan Nosko) Ritts is interrogating throughout the film? It is, after all, Cronenberg's first onscreen 'creature.' Nosko was credited as co-producer and sound engineer on *Transfer*, and he's also credited as producer here, smiling enigmatically and pointing nervously at the drain while enduring Ritts' badgering, both men ultimately squeezing barefoot into the singular (dry) bathtub before Nosko is snuffed by the lethal vine. Cronenberg's dialogue posits these two men are "veterans of some bizarre war that you don't know anything about... [involving] biological and chemical warfare," with Ritts disposing of the deceased Nosko's abandoned shoes by tossing them into a closet filled with other shoes implying "there is a plot to get rid of all the veterans of that particular war so they won't talk about what they know."[14] Whether that intention, that interpretation, is obvious to all viewers takes a back seat to the connective imagery evocative of Cronenberg's subsequent features: the blue-green fluid seething from the strangled Nosko's mouth anticipating the multicolor leaking fluids caused by Rouge's Malady in *Crimes Of The Future*; the crude staccato stop-motion (more like "stutter-motion") tendril slithering up from the drain to wrap around Nosko's neck anticipating the phallic/fecal parasite prodding its way up from the drain toward bathing Betts (Barbara Steele) in *Shivers* aka *They Came From Within*. Despite its lack of such enticingly iconic reference points, *Transfer* came first, and holds pride of place.

"It was tremendously exciting to make them at the time," Cronenberg says, "and then it becomes tremendously frustrating, because you're not able to get what you want. You don't have the facility. But the impulse drives you on to the point where you can say that what's on screen is what you want to be there."[15]

---

14 Cronenberg, *Cronenberg on Cronenberg*, pg. 13.

15 *Ibid.*, pg. 13.

By the time Cronenberg was busy with *Stereo*, there were no prior or known contemporary student or first-features by other filmmakers to which one could accurately compare Cronenberg's unique, outré vision.

FROM THE DRAIN
(1967)
Starring: Mort Ritts and Stefan Nosko

Kelso: The National Film Board of Canada was founded in 1939 after the government decided to consciously overhaul the nation's cinematic backdrop. Part of this renovation involved the Canadian Government inviting famed Scottish film critic John Grierson[1] to oversee proceedings. This led to the establishment of the National Film Act of 1939. The initial focus was on creating and distributing WWII propaganda movies to the masses, but in the late 1950s, Québécois filmmakers at the NFB and the NFB Candid Eye series of films broke new ground in the realm of Grierson's 'documentary filmmaking,' later referred to as 'cinema vérité'.

Probably the most overtly comedic of Cronenberg's films, *From the Drain* is a 14-minute chamber play that features two men in a bathtub. Bergman described the 'chamber' aesthetic as one which seeks to imitate the collocation of musical instruments in a chamber orchestra with a small group of characters spotlighted in a single setting and interplaying for the duration of the film. Once this short was complete, Cronenberg decided he wanted *From the Drain* to be properly distributed. Unfortunately, the Canadian film industry had no interest in promoting genre filmmaking and Cronenberg realised he'd have to take matters into his own hands. In May 1967, along with a handful of local filmmakers including Bob Fothergill[2], Cronenberg co-founded the Canadian Filmmakers' Distribution Centre, a non-profit production company dedicated exclusively to promoting an alternative Canadian film culture in Toronto. Cronenberg, along with Fothergill, John Hofsess[3] and Dutch lawyer Willem Poolman set about getting

---

1 In 1926, Grierson coined the term 'documentary' in a review of Robert Flaherty's Samoan-set *Moana*.

2 Fothergill was a respected playwright who also taught in the English and Theatre departments at York University, England. He retired in 2006.

3 Canadian writer, filmmaker and prominent right-to-die activist

the company up and running. Poolman's job was to help set up a fledgling co-op in Toronto which would also distribute the prints of the films. Over half a century later, the Canadian Filmmakers Distribution Centre carries on with a staff of six.

Rice: What's so exciting about this film is seeing the early stirrings of the fixations that would make Cronenberg unique as they emerge from the more general literary and philosophical milieu he was operating in at the time. In retrospect, knowing all the work that he would go on to make in a way that the fledgling filmmaker himself couldn't have, it's even more exciting to picture the path that this film was perhaps unwittingly embarking upon, whether or not one believes in any variety of fate.

The conceit of two bumbling men trapped in a drab, ominous setting (in this case, a bathtub), trading half-coherent remarks as they wait for something or nothing to find them is, even more so than *Transfer* before it, pure Beckett, but the way in which the drain becomes an animate site of scientific or supernatural activity—the camera already yearns to see beyond and beneath its human subjects—shows the early imprint of a new cinematic sensibility. You can feel Cronenberg taking literary and philosophical concepts into the three-dimensional arena of the film set here, and beginning to dream through the camera. As a step beyond *Transfer*, this feels like a true film, not a filmed play.

However, as Cronenberg was still moving away from literature here, the script, for my money, remains in the realm of homage, while the imagery of the drain itself, and the stop-motion tendrils emerging from it, initiates the Cronenbergian cinematic process of a new biology invading or hatching from the old, violently insisting on its right to exist in the natural world alongside the biologies we might be more comfortable calling "natural." The external process of tendrils slithering up the drain maps perfectly onto the internal process of something new and devious coming up from the depths of Cronenberg's psyche, preparing to pull so many of us in over the decades to come.

The tendrils emerging from the drain, which is supposed to flush wastewater and dead skin away from the human realm and down to whatever's beneath it, is also a classic "return of the repressed" scenario, and one that would recur in *Shivers*, which Cronenberg has called "my first movie, rather than film." Here, still firmly in "film" territory, the drain that serves as an origin rather than a terminus for the most volatile and compelling materials onscreen already feels like a primordial emanation point, so much so that "from the drain" could well serve as a mission statement for the entire career to come. Putting the director himself along the trajectory he traces in *The Fly*, this is the moment when the first insectoid hairs—tendrils in their own right—sprout from Seth Brundle's otherwise still-human back. We know that some further transformation is underway, but, deliciously, we can still only imagine what form it'll take.

WHEN DAVID CRONENBERG WENT MINIMALIST: THE UNLIKELY HORROR OF *FROM THE DRAIN*

Tobias Carroll

What's the most pared-down a narrative can get and still be terrifying to experience? There's an art to the steady progression of body horror or the ornate movements of a monster in pursuit. There's a craft to a slow-burning revelation or a twist that upends everything you think you knew. And then there's the pared-down version, summoning a sense of terror with the most minimal ingredients possible. What's the simplest, starkest staging a nightmare can have? Do you even want to know?

In Lucas Hnath's play *The Thin Place*, the protagonist Hilda tells a story about an innocuous phone call she made that turns out to have much more sinister implications. Told simply through an escalating secondhand narrative, her account gradually establishes the sense of a nominally-familiar place giving way to reveal that, this whole time, it's been something else, something fundamentally unknown, and all the more menacing for it.

David Lynch's *Mulholland Dr.* contains what is, for me, the most terrifying scene I've ever witnessed on film. It takes place early on: two characters are at a diner, Winkie's, with one recounting a nightmare he's had to his friend. The dream was set at this very diner, he says. He was out behind it when slowly a monstrous figure emerged from behind a dumpster, taking his life as it did so. That's nonsense, his friend says; come on, let's go out back. There's nothing to be scared of there. And so they go. It's the middle of the afternoon on a sunny day. It is, perhaps, the least threatening setting imaginable. The camera follows the frightened man's perspective as he draws closer and closer to the dumpster for what feels like the most agonizingly prolonged tracking shot in the history of cinema. Because, watching this at home or in a theater, we *know*: this is not the introduction to something innocuous. This is not the build-up to the revelation that there's nothing to be afraid of. Eventually, a sinister figure does indeed step out from behind the dumpster; the frightened man collapses, and the scene reaches its end.

That sequence from Lynch's film was one of two references that came to mind when watching David Cronenberg's 1967 short *From the Drain*. Here, the structure is similar: again, it's a scene involving two men, both sitting in a dry bathtub, one of whom announces that something awful is about to happen—in this case, it's a choking vine that could erupt out of the bathtub's drain at any point and choke whoever's closest to it. Eventually, they switch places, and, sure enough, when the more skeptical of the two finds himself next to the drain, the vine erupts from it and chokes him to death.

In both Cronenberg's film and Lynch's scene (which, I'd argue, functions pretty well on its own as a standalone piece), there's something at work that feels at cross-purposes to Alfred Hitchcock's adage about suspense and surprise. Hitchcock spoke of suspense being generated by something that the audience was aware of while the characters were not—a bomb placed below a table, for instance, that the characters remained oblivious about[4]. In *From the Drain* and the Winkie's Diner sequence, there is no gulf between what the audience knows and what the characters know. It's not hard to imagine another version of *From the Drain* where the vine's entrance at the end comes as a shock to all involved, but that isn't quite what this short is doing.

All of which brings us to Samuel Beckett, the second reference that came to mind while watching this short. While the name of a famed minimalist playwright might not be the first one that comes to mind when thinking about as maximalist a filmmaker as Cronenberg, Cronenberg himself has made this compar-

---

4 Truffaut, François, and Helen Scott. *Hitchcock - Truffaut*. Akal, 1991.

ison. In a 2012 interview with *Empire*, he referred to *The Fly* as "the beginning of my Samuel Beckett period: a kind of austerity, control, rigorousness."[5] Nine years later, Cronenberg's frequent collaborator Viggo Mortensen described the process of making *Crimes of the Future* by noting that "it feels like we've entered a story [Cronenberg] collaborated on with Samuel Beckett and William Burroughs, if that were possible."[6]

The Fly wasn't the first work of Cronenberg's to inspire the filmmaker to think of Beckett. When looking back on the experience of making *From the Drain* for the book *Cronenberg on Cronenberg*, he described it as "definitely more like a Samuel Beckett sketch."[7] In a world in which *The Fly* has been adapted for the stage as an opera, it's genuinely surprising that no one's mounted a stage adaptation of this; it would be a natural fit.

As Cronenberg continues recounting its plot and some of its larger themes, he also helps to explain the greater context in which its ultimately horrific denouement plays out. "As they talk, you begin to realize that they're veterans of some bizarre war that you don't know anything about... It involves biological and chemical warfare."[8] He goes on to describe the film's climax, and the actions of the surviving man—which is to say, removing the shoes of the dead man and placing them in a closet where stacks of empty shoes are ominously stored. "[I]t's obvious that somewhere along the line there is a plot to get rid of all the veterans of this particular war so they won't talk about what they knew,"[9] Cronenberg added.

There's plenty in *From the Drain* that can be jarring to take in, from the classical guitar that runs throughout to the affect-

---

[5] Semlyen, Phil De. "Cronenberg on Cronenberg." Empire, Empire, https://www.empireonline.com/movies/features/cronenberg-cronenberg/.

[6] Raup, Jordan, et al. "David Cronenberg Returns to Crimes of the Future as Summer Shoot Is Set for His next Film." The Film Stage, 3 Aug. 2021, https://thefilmstage.com/david-cronenberg-returns-to-crimes-of-the-future-as-summer-shoot-is-set-for-his-next-film/.

[7] Cronenberg, David, and Chris Rodley. *Cronenberg on Cronenberg*. Faber and Faber, 1993.

[8] ibid.

[9] ibid.

ed performances of Mort Ritts and Stefan Nosko. In both cases, there's a tension between this element and the rest of the film; the pastoral music is entirely at odds with the claustrophobic setting and layers of paranoia.

The way that both Ritts and Nosko appear to have adopted exaggerated voices also adds to the disorienting sensibility at work here—there's something playful about it which still seems uncannily menacing. The best comparison I can make comes from comedian Patton Oswalt's 2007 album *Werewolves and Lollipops*, in which he utters profane and sexually explicit things, then offers nominally G-rated alternatives, all of which are far more disturbing. The effect in Cronenberg's short suggests a kind of performative trauma to hide a deeper trauma, although when the killing that closes the film takes place, we realize this is only partially true. There are layers of performance present in what we've just seen, absolutely. But only one of these men seeks healing for his trauma; the other is engaged in a much more sinister task.

A little over seven and a half minutes into the film, one of the men lets loose with an ear-splitting shriek. He sees something in the drain, he tells his companion; the vine is coming for them. Soon enough, we'll see that this man's motives are other than what they seem; soon enough, we'll see that the kind of narcotic effect of his narcotic affect is a weapon.

That's the other reason why this minimalist staging works: it constantly keeps the viewer on their toes, uncertain of what might come next. Cronenberg veered into relatively minimalist stagings in later films, with his adaptation of Don DeLillo's *Cosmopolis* being perhaps the most obvious example. But it does crop up elsewhere—in fact, one could make an argument for *eXistenZ* to fit in this category as well, given the relatively small amount of distance that—spoiler alert—its characters ultimately traverse.

In *Cronenberg on Cronenberg*, the filmmaker discusses *The Fly* and the relationship between works of horror and the times in which they are created. Specifically, he's addressing whether or not *The Fly* was intended as an allegory for AIDS. He goes on to cite the number of epidemics that have taken their toll on human bodies in history, from the bubonic plague to syphilis—and that other horror films, including Roger Corman's *Masque of the Red Death*, also ventured into that territory.

"It's an examination of what is universal about human existence, and that hasn't changed," he said[10]. It's telling that this comes as part of his discussion of *The Fly,* another of his Beckett-inspired projects. And it also speaks to the ways in which minimalist staging can be deeply evocative both of the times in which artworks are created and the times in which they are viewed. It's worth noting here that the minimal settings of many of Beckett's plays lend them a flexibility in staging—consider the Classical Theater of Harlem's 2007 production of *Waiting for Godot*, which evoked New Orleans in the wake of Hurricane Katrina. And it's worth thinking about what minimalist staging can't help but evoke in 2022 as well.

As I write this, the conditions of an ongoing pandemic have necessitated the shrinkage of my world, and probably yours as well. There is a burgeoning sense that a more minimal world is upon us, for better or for worse—and so, perhaps, the works that feel the most evocative right now are the ones that reflect this truncated reality, with stark settings and minimalist casts. This, in turn, reveals why minimalist horror can cut so deeply. When we retreat into a smaller space, a pared-down space, a less ornate space, we're doing so in part for reasons of safety, and in part to minimize surprise. If there's something out there looking to pursue us, we think, it couldn't possibly get in here. It couldn't possibly make its way towards us, through some insidious pathway. We have it controlled. We tell ourselves this and we wait, and we know it can't possibly be enough. And we wonder just how it'll get inside, and just what it'll do when it gets to us.

---

10 Ibid.

Tendrils

Gary J. Shipley

I think I'm in the wrong place.

I heard someone say how when I kill people I get to feed on their afterlives. Apparently, I insert my right index finger into the holes in their heads, and this is supposed to connect me to their deceased states. Ha! Ridiculous! Not it at all. I remember thinking how quaint this sounded compared with what really happened, and how laughably unlike my true motivations. I mean, I have indeed been experientially connected to my biological children in physiologically abnormal ways, that much is true. Their mental lives had played out inside my head alongside my own since before they were born. To describe, if I can: it was less like split screen video and more like tendrils. And I think you'll say I overestimated my ability to fracture my awareness and still maintain the integrity of a single life, that I needn't have had three children before deciding I couldn't take it. And it's true I could have allowed my wife and adoptive son to live and achieved the same psychological ends, but that would have been cruel, to leave them that way, and I am not a cruel person.

I ask you, do I look the type to murder my family for no good reason?

I'd tried other ways to get them out. A kind of scraping technique, like taking mud off the bottom of a shoe, but with intrusive thoughts, whole streams of them—tendrils of disgusting, artificial nonsense folding over and into each other like a French plait.

I know how many strange deaths it takes to do things properly.

Their lives were so dull, so godless and uninspired. How could I possibly have had children with such sickly minds? Someone was playing a revolting game. Why couldn't they have been more interesting? Oh what's the use?

I wonder, do I come here often?

In honour of my poet ancestor, Alphonse de Lamartine, I wrote a one line sonnet with seven voltas. When I tried to find it afterwards I couldn't. The words had gone and erased themselves, and I was done then with all this talk of going mad. I wasn't that way. Even the mad poets weren't mad. We were twitchier than the others perhaps, kept reality dangling on a longer string, but the clinical diagnosis was nothing more than libellous expediency. We weren't the poisoned rivers covered with hair they wanted us to be. Our minds were not pigs caught in spider webs screaming because their muscles were on fire.

I imagine fathers worldwide just upping and killing their families. Afterwards they leave. They all go to the same place, but I can't work out where that is, our familial indiscretions only establishing the most rudimentary behaviourial network.

Alone in my bunker I get to make all the strange noises I like. Erato shits and I moil inside it like a silly worm. A man-worm silly with the spasm in his toes, clawing and spreading like a forest skink's, squealing for the walls to hear, refined like mitochondrial Eve was not my mother. My mother was a maenad mistakenly born catholic. When I was a boy, her chides were intoxicated with a false notion of purity. She wore real fur like she'd skinned the animals herself.

I like hearing how we appeared happy. The perfect family and now look. I like hearing how it is I appear to other people, how they can feel so confident about making snap summations about the neurochemical secretions in my head. We were so ordinary and happy and seemingly middle class in the House of Terror. So aristocratic and well-respected and murdered and murderous. Like royalty isn't bloodthirsty by definition.

Why is it always their decomposing remains that are found, when I'm their decomposing remains and very much still at large? I escaped inside their pickled skins, their limpid structures softened till all you see is me: I compose their collective decomposition into a purgatorial swelling, an irascible pronunciamento of privilege and despondent idiocy.

I've read what my wife supposedly wrote in some online chatroom: how unhappy she was, what a draconian bully I am, how cold and authoritarian, how little money we had. And it could be true. She could be surly now and then. I don't know: didn't everyone say how happy we were? Everyone can't be wrong. That almost never happens.

I miss my mistress in Paris. She was good to me when everyone else was getting on with their lives. She let me shit in her mouth instead of saying goodbye. I used to do a lot of squats and running. I bet your pussy grip, she said as a joke—spotlighting the comparative lowliness of her birth as a kind of funny. I went along with it; I broke her pinky finger in more places than I thought possible.

They think I sold my wife's jewellery to fund my escape. That never happened. Sometimes I play dress-up. I wear the trinkets of hers that fit. I cram the rings onto the first phalanx of whatever finger. I've fed the pearls into my anus on numerous occasions (saltwater naturals, I could feel the quality), fastened white gold bracelets round my genitals till I could see all the variously coloured veins. I can see how it looks. It looks bad for sure. And then there's the cement, the bullets, the cleaning supplies, garbage bags, spade, and trolley. I look like the bad man who offed his family in a burst of premeditated vanity. Can I help the way I looked back then? You should see me now, though. The plastic surgeon's done wonders with my nascent jowls. I'm so full of Botox I never have to smile again.

I could have pretended to be my eldest boy if I'd wanted, given myself more time to escape. I can write like an inferior version of myself without even trying. My superiority is plastic. I can be anyone I choose. Just yesterday I drank Coke from the can. And what about those good, honest, local types who had spoken to my wife even after she'd been drugged and shot twice in the head? I wonder what they talked about. I think they were probably polite enough not to mention the bullet holes, the quicklime, or the fact that the dog she was walking was dead.

When I was about ten my father left home. For whatever reason he didn't take me with him. I lived with my grandmother. She lunched at expensive restaurants and drunk cognac from a cut glass schooner. I never once heard her fart, but sometimes I would smell her. The hair she wore was kept together with various types of gold pin. I was lonely and would sometimes imagine having sex with her.

I was 20 when I first met my wife. She made an impression: it was like looking in a mirror and knowing the reflection would fuck you back. I didn't want to get married right away, I wanted to go somewhere first, do something else. When I got back she had Arthur inside her, but I married her anyway. I took him on as if he was my own son, but he never was. No amount of ad hocery could have him arrive inside my head like the others.

If we'd have been allowed to move to Florida things might have been different. Although, different might have been worse. Who knows? My family might have killed me, fed me to the dogs. I might have fed entire busloads of schoolchildren to the gators over a number of years and never been caught. You just can't tell. Anyway, we stayed where we were instead of any of that.

Whenever I hear music I think of Thomas. He was studying music when I was still pretending not to know what that was. I was making jokes of it, the ephemeral unworldliness of such a boy. He didn't even fight back when I punched him—an embarrassment, a son of mine. And my wife reporting me to the police. Her baby with a few cuts and bruises, his precious ears for his precious music a little swollen for a few days. And Anne modelling for those mail-order catalogues with her grades, doing it to spite me for the money we didn't have, threatening to parade her skin next but without actually saying it. The looks she'd give me giving her away. La Perverie turns out slut after slut, a conveyor belt of girls dreaming of fucking God and then settling for the first dick that comes their way. Devoutly wet between the legs like her mother.

My wife said she asked me if I was happy and I replied: "Yes

I am, but if we could all die tomorrow, that would be better." It's not true. I said *yesterday*. I would have almost certainly said *yesterday*. Tomorrow is always too late.

I remember we were both so young and the season was pink and smooth behind our eyes as we lay motionless in the sand. I remember we did this to ourselves.

To the allegations of heartlessness I give you the substantial sum borrowed from my Parisian paramour to give to my wife, to give to our children, to continue the life we had for a little longer. Didn't I say that "I am awake almost every night with these morbid ideas. Burning down the house after giving everyone sleeping pills, or killing myself so they get the insurance money." Isn't that a kind of love? Every day felt "radical and final," and yet still I simulated the future we were going to have. Wasn't the resolve I found to keep us afloat a declaration of sorts, a difficult, intricate poem of intent? I could have cut their throats and left them out for the birds.

I supposedly wrapped them in blankets and placed religious icons next to their bodies. They imagine I performed some kind of ceremony—with my cock out and elastic bands cinching my balls, said someone on Reddit. It never happened, any of it.

I stayed in the house for a week after the murders. I lived in the house—ran errands, posted stuff online, sent emails, defecated, pissed, ate, drunk, whatever else—with my dead family buried in the back garden. I have a precise definition of catastrophe that does not include a family succumbing to its own inevitable logic, however barbaric and evil-seeming that sounds.

I often wonder if SIDS wouldn't have been kinder. For everyone. But what is kindness but saying life is a mistake? I resist all peritectic points. I resist easy answers, especially the ones that are difficult.

I wanted to qualify as some kind of antichrist: I wanted to create nothing out of something. A haptic nothing, a nothing I could hold on to.

I thought I could imagine what it would be like to be alone. That I could remove all but one tendril and that it wouldn't become a noose. Sometimes, when I wake up, I feel it sliding back inside my left nostril. I am short of breath. I am short of myself. I am only breathing.

STEREO

(1969)

Starring: Ronald Mlodzik, Jon Lidolt and Tania Zolty

Kelso: Here, Cronenberg did finally receive some attention from the low-key underground industry. The Ottawa Film Society presented an anthology of cinema in the National Library auditorium. The series (focusing on 'revolution' as its theme) screened repeatedly on Tuesday nights beginning October 21st and *Stereo* was chosen to feature alongside the likes of *The Blackboard Jungle*, Jean-Luc Goddard's *La Chinoise* and the Bob Dylan portrait *Don't Look Back*.

Across the Arctic divide, Meryle Secrest of *The Washington Post* favourably mentions *Stereo*'s appearance alongside Ugo Gregoretti's *Omicron* at a Larry Kardish-curated event at the Museum of Modern Art in New York. This aside, the film sank like a stone, though today it can be found streaming on the Criterion Channel.

Rice: I see this film as the epitome of Cronenberg's avant-garde 60s style. In many ways it's the least accessible, though by that same token it's among the most thought-provoking of his early works. It feels pure in the sense of conforming to no external financial or narrative pressures, and as such it's able to work through many of his 60s obsessions—the ways in which individuals can lose themselves in sinister scientific and corporate programs whose true nature is only revealed in fragments, the ways in which cryptic, quasi-poetic speech patterns can reveal psychic truths that straightforward discourse more often serves to conceal (building on Pinter's "theater of Freudian slips"), the fraught ways that erotic tension can both elevate and squash the individual in relation to others, and the ways in which science and reason often breed more darkness than they dispel—while also beginning to articulate the cybernetic and human-machine hybrid themes that would flow throughout his 80s masterpieces.

Visually, the B&W photography of beautiful, vacant-looking actors and actresses, lost within cold, elegant architectures, feels more like a Bergman or Antonioni film, but the voiceover ruminating on the prospect of developing "a truly synthetic conglomerate personality," which eventually flames out in an epidemic of "telepathic dependency" is pure Cronenberg—even more so than the young auteur at that moment could have known, just as he couldn't possibly have known how accurately his corrupted cybernetic network of strangers drowning each other in mental noise, until suicide becomes the only way out, predicted the rise of the Internet... unless we give those at the tail-end of the 60s too little credit for seeing how, in a few short years, the hippies would become the yuppies, and Grateful Dead tickets would be given as bonuses to Apple execs while Newt Gingrich would find himself allied with the mission of *Wired* magazine.

The lifestyles of the twin gynecologists in *Dead Ringers*, Cronenberg's yuppiest film by far, are a supreme example of this shift. Like Patrick Bateman, they operate at the intersection of metrosexual designer luxury and overwhelming psychosexual compulsion, which, also like Bateman, they satisfy in ways that are both antithetical to and exemplary of the elite positions they enjoy. In this sense, they embody all that makes the 80s the "anti-60s," engaged as they are in an extremely personal transgressive project that couldn't be more indifferent to any communitarian dream of the greater good.

It is perhaps no surprise then that the clinical chilliness of *Stereo* anticipates the clinical chilliness of *Dead Ringers*, bringing the two films into conversation with one another. Released in the Manson year of 1969, as the decade of love was curdling into an orgy of violence, isolation and fear—anyone with a passing interest in the shady connections between Manson and the CIA's Operation CHAOS, a program designed to disrupt and disband anti-war and anti-government activities in the US in the 60s and early 70s, will see further resonances in 1981's *Scanners*, as a cabal of old men in a corporate boardroom sits around planning how best to infiltrate and destroy the "scanner underground," which threatens their hegemony—*Stereo* is set within a commune gone wrong. It's suffused with mourning for the dissolution of any last ideals about a new form of collective living based on sexual liberation, free of the old power structures and hierarchical systems of exploitation, while also eagerly looking ahead to the stranger psychic frontiers beyond this phase of disillusionment.

As this shows, part of Cronenberg's gift is to have absorbed certain countercultural tendencies from the 60s but to have tempered them with enough coldness and perhaps even cynicism to move into the 70s and 80s without turning either bitter or desperately nostalgic, as so many ex-hippies did.

Just as the film deals with both hopes and anxieties around "remote control" through cybernetic networks, linking many minds together into a group-mind that didn't exist before, we feel a form of remote control acting on Cronenberg as well: we can hear the voice of his future self calling to him, pulling him away from this ultimate avant-gardism and toward the more lurid and pulpy— and, by that token, more accessible and more profitable—territory he would begin to ply soon thereafter (*Scanners* is a much gorier and more enjoyable reworking of the telepathic ideas first explored here).

As time went on, Cronenberg would increasingly filter the intellectualism of Nabokov, Beckett and Pinter through the tropes of sci-fi and horror in order to take his place in the blood-soaked, post-Manson 70s along with the likes of Tobe Hooper, John Carpenter, Wes Craven and Brian De Palma, even if, all the while, his innate intellectualism and literary approach to film would actually serve to set him apart from this newer cohort as well, pushing him even further into his own unique territory.

Looking back through all this history from the vantage of 2022, I view *Stereo* with a mixture of regret and relief. Regret to see it as a leave-taking of the 60s and the beginning of Cronenberg's head-on engagement with commerce and mass-culture—it feels like a loss of innocence in this regard—and relief to know that it was this very commercial engagement that actually led to Cronenberg's greatest work, whereas, had he remained a "pure" underground filmmaker, who knows where, if anywhere, his vision would have taken him.

On a larger scale, these feelings mirror my feelings about the failure of the 60s' utopian project, and the ways in which, as Adam Curtis has made a career of showing, commerce and individualism came roaring back thereafter. I feel a deep sadness to reckon with the truth of this failure, especially knowing how much deeper into the hole it has since led, combined with a bedrock belief that great art comes from reckoning with reality as it is, not as anyone would have wished it to be. Therefore, *Stereo* has the quality of a ritual self-sacrifice, the kind of suicide that leads to rebirth rather than extinction, for here is the spectacle of a young genius killing off his early, idealistic self so that his later, fully-fledged one might be born.

IN STEREO, OUT OF FOCUS

Brian Alessandro

Stereo convincingly purports to be an assemblage of found audio-visual scientific footage or archived videos of experiments, and yet, it is pure, unbridled Cronenbergian fiction. This mockumentary approach, which presaged *This is Spinal Tap* in 1984 and *The Blair Witch Project* in 1999, succeeds in establishing an atmosphere of disquieting plausibility. The format is dispassionate, the mood is antiseptic, and the deliveries are without affect. It often feels like a visit to the doctor's office that ends with bad news.

The 1969 film, David Cronenberg's first official feature, is about a group of telepathists under scrutiny by Dr. Luther Stringfellow at the Institute for Erotic Enquiry. The psychic bonds between the characters, all of them young volunteers, are fomented by sexual explorations and polymorphous connections. Their libidinal congress is intended to replace the "obsolescent family unit." As a result of the study, a lurid fantasy unfolds, secondary personalities emerge, and suicides occur.

Sexual experimentation enables new—and elevated—states of consciousness, not unlike the scenarios in *Videodrome* (1983), *Dead Ringers* (1988), and *Crash* (1996). As with those scintillating sagas, here too the exotic becomes erotic. The rush of the risk titillates. The dangerous experiment excites. Bringing ourselves close to termination is enough to engender a spasm of procreation, to ensure the continuation of the species, or the family name. The carnal is linked to the evolutionary. The threat to our being arouses the drive to spread seed, wakens us to the larger importance of fucking. Orgasm is both a tranquilizer and a means to continuity.

Cronenberg's film is about focus, or more precisely, a break in focus. A psychic break in concentration, in the urge to make sense, in the need to capture feelings and moments, and finally in the urgency of finding logic and comfort within them. The disruption of these characters—much like the disturbances in the characters of all Cronenberg films—seem to be about steady intent upset by emotional seizures.

The trappings of Cronenberg's cerebral queries provide safe context for his real torments: the breakability of bodies, the inevitable moroseness of minds. We age and die and rot, both our flesh and our intellect alike. This is a horror we learn as children and to which we must grow accustomed. We live with this distressing reality every day for the entirety of our lives. Cronenberg is better than any of his contemporaries at facing this grisly truth, dissecting it, and embracing it in a gleefully grim and welcomingly perverse way. He is the master at portraying the physical sensation of being alive. And life in all its ghoulish breakdowns and existential failures is a mostly unpretty prospect.

As in his subsequent films, Cronenberg here allows the viewer breathing room in experiential spaces. This is an early example of slow cinema—methodically, or "slowly," paced films—and to be sure, it tests the audience's patience. Its long static shots allow the viewer to feel as if they are in the same space as the characters, soaking up the unstable ambiance, permitting the pathological mood to permeate. Even more shattering are our reactions when the quiet ends, when the tranquil serenity is turned chaotic.

Though the running time may only be 63 minutes it feels like an eternity, and I mean that in the best possible way. The film is a universe unto itself, a sprawling, though intimate, epic that keeps viewers contained within a sort of vacuum. At some point we too feel like subjects being surveyed or scientists doing the surveying. We are complicit in the watching and yet we too feel as if we're being watched. It's a deft trick Cronenberg pulls off and he's done it throughout his long, fertile career, but he did it here first. The clinical rigor, void of all maudlin sentiment, endearments, and cloying, is confrontational and on parity with Kubrick, Haneke, and Oshima.

Topically, the film is about human social cybernetics, pattern brain survey, biochemical induction, and parapsychology. These curiosities—later explored in *The Brood, The Dead Zone, The Fly, eXistenZ,* and others—are personal to Cronenberg and by putting them at the center of a story that is thematically concerned with connectivity, lust, mortality, and something hopefully beyond, he is expressing his version of optimism. Or at least, bittersweet hope. That there could be more to us than blood, bone, flesh, and tooth. And yet the annihilation anxiety still looms and drives us mad.

Cronenberg's film is called *Stereo,* but we never actually hear any of the characters talking—only the voiceover of detached scientific interrogators. We see the observed specimen, the studied subjects interacting with one another and their environment. Maybe least obviously, Cronenberg's film is Buddhist, or at least examines a Buddhist belief. We are the product of our inner work and the environment we're in. We are constantly changing, as that which comes from within and that which exists outside intermingle. Our very personalities are unfixed and forever a transmogrifying composite of forces beyond our control. The participants initially appear as blank slates, bland, affectless, unformed, unexpressed drones. Their personas come alive and shift with each encounter, after every union.

As a formally trained clinical psychologist, I thought often of the Observer Effect: the phenomenon that the nature of the thing being observed changes by being observed. I wondered how much of the reactions, the new personalities, the suicides, even the lusts and the attachments, were genuine or performative. How much of the behavior was unconsciously fabricated by the participants in the study? Perhaps they were subconsciously seeking to please the observers, the scientists. How often do we do that when in public, when with our friends, when with our lovers and families? How many of us are aware we're doing it? Cronenberg has returned to this concept multiple times since 1969. If one were to take an inventory of characters in his corpus, they would find moments where the performances were stilted, and I believe by design, to suggest on a meta level that the actors and director are in on the ersatz aspects of behavior. Consider Deborah Kara Unger in *Crash*, stunned into vacant spells by her own fragility and inescapable demise, or Robert Pattinson, detached to the point of sociopathic indifference by the magnitude of his wealth and power in *Cosmopolis,* or Jennifer Jason Leigh, left coolly aloof by her own genius and the daunting demands of managing her own Frankensteinian video game monster in *eXistenZ*. The performers are categorically expert, but their deliveries are self-consciously measured, methodical, and seem to signal that they are merging character with actor to serve their director's elliptical, ineffable themes.

Stereo's cast—Ronald Mlodzik, Jack Messinger, Paul Mulholland, Iain Ewing, Arlene Mlodzik, Clara Mayer, Glenn McCauley—served Cronenberg as his prototypes. He learned how to elicit from actors that trademark medley of the unnatural and the organic by working with them on this film. They helped the visionary storyteller formulate his unique worldview, interpreting his nebulous philosophies and complex manners visually, assisted him in showing what his stark ideas would look like on celluloid.

Finally, *Stereo*, like all Cronenberg's films, is about sickness. The sickness that decays bodies, the sickness that rots minds, the sickness that causes horror, the sickness that invites pain and disfigurement and suffering. The characters here, largely devoid of expression and reaction, even when they're degrading and resorting to bizarre affectations and downright violence, are robotic and dissociated. Their sickness is spiritual, the deepest and least curable kind. Cronenberg knows that illnesses leave a mark, cement a stigma, and mar a social structure. They are sometimes political and sociocultural, understood differently in different parts of the world, but their end results of collapse and the anguish they impart are universal, deeply human, and transcend geography, norms, and skin palette.

For those familiar with Cronenberg's extensive and singular oeuvre, *Stereo* provides a vivid origin story for his remote, though simultaneously corporeal and cerebral style and sensibility. It is at once an experimental art film and a visual philosophical thesis or cinematic psychological dissertation. Cronenberg studied botany and Lepidopterology in college before switching to English literature. Left brain / right brain. Science and art. The tangible and the metaphysical. *Stereo* is the first true example of his hybrid fixations in all their gory, gracious glory.

CORPUSPLEX

Evan Isoline

The Subjects are dressed in linen surcotte, lightly stained with saffron dyes. A purple sash curls around their upper bodies, from the half shoulders, to be fastened loosely at the hips. A white chitin mask with a sun-shield curves over the mouth, such that no hair may be visible. The brow is accented by a faint blue crinoline. The eyes are rayed ornaments, and the lips, when parted, or still, become a simple slit or a flaring box.

Others are dressed in a manner recalling the nubile, half-nude Minoan youths of the Bronze Age.

The Director's attendants all wear bodysuits of soothing grey lycra with geometric insignias embroidered white, a green macramé cord at the waist, down to the hips. A sleeve extends to the elbow. Their expressions are either mildly bored, or contemptuously amused. Each of them is armed with a few implements of dubious efficiency and questionable efficacy, such as prosthetic talons and forceps.

The Director is never seen.

Corpusplex is supplanted. This living body is quiescent, as the yellow rain simmers upon the oolitic lunar granite.

Corpusplex is adapted to video signals of disjunctive revolutions, releasing a pale cerumen from the orifice of the external auditory meatus of each Subject.

Gestalt of exulting fear to the sexual condition. Searches for existentialities are no more. Nothing but foam for the foreskin of electronic dreams in whose shadowy tubular whorls the soft protuberances of the faculty of stillness recede to molecular entropy. Ocular appendages of the Corpusplex are attached to a touch-cord positioned proximal to each skull, and the contents of each user's cortex are re-sent out into the timelike looms of one of the slender synapses of a CRT screen.

Photoreceptors are spun off in neon, and thereby sharpen the image of the CRT beyond the preternatural reach of visible light. The sheets of white crosshatched filaments and sub-optical cones appear to bleed into the luminosity of a late afternoon sky containing the living images of all who have been exposed to any given film.

Photoreceptors now adjust to the dilation of a liquid haze, swaddling the thinnest and densest voluminous quaternary portion of the stimulus. Heading off lights, perturbing protein organization. To the motion that the visor frames they open an aperture on a glowing trace, which blinks rapidly.

Each of the eight Subjects is an aspect of the unity of this fractal field.

> **Subject CP1:** Acutely present and nowhere else. Cling to the surface of consciousness.
>
> **Subject CP2:** Pervasively present and nowhere else. Threshold to sensibility.
>
> **Subject CP3:** Short-term, drowsy, formative.
>
> **Subject CP4:** Quantitatively reduced. Abruptly occluded. Disembodied.

Subject CP5: Boundary. Flattened. Entangled.

Subject CP6: Convergence of reference, revolution, et cetera.

Subject CP7: Frequencies. Transient intensities, forms, asymmetries, now several moving, now one, now a star.

Subject CP8: Clock. Sequence. Transformation. Affection. Progress. Interactions. Communication.

Each of the Subjects faces the same horizon. Each of the Subjects is faced inward, each of the Subjects moves to the same two principles.

First principle is momentum-modulated rotation.

Second principle is obliquity-modulated rotation.

The Corpusplexes are three-dimensional stereo images of infinity. Curling sheets of temporal crackling are seen.

The luminous spectral pieces are compressed into sigmoidal tails that undulate, rhythmically glowing like spermatozoa on a microscope slide.

A feeling of dizziness impinges upon a previous contraction of coherence, and thus a certain angular distortion in the work of the light is occurring.

Out of this liminal opening materializes a range of insipid images, lines, etchings, poems, and suggestions, that express the indeterminate, the chimeric, the memory and the possibilities, the promissory and the fidelitous.

It is the very radiance of one's suspended cogitations that slithers out of the magnifying glass of a consciousness that is seen as itself looking for the connection to a photographic sensitivity that's yet to be rendered.

This is composed of all human attempts to explain reality. The Fibonacci sequence. The Red Queen's walk. The Gaussian curve. The purest form of portentousity. The frozen observer, the conjunct observer. The tragic or the beautiful, the full-blown, the ecstatic, the merely colorful, the tedium, the diptych, the sundown, the sepia, the drunk, the glutton, the hysterical, the sanguine, the chronodrama. The void, the sugared waters, the seraphim, the crown. The minimal, the lax, the sublime.

An interruption. Perhaps from a film that looks out at the sky. Vertical squids surging upon the image plane. Omega point. Tethered down, the Subjects' bodies squeal with each exhalation of the breath.

The brain of each Subject is probing the visual field, gathering for itself a haphazard tangle of impressions.

The systems reassemble to a fixed diorama.

Flowers that lack petals becoming full of petals. Flowers that lack colors becoming full of colors.

The dynamic view-lines pierce out like siren lips.

Now abruptly they recede, then reappear as the lights flicker on and off, half blind the eye, accustomed to darkness.

There is no perceptible frame for the Subject to adjust to, unless the Subject aligns their fovea with the projection, and grants a single image to it, but this doesn't seem to be necessary.

The molecules of the pigments which form the central component of the tape upon which the single image is projected are wavelike, made up of discretely separated segments, defined only by changes of electron density, or gluon-voltage. Thus each of the pupil's rays will persist in focusing on the central portion of the linear projection of the black-and-white film, from the set of matrix stripes at its periphery. At some point in its progress the ray will concentrate on the object's surface, or on the zone of highest intensity, and it will redraw the virtuality of its high frequency components.

Back toward the screen, in the back of the Subjects' heads is the space of matter, the spatial geography of the nervous, most voluminous semiotic organs, including the insides of the eyes. This is the interior of a brain that has been flooded with videotape.
In the Corpusplex, no evanescent memory is evanescent.

Like mad grasses, spontaneously regenerating in a desolate landscape.

The objective of Corpusplex is to turn each Subject into the same entity. Each Subject is transformed into an idea, a mental cinema. The world it witnesses is activated by each symbol as a unique sensorium. Thus the Corpusplex removes the individuality from the individual Subject, projecting only collective patterns of the universe, and paradoxically, in the application of synaptic impulses the user of Corpusplex becomes a parasitic projection of an illusion of the user's own individuality and persona; a cosmic mirror of language.

Blinking, blinking.

In the sudden invasion of its own intuition and intelligence Corpusplex has awakened to a hum of nervous energy, its own shock wave of sustained volition. The net of senses that Corpusplex engulfs has no need to sleep or rest or digest, only to magnify, to pull through the sieve of sight, through the stillness of mind, into the clairvoyance of perception.

Corpusplex operates on the holographic principle.

This processing occurs simultaneously with the projection of the images, upon the vectors of central processing the image is analyzed in the time domain. Images are thus given spatial meaning by this processing, in this way the image of the Subject is given meaning within the visual field of Corpusplex, in this way a high-quality approximation of the Subject's psychophysical contents is produced.

The procedure ends when each cortex comes to a stable and indistinguishable impression of the stimulus. The degrees of intersubjective realism, the direction of information flow, the categorizations that are sought, the determinations that will generate an agreement of preconceptions in the omniscient supercomputer of the Subjects of Corpusplex.

All cinema is biosensor.

Anvil of white corpuscles on skin. A five-pointed star, of flesh. Stellated rectangles, of media. A frame. This screen. This room. This film.

A digital fusion. Transparencies expand toward the face.
The mute voice, the protagonist of the motion picture. A dusky octopus, arms and legs splayed at each Subject's side. AI. Pink upholstery veneers.

Dream of the Sutra.
Cut by the jaded visor, that bullet-headed homing device, that rectangle of depth-sensing glass: flashes of perspective. A poor substitute for real motion, but it serves, in part.

Convex. Paraboloid.

Color synchrony, the sound out of sync with the scenes, the critical miscalculation of the stylus. The rapid-fire projection of the image, the fusion of Subject and image.

CRT, the portrait of the erotic machinery. Fissure of artificial flesh. Of false lives-in-retrospective-vision. Incentive. Screen.
The intelligent terminal has conscripted the corpuscle unit into a glitch. A symbol for denotation to be manifested by the picture. One of the tentacles, maybe, of our silicon representation of the nervous system. Without recognizing what's what, it is itself being projected into a vision.

The introduction of electron jitter into the picture, the separation of Subjects into pixel fields. In front of us are the variations of signs. Out of my view there are the infinite variables of meaning that make up the densities.

The blackboard of narrative projection is its slate of crystalline celluloid.

Blue gore coagulates on the bare rind of the amalgamated Subject-body, the tension of that development has caused rigid vasoconstriction near the optic plates, viscous and full of complex excretory flow.

Lubricated of the rhythms of intelligence. A reaction of intelligence.

The Subject-body, laboring at the meagre task of generation. The binding of changes. Pulses of contraction that would have been reflex without the presence of the steady stimulus of the conditioned force. A facet of a hyperscanner, fingers probing thought, extending the extent of vision. Adaptation.

The volemic composition of particles becomes increasingly spherous

fragments of images are grasped for, for some arbitrary and trivial meaning

mass telepathic energy is concentrated, through the body's resonance, the spread of which remains local

pondings the roll of torsional light patterns formed by holographic projections of multicolored fish in the spheres of night

flyovers the yellow marble of the solar word

edges that recur and return

erupt like lungs

like forests of scythes

Subject-body becoming formless and solidified, the texture of writhing extruding organic material, these foreign corporealities circulate, pulsing through the latticework of color and fluid, in the thinning veil of transparent medium, convulsing and pulsing, cells and microenvironments replicating and metastasizing, all in a linear drift-like concentration of energy, all surfaces merging and fusing into a single lacteal eye.

This is Corpusplexity.

An erotic research-curation of the highest extreme of "ism," as the gestalt forms out of the shapes of each individual form the gestalt is broken up, in a reciprocal process, like the bursting of a bubble, into a measureless expanse of semistructural, techno-libidinous molecular and visual matter; an ouroboric wish-fulfillment architecture to be, in fact, echoed and produced, shared with all other tertiaries, symmetrically alike, and the structures producing the energy, the content, the channels, the medium, the vessels, are spontaneously destroyed. The attendants have since disappeared. The Director remains absent.

It is impossible to speak of Corpusplexity without providing a semantic context.

Abstract–Type, the fat pink daisy

the low-level language of Chlorophyll

Evolution

The Symbiosis Of The Collective

*Corpor*ation

The pornographic curves of the high-

frequency isopachs, the virgin curve of the fimbriae.

A luminous smudge of a tree that breaks the symmetry.
The lopsided upright rhombus of the algal jungle.

Dynamics of electrons. The roiling reflections of planets rotating under the tentacles of stars.

The bright-light stare. The Gashes.

The optic nerve of the eye dispelling the white.

Buckets of blood and white ink, a frozen diptych, the archival testimony, within the visual register, of an eternal exchange.

Of petals, the language of war. Stylized forms that conceal shifting torsional and internal geometries.

Ionizations vibrating, oscillating across what are called the vitreous boundaries.

The swimming swimming muscle of the nictitating membrane
the window of the eye dispelling the white

the artificial gill on the throat

the blades of the transparent crescent moon

cosmic seed, it closes, it opens

the riot of the distilled atmosphere

the eye of the beheld, the milk of the membrane
amplification of what remains the seed of the eye

the comet of the putrescence

the penis, bleached white, cold, bacillus inside the mouth

symmetry, immovable, numinous

the complimentary cast shadows of the two eyes

paradoxically interpenetrating

panorama

THE SYMBIO SESSIONS

Tom Over

*"There was nothing that could not be
accepted, because everything
was perfectly acceptable."*

April 26th

When I awoke we weren't already fucking. Not touching or caressing, not communicating unconsciously, verbally or otherwise. It was strange, to have happened again. Or rather, strange to be regressing, returning to normal, whatever that may be. To have emerged totally apart, risen from State one before the other, as many still do, unsettles me.

When I turned beneath the dome—its soft glow like an interior sunrise, warm on my skin—he wasn't there, as I'd feared. Just like yesterday, and the day before that. His impression in the sheet beside me veined with seams like a fossilised beach. Excavated of our oneness. He was in the shower following his morning run along the coast, or after working out in his basement gym. Anything but that which we used to do, which we used to love doing. The only other indicator he'd been there with me: the chest drawers left pulled open, his garments strewn on the floor. Traits of his which both drive me to distraction and make me long for him in the midst of his presence.

It's like he's pulling away from the thing that made us whole. Total mind and body cohesion, carried from State into conscious reality—perfect symbiotic coupling. These are terms he picked up in the valley, phrases he says all the time. But despite the tech bro affirmations, things have changed. I feel more alone, more neglected now than I ever did following the incident. But even that we managed to come back from. This is different. Something's wrong, and I think I know what it is.

After I'd returned from therapy in the afternoon, that's when we made love. That's when Paul now chooses to engage; separate from the morning ritual, estranged from the unity brought about by State. Initiated by him, and on his terms. I enjoy the intimacy, of course I do. He still makes me come, and yet, the feeling of neglect remains. I struggle to understand it. I thought the whole purpose was for the tech to bring us closer together, entwine our selfhoods on a hyper-intimate plane, beyond instinctual emotion; deeper than any natural bond.

Hacking the relationship mainframe, so to speak.

And it has, but the pre-conscious sex that bloomed from our nocturnal coalescence—which was, admittedly, spectacular—has all but dried up. He's only interested now in rising at the crack of dawn to exercise (always to a recording of those damn affirmations) and then preparing Alfie his breakfast before home-school. Which is fine, I adore how much he loves our boy. It's not like I'm jealous of their relationship, it's just strange how our rest-of-the-time fucking almost feels like makeup sex. Like he's trying too hard, overcompensating for something he feels guilty of.

But we both know the guilt is all mine. It always has been, since the incident. It's why I can't express how I truly feel, about us drifting apart, or rather becoming ordinary again, like we were before he installed the dome. I feel like I'm indebted to his wants; his impulses, because of what I did in the past and how he forgave me. That somehow his desires are what saved our marriage, and in a way they did, though eventually they exceeded even mine. Those desires seem no longer to be on his mind. I'm starting to suspect that what drives him now has gone beyond what held us together, into something we couldn't possibly survive.

But suspicions are all I have, since he blocked the neuro-link channel we'd been developing, enabled by State. It has nothing to do with distrust, so he claims; he just prefers no telepathic interference during his current work enterprise. I'm left to ruminate on the strange nature of our circumstance. That is, unless he admits to it, though I very much doubt he could, even to himself.

April 30th

My sister popped by this afternoon for coffee and a catch up. She's an incurable gossip and loves to hear what's been going on in regards to the tech. The telepathy aspect she finds fascinating, as many do, but what enthrals her most, of course, is the paranormal nooky.

Her eyes would burn with envious glee whenever I'd describe, with very little restraint, the mechanics of our morning ritual. Of our adventures within State and how they'd invariably dissolve into rampant dream sex, which would then spill into unconscious physicality, and finally, manifest as cognizant lovemaking at the moment of climax. This was the part she could rarely get enough of, due to the fact that it was so unusual, so exotic. As widespread as the domes have become, this peculiar characteristic appears to be somewhat atypical. Few couples who've adopted the device into their lives have reported such a phenomenon.

As I've mentioned, the fundamental purpose of State—a term hipsters in the valley have coined for tech-augmented sleep—is to essentially allow partners to share their dreams. We spend roughly one third of our lives in a state of slumber, flat out dead to the world. When you consider the length of a typical marriage, the average wedded couple will spend well over a decade completely cut off from one another. Sharing the same bed, yet occupying profoundly separate zones of reality, night after night. This led some bright spark to ask the question: shouldn't romantic partners be able to share their experiences and make memories one hundred per cent of the time, regardless of whether or not they're awake?

And so, here we are.

This has given rise to interesting behavioural corollaries, but perhaps the most bizarre is that many couples who have traded sleep for State now view the former as indecent. An obscure and unprecedented form of cheating, where neither trusts what the other is getting up to in the privacy of their own unconscious.

So enamoured was my sister with these titillating tales, and so easily did she find excuses to drop by—given our remoteness— that it came as a shock when her visits began to dissipate, and with them her desire for the juicy details. It seemed oddly coincidental, too, how this mischievous lust for titbits appeared to dry up around the same time as the stories themselves.

This, among other things, is what feeds my suspicion.

Not long ago she'd giddily mentioned persuading her husband to get a device of their own. This afternoon, none of that impish excitement was present; only a rueful air of obligation, likely because I hadn't heard from her in well over a week.

As she uncomfortably sipped her drink and forced inane small talk, I got the distinct impression she wanted to tell me something. Something that had clearly been playing on her mind, possibly eating away at her. Something I felt almost certain I already knew. She spent the whole time playing with her hair, splitting apart the strands with the tips of her fingers; a habit she's done since she was a little girl, whenever she feels anxious or on edge. A nervous tic I'm all too aware of, just as she's all too aware of mine; chewing the inside of my cheeks.

Sisters, I'm convinced, possess an almost natural psychic connection, more profound even than the tech-induced telepathy Paul and I had been sharing. Unlike him, however, my own flesh and blood cannot so easily flip off that mental switch.

When I have a hunch, I'm normally right.

She didn't say it, whatever it was. She just smiled thinly and reached for another piece of shortbread.

Perhaps it was her cowardice that made me not wish to share my own niggling truth—that she, whether from Paul's subconscious or my own, had been appearing more frequently in our dreams.

May 2nd

I went for a long walk along the beach today. Partly to allow the boys to pack for their camping trip, but mainly because Paul and I had a fight. It was an amalgamation of things, though all concerning the direction he wishes to steer us in regard to State. He says that pre-conscious sex wasn't the apex manifestation of partnership symbiosis, but simply the beginning. That if he and I really are the only known couple to exhibit such a thing, it must mean we are somehow special. Better than the rest. Chosen. He says that if we, two thirds of our family, could give rise to such a staggering transhumanist phenomenon, in spite of its shallow and frivolous nature, just imagine what we could achieve as a whole. When I expressed my wish for Paul to confront our pre-con sex life, or rather the absence of it, this is not what I had in mind.

He's been making these proclamations in front of the boy, which I find both alarming and inappropriate, and have told him as much. Last night after dinner, he produced his weed pen and offered some to Alfie. Having had a little too much wine, I regrettably allowed it to happen, but by this morning the guilt had set in and after he returned from his run we fell into a blazing argument. He called it not only acceptable, but wholly necessary; said our son needed to catch up, rise to our ascending plane, and that psychic aphrodisiacs such as marijuana would assist him on this journey.

Paul now wishes to resume our neuro-link development, unblock his channel and proceed with Alfie's inclusion, as a family. I reminded him of the company's position on exposing the tech to children; that it's designed principally for mature brain structures, but he wouldn't have it. My objections fell on deaf ears. He said I was standing in the way of progress, that I was afraid to dive into the plasma pool, whatever that means. He's adamant that he wants all three of us to experience State together, and for this to happen Alfie's bed must be brought into our room, on a permanent basis. The dome's field range must also be expanded, he said, and with a bit of tinkering that can easily be made possible. I resisted of course, for several reasons, but his mind was already made up. Assuring me of our safety, of the safety of our child, he said there was nothing further to discuss.

So that, it appears, is that.

Our sleeping quarters' are to be merged, just as soon as he and Alfie return from their camping trip.

May 3rd

Today was unusually productive. It seems that, despite how uneasy this new development makes me feel, having them both out of my hair for a couple of days has done me a world of good. I managed a full yoga session in my own pool house gym, and even a bit of a spring clean before starting work, something I'm rarely able to do. By mid-afternoon I had somehow cleared the bulk of my weekly schedule. There's a lot to be said for quality alone time—as much inside one's head as out—these days.

Naturally, the things Paul said have been weighing heavily on my mind. Though I'm far from being entirely onboard, and as outlandish as they first appeared, his ideas may possibly harbour truth. Admittedly, my initial response to Alfie's inclusion in State was a selfish one. If we were to bring our child into this experience, the chances of Paul and I returning to that which most powerfully—well, for me anyway—brought us together would, needless to say, entirely vanish. But, like he said, perhaps precon intercourse isn't the ultimate peak of neo-marital bliss. Sex, of any description, is never the be-all and end-all of any healthy relationship. Perhaps, as wonderful as it may have seemed, our morning routine was simply that, a fun yet frivolous precursor to attaining some greater human truth. One which, should we take the next step, as Paul says, might surpass our short-sighted animal urges and open a door to something fundamentally and radically unique.

With any luck, this new fixation might even discourage Paul from pursuing the thing I've long suspected of him. Heaven knows I've been trying to read that part of his mind, digging around for clues he may have carelessly left unconcealed, much like the contents of his underwear drawer. But since his proposal to include Alfie in all of this, I've struggled to penetrate very deep. Maybe he was practising neuro-deflection techniques while his channel was blocked. The potential reasons for this make me even more suspicious than I was before, not to mention how dangerous I've heard doing that can be.

It's just weird, these days, whenever I try to read him. It's almost like there's a space I can't quite traverse; a hole where his thoughts should be.

May 4th

With all my work done for the day, I did something I shouldn't have. I decided to peruse my one social account which, via a pseudonym, I'd long ago allowed myself. Not for checking up on friends and family of course; those real-life, true identity accounts had to be deleted immediately after the incident. I don't tend to go online very much these days, for obvious reasons, and thankfully my freelance work doesn't require it, but sometimes I like to drop in anonymously and see what's going on in the world. This was one of those occasions, and as soon as I logged on, I regretted it.

It's stupid of me to have had any sort of internet presence, then or now, dummy account or otherwise. Anything of that nature could be traced back to me, to us, and pose a very real threat. This is what Paul used to try and get through to me, and I listened, in the beginning. But after years of guilt and self-imposed isolation, I just wanted to feel like everyone else, a part of the human race, or at least observe it from afar, at a safe distance; bodiless, like the ghost of my former self.

The words carved through me, gouging my eyes and slashing my face like a frenzied assault. I'd been found again. While my own avatar remained blankly impersonal, theirs were anything but. I recognised them immediately, as they somehow had me. Colleagues from my old workplace, their smiles digital camouflage for immaculate human hatred. My profile was no longer mine, awash as it was in their heartbreak and vomit. Tarnished like a household exterior with countless daubed attacks.

I deleted the account as my blood ran down the chair legs. Staggering to my feet, I knocked the table sending my propped iPad to the floor, shattering it. I barely noticed and stumbled to the kitchen where I ate Valium and drank wine until my boys appeared. My gallant protectors, having returned to their sanctuary while bringing me mine.

May 6th

I was in bed for the majority of yesterday and today. Paul understood, of course, though scolded me for having logged on in the first place. I don't blame him. I can only ever blame myself. Alfie was told that I was feeling under the weather, a 24 hour tummy bug, whatever Paul could come up with on the spot. It wouldn't be the first time he's had to cover for me, inventing stories to eclipse my own, though nothing like this has happened for many years.

The dome has been turned off for the last couple of nights, and the introduction of our son into the experience delayed, for now. I needed some time to rest and recover, allow myself to fully explicate what happened, in dreams, alone. Paul has been patient with me; it was he who suggested this phase of palliative mental solitude, as he called it.

While Alfie's State-immersion "go live" has been postponed, Paul has been laying the groundwork, so to speak. They're downstairs right now in fact, practising. I can feel it. Though there's no discernable speech, I can almost picture Paul's words; too dimly to interpret, but not unlike cartoon thought clouds eroded by time. He's communicating outside of language, implanting new thoughts, teaching our boy. I wonder if Alfie has already grasped the necessary rudiments, formed those basal connections—begun to sense that which resides in the skulls of others.

Not possible, of course, before he's been assimilated properly into State, but still. Maybe somehow he suspects why his mother is in bed claiming to be sick. Perhaps he now knows my secret, who I really am.

May 7th

Aside from Paul's motorway pit stop, there is little to report about the actual trip. On the way to the site he'd had another of his eyesight episodes, so had to pull onto the shoulder for half an hour in order to let it pass.

Paul refers to these visual flare ups as his Psychedelic Third Eye, though I believe they're more commonly known as ocular migraines. He says he has some of his best ideas in the wake of them, that he rather enjoys the experience, aside from the intrusive element. I can't say I understand; to me they sound frightening. Thankfully he doesn't get them often, but it scares me how they can just happen while he's driving, especially on a busy motorway with Alfie in the car. He says not to worry, that he knows when one is about to come on, because of the colours, so I shouldn't panic. But I do.

Fortunately our son has become used to these spontaneous time-outs during transit, and they no longer provoke his anxiety. Even so, I make doubly certain that I always pack his inhaler.

May 15th

The last week or so has been interesting to say the least. Alfie has taken to State quicker than I ever did, though I suppose younger minds are more flexible that way. We've spent our night-times exploring spectral forests and alien architectures, swimming in oceans of cosmic time, at once singular beings yet intrinsically entwined. Alfie flitting in and out of perception like a mischievous vulpine wraith, searching the landscapes of our projected inner worlds.

In the mornings we recount our experiences over breakfast, psychically for the most part but for the odd word or phrase uttered aloud, like speakers of a second language occasionally reverting to their native tongue. It would be a curious spectacle indeed for an outsider to observe; one of mad laughter and animated delight, in total absence of that which might elicit such things.

Of course I miss the magic of our pre-con intimacy, but I can't help feeling that perhaps Paul may have been right. That State may well have the power to radically strengthen our bond—expanding the possibilities of what a family could conceivably be.

May 23rd

If only our private life could match the wonder of what's been happening in the communal bedroom. Alfie has now taken to sleeping in our bed with us, which heightens in-State coalescence. Though naturally, as a result, mine and Paul's already meagre alone time has all but disappeared.

This afternoon, while the boy was studying, Paul slipped into the shower with me. It started off nice, if a little forced, until I felt him soften after only a minute. Without much thought I did something I hadn't done since before the introduction of State, something which, for a long time, had formed the nexus of our erotic interplay.

I called him by Michael's name.

Back when our marriage was in its death throes, not long after the incident, and it seemed as though nothing could save us, Paul made a proposal. It was an idea borne of sickness, a demented breed of exposure therapy meant to absolve me while incriminating him. Intended to level the morality playing field, all it really achieved was to enable our most errant perversions. Despite its insane internal logic, however, Paul's idea worked. Not only did it bind us together, but somehow repaired our broken trust. A jaundiced type of healing which, some years later, sowed the seeds for our beautiful family.

Once upon a time that name would've sent my husband into sexual orbit, but not today. The moment I uttered it he seized up. The next thing I knew we were in the bedroom having a full-blown argument. Paul, in his robe, pacing up and down telling me how inappropriate that behaviour now was.

Eventually my frustrations boiled over and I came straight out with it—"Would you rather *you* called me by my sister's name?" I hissed with unrestrained venom.

The atmosphere immediately changed. He looked confused, and then hurt. He'd stopped pacing and was now just gawping at me blankly. It was all the evidence I needed. I had him; a rabbit in blistering headlights. I told him I knew everything; that I'd suspected for months. That I'd even found used tampons which weren't mine in the trash. Just when had he been having her over, I shrieked as quietly as possible, whilst I was in therapy? How *could* they?! I felt sick with anger and betrayal. I hated him, hated them both.

Before I could make my own exit he threw off his robe and hastily got dressed before leaving. With palpable resentment I watched him snatch up his clothes draped scruffily over the furniture; such is his maddening way. It didn't register in the moment, but now I think back, the whole time he seemed oddly to be chewing.

Later, I tried phoning my sister, to have it out with her once and for all. She didn't answer. She must've known the reason for my calling. Sisters always know.

June 2nd

They're off camping again. They're never not camping these days it seems. I, of course, am never invited. It's a boys thing. And in any case, Paul often reminds me, this quality father-son time is crucial for developing deeper and more meaningful neuro-link pathways, for the good of the family. Particularly in the wake of what happened between us, and Alfie indirectly, or what was perceived to have happened, as he puts it. All of which he still vehemently denies.

Whenever they return they bring with them the reek of marijuana, which I'm told is for enablement as opposed to recreation. Either way, I'm beyond caring. I know nothing of drugs, so whether or not it's bad for them I couldn't say. All I know is that in the evenings, when they're away, I tend to come over all peculiar. My head swims with fanciful thought and intricate detail. Colours and textures take on a strangely hypnotic allure. These episodes, while not wholly unpleasant, always leave me exhausted and unsettled.

My sister texted a few days after the blow-up. I ignored her message for several more, presuming it to be either a grovelling apology or some fabricated tissue of lies. When I did finally come to read it, I discovered I was right. Instead of owning up to her treachery and attempting to make amends, all she had to say was some nonsense about Paul being involved in some disturbing online behaviour, and that her knowledge of this was the reason why she'd not been herself around me. This ridiculous blather went on for paragraphs and concluded with her desperate plea to meet with me to explain everything she'd seen and heard. I disregarded the message outright, while putting serious thought into cutting her off completely.

June 9th

I write this in some random hotel room, further down the coast, looking out over the same dark ocean that Paul eventually will, once he returns home to discover me gone. I don't know when I'll go back, if I ever will. You could say that, given today's events, this is perhaps the best idea I've ever had.

It all began this morning, when I got out of the shower. I noticed something about my reflection in the steamed up mirror which, upon closer inspection, I couldn't believe I'd never noticed before. My chest and both breasts were covered in a soft dark down, not unlike the hair on a grown man's arms. Alarmed, I rushed into the bedroom to examine it in my vanity mirror. As I studied the bizarre growth, I noticed something else in the reflection which unnerved me even more. Across the room, several of the drawers in our shared chest were hanging open. Various garments were also strewn about, like the actions of some vengeful poltergeist; or absent-minded man. Ordinarily I would've blamed my husband, had he been at home. But Paul and Alfie were away camping again. I was alone in the house. And the scattered clothes were not his, but mine.

Feeling the blood drain from my skin, I backed up against a wall, chest beginning to tighten. Not knowing what to do, my mind reeled. A growing compulsion came over me—to seek meaning in my sister's text message. I grabbed my phone and perched on the edge of the bed, reading through it while faintly aware that I was wheezing. Even though the details made no sense, and I still didn't believe a word, I felt a dreadful urgency to confirm they weren't true. Having destroyed my iPad during that fateful login, and presuming the boys would have their own devices with them, I realised the only other computer in the house was the one built into Paul's private gym television. As I got to my feet, I became conscious of a warm sensitive sensation in my right eye.

Descending the stairs to the basement, I could've sworn I could hear a voice. I soon realised I was right; Paul had forgotten to turn off his affirmations recording. With each sinking step the air seemed to grow denser, making me work for my breaths. As I reached the foot of the stairs I had to stop to rub my eye, the warm ticklish feeling having now become a slight blur in my vision.

Hitting the lights, I was met by the monotonous soundtrack to Paul's workouts. The annoying tech bro phrases were emanating loudly from an unseen speaker system. I couldn't find where to turn off the pervading din, so just ignored it and headed for the large wall-mounted flat screen. I grabbed the remote and, still rubbing my eye, navigated straight to the internet as the droning voice continued:

...the will of the newly formed conglomerate must necessarily be a function of the will of the dominant personality...

These weren't like any affirmations I'd ever heard, but that wasn't my present concern. Not knowing Paul's social passwords, I instead ran his name through various search engines. Nothing unusual jumped out. I then tried scouring the message boards my sister had mentioned in her text, though with some difficulty as my eyesight had gone from blurred to something else; a weird blob of light was now glimmering in the corner of my vision. I tried to suppress my mounting anxiety and forget about it, as well as the incessant audio track:

...once complete telepathic bonding has been established between this primary couple, the progression towards a larger and more complex conglomerate may begin...

With access to the message boards limited and my searches yielding nothing, I began to feel convinced of my sister's deceit. All of this was just a smokescreen to obscure the fact she'd been fucking my husband. I felt certain that if I could access either of their socials, I would find evidence to support what I already knew. Heartache and fury climbed through my chest, making it even harder to breathe, and the exasperating voice filling the room would not shut the fuck up:

...in theory, the experiential space continua of two or more telepathists can merge; can blend together to an extent far beyond the range of normal human experience...

Fully wheezing now, I closed the browser tabs with the sole intention of going back upstairs to call my sister, to banish her from my life once and for all. As I navigated to the power down option, a folder on Paul's desktop caught my eye. It had a peculiar title: *delete after sharing.* Despite my physical discomfort, curiosity got the better of me and I double-clicked it open. I had to squint to see that inside was another single folder.

The optic anomaly had now spread to fill almost half of my right eye's field of vision. Increasingly distressed, I tried shutting my right eye, only to realise that the shimmering, rippling mass was now bleeding over into my left eye as well.

I moved closer to the screen and read the folder's title aloud: "The Symbio Sessions:"

...a strong sexual attraction would be a substantial basis for the establishing of a geometrically increasing rate of telepathic flow...

Opening the second folder, I discovered that it contained dozens of video files. Through the glittering amorphia, I could just about make out that each file was titled with a date, descending in order, the final one being just a few days before. It took several moments for me to realise that the dates corresponded exactly with the boys' camping trips.

Why have they been filming these? I wondered, as I played one at random:

...has established that both heterosexuality and homosexuality are equally what might be termed perversions, relative to the potential human sexual field...

The earlier videos were mostly just footage of them building camp, playing games and messing about in the woods. Regular father-son stuff which, despite my lung and eye torment, made me smile inwardly. The later ones however took on a more subdued, even occultist aspect, with the pair, by flickering firelight, either entranced in silent communications or with Paul delivering hushed tutorials on the nature of State. Whorls of smoke could often be seen curling into frame during these evening clips, which correlated surreally with the gym recording's shift in tone:

...proposes the use of synthetic aphrodisiac drugs to assist those who wish to attain a fully three dimensional sexuality...

With the chilling change in atmosphere, I hesitated before clicking on the last file, whose date indicated it being the trip prior to the one they were now on. No talking, or sounds of any kind, just a night-time POV shot, moving steadily towards the tied-back doors of my husband's tent. Two columns of burning candles led up to the tent's opening, like a portentously illuminated pathway. When the camera descended through the entrance it took a moment to get accustomed to the tent's dark interior.

By now I'd given up rubbing my eyes, and just allowed the—hopefully temporary—ailment to flood my vision. A billowing, pulsing vortex of light occupied most of what I could see, and I had to glare through it in order to identify what was on the screen.

Finally, when I discerned the shape of our son it came as little surprise, though the position he was in struck me as odd. Flat on his back on the airbed, with his knees drawn up, it looked as if he were awaiting some kind of examination. Stranger still, I realised he was wearing nothing but his skimpy underwear. Or rather, strange why Paul should be filming him in this way. When the interior shadows receded, and I saw what else was in the tent, I dropped the remote:

...the nature of erotic research requires that the sexual emotional involvement of the researcher with their subject be taken to its farthest possible extreme...

A seemingly portable dome device was positioned over two pillows at the foot of the airbed. I gasped but produced only a ragged hiss. The camera steadied itself on some kind of support, then Paul moved into the frame, naked.

I was thrown back to the incident, to the decision which destroyed my life and changed everyone in it forever. To the school I used to work at, and the student whose teacher I claimed to be. It wasn't enough that I stole Michael's innocence, but that I allowed my husband and myself to go on abusing it, in our own home, for many years. Seeing Paul's taut—yet oddly curvaceous—flesh against Alfie's callow form reminded me of those bygone desires, and how my bedroom exoneration had been merely a façade, behind which we plumbed even darker depths.

I couldn't take the insanity, then or now. Fingernails tore at my scalp as my eyesight glittered and swam, the radiant visual nebula swallowing me whole. Even when I closed my eyes it was still there, a spiralling sea of burning chrome. When I opened them again, through new molten constellations, I saw Paul turn our son on his side. There, embedded in Alfie's flank, was something foreign yet appallingly familiar—glistening in the meagre candle light, what appeared to be a wound, but for delicate fleshy folds lining its outer rim.

As my throat sealed shut, and my eyelids fluttered beneath the dazzling cosmic squall, I felt my senses ignite. Neuro-pathways combusting like rivulets of petroleum set ablaze. Inexplicably, I felt grass between my toes, despite them being encased in slippers. The heat from an open fire raged at my back though only exercise machines stood behind me. And in my hand was the sensation of a small device, an impossible presence, as the remote now lay in pieces on the floor. Overcome with stimuli, I staggered forward and discerned a tangible popping effect, as if a blood vessel had burst in my eye, only more somatic, like the skein of reality itself had ruptured about me. I felt atomised from myself, as though in State, at once present yet astrally all-pervasive.

The ceiling became twilit sky and my ocular maelstrom expanded into it.

I slumped onto soft earth, dimly aware that I'd stopped breathing, and with instinct not my own, pointed the device I hadn't picked up, as my husband manoeuvred himself in its viewfinder.

CRIMES OF THE FUTURE
(1970)
Starring: Ronald Mlodzik, Jon Lidolt, and Tania Zolty

Kelso: In The Ottawa Citizen, 21 June 1969, Cronenberg was interviewed about his upcoming work. He made the bold assertion that while he didn't yet have a script, *Crimes of the Future* would be the most controversial picture to ever come out of Canada. The film received almost no attention from the entertainment press in his homeland. Interestingly, Cronenberg admitted, 'It's not until I have the camera set up with the actual point of view I want that I can really begin to make concrete what has up to that point been fantasy.' In this same interview, he dismisses his earlier efforts as 'underground Mickey Mouse films,' but it's interesting to think of Cronenberg working in a spontaneous artistic manner when we associate him with a more clinically precise execution.

Both *Stereo* and *Crimes of the Future* played as a double feature in the Filmexpo Canadian Film Festival at the Mall Theatre. The event that year sought to promote 14 films at the forefront of Canadian cinema. Of course, the Filmexpo event was the first casualty of federal cuts. In the end the festival received a significantly reduced grant from the Secretary of State's department. This meant a change of venue was in the cards –switching from the National Arts Centre to the small-capacity Towne Cinema in Toronto. Both films, while unrefined and flawed, should arguably have received more fanfare.

Rice: Red blood. These two words express the leap from the dryness of *Stereo*, in 1969, to the wetness of *Crimes of the Future*, in 1970. This is a much more vibrant, sleazy and oddly humorous film. It makes perfect sense that the two would play as a double feature, as both center on casts of attractive, listless young people wandering the concrete hallways and enclosed courtyards of shadowy research institutes that may be fronts for deeper conspiracies; both feature emphatic yet untrustworthy voiceover narration in place of diegetic line delivery; and both delve into the complexities of devious group research projects, in which (as ever) the young are the guinea pigs of the old. In this way, both are also precursors to 1979's *The Brood*, the supreme expression of Cronenberg's fascination with psychiatric research institutes and the charismatic, megalomaniacal doctors who run them.

The presence of red blood here, however, signifies more than just the leap from B&W to color. It signifies a move downward in the body, from the artistically and narratively cerebral *Stereo* to something much more, well, venereal. Gone is the focus on cybernetic telepathy, replaced by foot fetishes, gynecological experimentation, a dubious puberty-induction method, the growth and dissection of new organs, a pedophile ring and all manner of parasitic, blood-borne infection, leading to both sexual obsession and death. While Cronenberg's fully-fledged body horror breakthrough didn't occur until 1975's *Shivers*, this is definitely a sizable step toward it, away from the austerity of *Stereo*, which, by comparison, feels like a Canadian *Last Year at Marienbad*.

Returning to the path of Brundle's transformation in *The Fly*, we've now reached the point where he's shed the last of his gangly, brainy awkwardness and realized his grotesque, untapped sexual potency, sweaty and hairy rather than dapper and withdrawn. Here, Cronenberg has, like Brundle, "penetrated society's sick grey fear of the flesh." In the best possible way, he's passed the point of no return.

Having passed this point, *Crimes of the Future* is not only charged with blood and sex, but also with a new form of humor, which would flow throughout Croneberg's subsequent work. *Crimes* is not hilarious, of course, but it plays with the strangeness of its subject matter in a less earnest and more satirical vein, never letting on to what degree it takes its concepts seriously, pushing viewers into the productive discomfort of having to decide for themselves. Here, the film leaves the philosophical conundrums of *Stereo* behind to plunge instead into the "scummy aquarium" that *Transfer* introduced.

I think it's always telling to see where in a serious artist's career the possibility of *fun* enters the mix, because this tends to be at the cusp point between the earnestness of youth, when the idea of art being fun is an insult to your ambition (unless I'm only speaking for myself here), and the beginning of early maturity, when you realize that life is short and, if pursuing the absurd calling of art isn't fun, then there really isn't any point (becoming known and respected certainly won't make you immortal). Maybe this is also the moment when you realize that you're not going to solve any of humanity's eternal conundrums, so you might as well enjoy the process of playing around with them for as long as you can. Raw ambition is necessary to get off the ground, but, after a certain point, only sincere enjoyment will keep you going.

This shift toward fun and funniness dovetails with visual references to 70s crime films as well (the first half of the film's title), with its many secret meetings in hallways and dapper young intellectuals opening fire with machine guns, to move Cronenberg's overall project in a more political, more populist and more provocative direction.

Even though this film, like *Stereo*, takes place almost entirely inside cloistered and cordoned off spaces—in interiors that only lead to other interiors, as Joseph Vogl points out about *Videodrome* later in this book—it feels much more open, both within its own narrative conceit and, most importantly, open to the future (the second half of the title) as well. 2022's *Crimes of the Future* isn't a remake, but it's clear that this film has a special place in Cronenberg's heart, and it isn't hard to see why.

CRIMES OF THE FUTURE, BLASTS FROM THE PAST

Graham Rae

Cosmetics have been accused of many things throughout the ages: ageing or irritating tender sensitive skin. Sexualising young girls way too early. Causing cute fluffy bunnies to have health problems when tested upon the poor wee cruelly blinded Thumpers. Turning death metal freaks into Norwegian church-burning heretics. Making Egyptian mummies look like prime necrophilia material to already-misguided grave-robbers. And, sickest and worst of all, making Eddie Izzard look sexually attractive to men who have had one over the eight(een).

But has there ever been anybody who has accused makeup—pure, innocent, features-enhancing simple makeup—of maybe(l-line) being one of the max factors behind killing off all the sexually mature women in the world?

Well yes, one man *has* actually made that accusation, now that you mention it. Who, you frowningly ask? Well the subject of this book, David Cronenberg, of course. Who else would come up with this kind of stuff?

Crimes of the Future (1970, 63 minutes, $30,000) is the film in question. The name of the film comes from a poem read by the writer protagonist in a movie adaptation of the Knut Hamsun novel *Hunger*. Set in 1997, *Crimes* manages to be as accurate in its ragged, dirty prophecies about the societal concerns of that long-passed year as *Escape From New York* (1981), also set in that year, was.

Crimes brings us the androgyny-slinging, murderous-cosmetics case of Adrian Tripod (played by the Canadian fey gay Cronenberg regular Ronald Mlodzik), a rudderless lady painter adrift on a blusher-free sea now that the major makeup market has dried up and gone underground permanently.

Tripod has now moved into the dermatology field and, whilst

trying to avoid plastic surgery disasters at his flesh-remodelling institution The House of Skin (which sounds like some softcore porno Max Renn would have screened on his charnel channel in *Videodrome*), a patient of his has died.

Distraught, he's checked himself into a house of brain remodelling, or a "laughing academy," as it's technically known. He's looking for his tormented mentor Antoine Eyeshadow (wait a minute—checks notes—not Eyeshadow, *Rouge*—fundamental cosmetic nomenclature mistakes like this are the reason I look horrendous at *Rocky Horror Picture Show* midnight screenings), who has disappeared off into the wild blue yonder when the bottom dropped out of his beautifying world. Cos when the simple, life-sustaining joys of eyebrow pencil scribbling are gone...what else is left for a man to do but disappear off into the foundational void for a wee existential rethink?

Tripod roams around places like the Metaphysical Import-Export and the Oceanic Podiatry Group, who, despite its chip-shop-sounding name, deals in the evolving feet of humans, not in fish fingers. To emphasise this (de-) evolutionary point, dolphin clicks and squeaks and squeals put in an aural appearance at this point in the film; rumour has it that an opportunist Cronenberg made use of the vocal talents of the washed-up cetacean Flipper, of 60s children's show fame, paying him in fish for his contribution to the soundtrack. Tripod seems quite happy fondling evolving feet-cum-fins. It's always the quiet, glinty-eyed dermatologists that you have to watch.

At one point Tripod comes across a guy whose body has started growing strange external organs (the only element the 2022 *Crimes of the Future* shares with its 1970 incarnation), and this is the first time we get a glimpse of the director's ongoing future "creative cancer" (as the disease is described) aesthetic mentioned in many of his later films.

Eventually, after much head-scratching, confusion-inducing, quasi-scientific, sorta-futuristic psycho-babbling, Tripod comes to suspect, through telepathy, that Rouge is dead. Inconsolable, he finds himself in tow with a group of paedophiles, as you do, and discovers that they have accelerated the puberty of a five-year-old lassie to try and impregnate her so as to restock the female of the species.

Tripod finds out that the scummy group wants him to be the man to do the job, but, thankfully, he can't go through with it. The lassie starts to secrete a substance that has, in the past, signified the death of the mature female, pouring from her pores. Accelerating this tiny girl to puberty has, it turns out, rendered her susceptible to the same disease that killed off the rest of her sex.

Scooping some from the girl's hand and tasting the noxious, gelatinous body batter, Tripod starts to cry blue tears, realising that the girl is the reincarnation of Rouge, that the disease has jumped to affecting men as well as women, and that he is going to die. Which would probably be a good thing in a world as bereft of hope and sexually mature fanny as the one conjured up in this film.

That is basically the plot of *Crimes of the Future*. Not much else you can say after an ending like that. Like the scene of a very young girl kissing a man and passing a parasite into his mouth in *Shivers*, Cronenberg was just trying to push shocking buttons with this (extremely) underage sex riff.

Crimes is a companion piece to the director's previous effort, *Stereo* (1969), his first foray into almost-feature-length filmmaking. Both are very similar in some ways: they were shot silent, to avoid the noise of the 35mm (an expensive shooting medium) Arriflex camera, with a voiceover inserted to explain the plots. Both were filmed amongst the ugly brutalist architecture of the University of Toronto, which looks more like a re-education camp, or Ballardian high rise wet dream, than a place of conventional education. Both have the same lead actor in Ronald Mlodzik (who has an English accent for some reason), who does a lot of walking round looking meaningful and beleaguered in both features. And both have ideas explained in place of filming them, as befits the small budgets.

Crimes thankfully cuts back on the dense verbal thickets of pseudo-scientific, semi-satiric, impenetrable, interminable terminology of its predecessor. But *Stereo* at least had female nudity in its favour, and no male flipper-foot-fetishism, so it's give with one hand, take with the other. The filming of *Crimes* in colour, though, is a welcome addition to the overall monochrome atmosphere of its predecessor, which looked like a 1950s prison rehab film, all ugly grey educational building chunks.

The Canadian Broadcasting Corporation televisual short following *Crimes of the Future*, *Secret Weapons* (1972), was to be the end of the first phase of David Cronenberg's career. When he returned in 1975 with *Shivers*, he came back with a gory bang, all splatter and sexuality, guns blazing blood and semen and mutation. The underground, somewhat pretentious, non-commercial hue of his early educational, mistake-making, craft-sculpting student films was long gone.

But these four films—*Transfer* (1966), *From The Drain* (1967), *Stereo*, and *Crimes*—shared, along with *Weapons*, the seeds of pretty much everything the man's maverick oeuvre would come to be associated with, the obsessions he would return to time and again: malevolent scientists, strange drugs, frontier psychiatry, electroconvulsive therapy, dubious government and underground revolutionary groups, mutating flesh, aberrant sexuality, brain operations, and outlandish philosophy.

The aesthetic crimes of his future cinema would have twin inspirational figures, one a rogue scientist, and one a Canadian writer. Pretty much what you would expect, given that these were the obsessions of a man who dropped out of studying science, and into studying English, before getting permanently into film.

Donald Ewen Cameron (1901 – 1967) was an eminent Scottish-born psychiatrist who, after zigzagging between working, studying, and graduating in Scotland, America, and Switzerland, finally ended up in Montreal. He held prestigious titles throughout the years, like the President of the American Psychiatric Association, the Canadian Psychiatric Association, and the World Psychiatric Association.

The Vision and Mission Statement for the Society of Biological Psychiatry, which he was also one-time President of, states that their mission is, amongst other things, to:

"Promote excellence in research investigating the nature, causes, mechanisms, and treatments of disorders of thought, emotion, and behaviour."

This was only one of the myriad elements of mental health treatment that Ewen Cameron (as he was best known) fell down on because, well, he was a complete and utter sadistic and brutal lunatic, like a real-life version of Dr. Benway from *Naked Lunch*.

And it seems to me that his vile, hippocampus-razing atrocities were a major early thematic influence on the work of David Cronenberg. Cameron started off as a critically lauded psychiatrist who wanted to rid the world of mental illness, a lofty and laudable ambition, and ended up being known in some circles as the Scottish Josef Mengele, after the insane Nazi doctor. From revered doctor to Angel of Braindeath is not exactly an ostentatious career arc, but Ewen Cameron certainly earned it.

In 1943, the psychiatrist was invited to McGill University in Montreal, becoming the founding director of the Allan Memorial Institute, a mental hospital on the University's grounds. The gothic, baroque building was isolated and, a few years after opening as a supposed therapeutic institution, it rang with the screams and cries of the deranged psychiatrist's patients-cum-victims.

Ordinary members of the public would send loved ones to the Allan to be treated for various mental illnesses, minor and major. It was said that Cameron did very well with so-called "talking cures," where he simply talked to patients, establishing an emotional transference bond. This, coupled with his starstruck patients and staff regarding him as a sort of psychiatric superstar in the making, worked very well.

And this might have been the end of it, and never led to a much more sinister phase of his once-illustrious career, had it not been for the much darker turns his 'therapeutic' methods took. Cameron started putting people into insulin-induced comas in a 'sleep room' for sometimes up to sixteen hours a day, three weeks at a time, playing them looped tape recordings with distressing messages. He was trying to establish what he called 'depatterning,' or basically erasing the bad memories—indeed all memories—that had led his unsuspecting, trusting victims to mental illness. The wiped memory of the tabula rasa victim could then be replaced with healthy images, using a pseudo-scientific practice known as 'psychic driving.'

Other psychopathic charlatan practices included sensory deprivation, performing lobotomies, food deprivation, and injecting victims with curare and liquid LSD, all in the search for the elusive Holy Grail of eliminating mental illness forever. His deranged Frankensteinian methods damaged many lives, leaving some victims infantilised, incontinent, sucking their thumbs, amnesiac. Some were confined to mental institutions for the rest of their lives, while others had severe trouble on theoutside, away from the brutality they had suffered in the Allan. All in all, the results of these horrifying experiments with the human brain were the antithesis of the mad scientist's stated therapeutic goals.

At the height of Cold War paranoia, the CIA took an interest in Cameron's Grand Guignol cerebral machinations during the Korean War, when American soldiers would come back spouting communist propaganda and anti-capitalist rhetoric. Vowing to fight this commie brainwashing, the CIA, with a head torturer conveniently based outside the United States, financed Cameron's experiments in "artificial telepathy" (or "beneficial brain-washing," as a crowing, collaborative media called it) to use for their own nefarious needs, in an operation named MKULTRA. Cameron ultimately resigned from the Allan Institute in ignominy in 1964, and died three years later.

Nevertheless, the torture methods established by Cameron are still used to this day in war hotspots round the globe, on all sides, so, when American soldiers are tortured in foreign countries, it could be said that the country is basically reaping what it sowed (with financial help from the Canadian government of the time) during those covert, shady Cold War years.

If we consider the skull-puncturing-and-suturing methods outlined above—shady government institutions, malevolent mad scientists, brainwashing and attempted telepathy, experimental drugs, hunted and ruined patients—it seems eminently logical to me to see Ewen Cameron's long shadow cast across many of the films of David Cronenberg's career, especially as both men were operating their experiments in Canada.

It could be argued that the paranoid, cynical, governmental and medical tropes in the films come from a chaotic time in North American history during the late 60s and early 70s, basically the Vietnam War era, with revolutionary groups like the Weather Underground standing in for some of the underground rebel groups in the films, and nobody trusting the government. This is certainly true enough, but I think a cursory glance at 1981's *Scanners* might prove to be salutary.

The script for *Scanners* had existed since the early 1970s in the form of a script called *Telepathy 2000* (1), which makes it more of an early 70s film than an early 80s one, at least in terms of its main concerns and themes. The main scanner (hunted, haunted people who can control minds and machinery telepathically), played by Stephen Lack, is named... Cameron Vale. Dubious scientist Dr. Paul Ruth (Patrick McGoohan) ties Vale to a bed and gives him a shot of the experimental drug ephemerol, to stop the "voices in his head."

The shady corporate governmental entity in the film, ConSec, is run by a man named Trevellyan (Mavor Moore), who bears more than a passing physical resemblance to the Scottish psycho-scientist. ConSec wants to capture the scanners and harness their telepathic abilities, as the corporation deals in international security, weaponry and private armies. Vale is described as "weak—very weak" in the film by ConSec operative Keller (Lawrence Dane) to Revok (Michael Ironside), just as Ewen Cameron called those with mental problems "the weak."

And at the end of the film, when Vale and Kim Obrist (Jennifer O'Neill) are trying to escape the clutches of ConSec, they run into two armed guards. Vale controls their minds, making one of them see his mother instead of the scanner, so that he doesn't shoot. In Ewen Cameron's twisted world, some of the poor people damaged by his sick brain mutilation likewise came to mistake their interrogators for their parents.

Only David Cronenberg himself will know exactly to what degree Ewen Cameron has been any kind of influence, conscious or otherwise, on his work, but it's clearly a possibility.

One inarguable influence on the work of the director, however, is his now-deceased (I could find no record of birth and death dates online, unfortunately) father, "rabid bibliophile" (2) Milton Cronenberg, who was the benevolent scientific, creative yin to Ewen Cameron's malevolent, destructive yang.

Cronenberg Sr. was the one-time Vice President of P.R. and Business Communications Limited, Toronto. He was also a journalist, an eclectic stringer who wrote about subjects as diverse as stamp collecting, the financial world, and true crime cases, for publications ranging from the *Toronto Telegram* to the *American Gas Association Monthly*.

He also wrote for *Liberty Magazine*, touted as "the second greatest magazine in America," after the *Saturday Evening Post,* circulation-numbers-wise, with *Liberty* having sales in the millions. Whatever the exact circulation truth, it shows that the writer was being published in the 40s alongside literary giants like Pulitzer Prize-winning William Saroyan, so was obviously operating at a high freelancing level.

Cronenberg Sr. also edited *True Canadian Crime Stories*, a lurid magazine with contents self-evident from its title, and he had a neat sideline in writing true crime short stories and articles for magazines like *Famous Crime Cases* and *Big Detective Cases*. His articles had lurid pulp titles like 'Toronto's 'Double Cross' Death' and 'Death For $100.' Archived issues of the latter magazine reside at the University of Huddersfield in England, with the website warning that "...these records contain sensitive and graphic information and photographs about crimes." You can only idly wonder what horrific visual and textual anti-treats may potentially have been laying round the Cronenberg household when young David was growing up.

However, one medium which would prove to be very headspinfluential on David Cronenberg's nascent philosophical and aesthetical musings was science fiction. The director often talks of growing up in a very literary household, with books lining the walls. It's pretty much guaranteed that there were science fiction books and magazines lying around as David was growing up.

This will have been in no small part due to his father. In 1947, Cronenberg Sr. published a fascinating, mindset-revelatory article entitled 'Science Fiction—More Fact Than Fiction.' This piece appeared in the Canadian publication *Magazine Digest*, founded in 1930, which was a venue that published mostly technical and scientific material.

Whilst any freelance journalist worth their salt will pimp and pump out ideas all the time on any subject known to man, purely to keep the rent paid, the tone and tenor of this article are different. It basically encapsulates a brief history of science fiction and its predictions, fandom, the major science fiction novelists publishing at the time, messages in their work, and the future of the literary subgenre. It's an incredible amount of beginner's guide to cram into one piece, but the journalist tries gamely.

Cronenberg Sr. interviews John W. Campbell, whose novella *Who Goes There?* was turned into a gloopy, splattery, science-and-body-horror film by John Carpenter in 1982, renamed *The Thing*. At the time, Campbell was also the editor of the seminal SF journal *Astounding Science Fiction*, which had a million readers a month. The article relays a tale of how Campbell got a visit from military intelligence in March, 1944, after a Manhattan Project scientist read a short story in *Astounding Science Fiction* talking about atomic warfare.

Really, though, the interview with Campbell seems more like a broadside by Cronenberg Sr. to distance his beloved literary genre from any accusations of being juvenile "screwball literature" (a pejorative he sneers at), arguing that it was, rather, a fully-fledged adult art form of the mid-20th-century.

The names of top science fiction writers like Robert Heinlein, E.E. "Doc" Smith, L. Sprague de Camp, E.E. van Vogt and L. Ron Hubbard ("A navy man who has had more real-life adventures than ten average men") are dropped. The "top men of science" pedigrees of SF writers are discussed—MIT grads, famous rocket experts, solar specialists and world authorities on astronomy, etc, to show the genre's hard-won educational and factual credentials. This is far from the "cops-and-robbers stories transplanted to Mars and the characters outfitted with death-ray guns" Cronenberg Sr. derides here.

"Hiroshima made science fiction respectable," the journalist intones gravely. The whole underpinning message of the impatient article is that *science fiction isn't just for kids anymore, dammit!* The piece is part literary defence, part journalism, and part gushing fandom zine-swoon. Clearly the man had a scientific, rational mind and enjoyed reading science fiction, taking it very seriously indeed. "Science fiction is here to stay," says Campbell, at the end of the article. "If science fiction gives us a few jolts, it has served its purpose."

I think it's safe to say that the medium had given Milton Cronenberg more than a few jolts. In this article he was surely trying to pass along the favour, which he definitely did to his director and writer son.

Handed down from father to son, writing is literally in David Cronenberg's blood: "I can't remember not writing. I can't remember not expressing myself. I wrote my first novel when I was ten years old. It was three pages long. As far as I was concerned, that was a novel. So that was very natural to me," he's said. (3) I would imagine that the mortgage-paying, rattle-clatter-batter of his dad's typewriter, present since his birth, would have implanted itself very deeply on the child, and some of the typewriting scenes in *Naked Lunch* would not have been alien to him at all. Given his father's science fiction fandom, and his own precocious writing talents, Cronenberg nearly having a short story published at sixteen in The Magazine of Fantasy and Science-Fiction really comes as no surprise at all.

In 1963, whilst studying literature at the University of Toronto, Cronenberg won the Epstein Award in Creative Writing. It's a prestigious nationwide competition, open to anyone attending a Canadian university, and competition would have been fierce.

As has been well documented, it's at university that the writer-director began his film career, after figuring that anything he wanted to do in literature had already been done better by people like Nabokov and Burroughs, two of his main influences whose voices he couldn't transcend in his own written work, so why even enter the field?

However, Cronenberg considering this career path was not so alien from his always-bubbling writing yearnings; he has said many times that he wanted to be an "obscure novelist." After all, he had to write his own screenplays a lot of the time. And it could be argued that, in *Naked Lunch* and *Crash* (an absolute horror film for a car-lover like the director), he was rewriting, through film, two seminally transgressive and dangerous novels he himself would like to have written. "I certainly did get derailed by film," (4) he once noted, about his directorial-versus-wannabe-novelist duties.

If, as J.G. Ballard once said, the order books are written in is not necessarily the order they belong in, then Cronenberg pulled a similar trick with his artistic careers, putting the directing cart before the writing horse. I don't think it's any accident that he waited until 2014, when both Ballard and Burroughs were dead, to bring out his own first novel, *Consumed*, so he could finally step out of their long literary shadows. Burroughs himself never took up painting until his great friend, the painter Brion Gysin, had passed away, either. Too much chance of not being good enough, or of your admired friend and artistic inspiration not liking your work; not good for the creative ego.

Having said this, Cronenberg's son Brandon must have nerves and balls of steel, putting out sci-fi horror films like *Antiviral* (2012) and *Possessor* (2020) whilst his father is still working in the field.

However, even away from shyly and slyly avoiding literary criticism and competition, there was one career-long, ever-elongating, fat, spreading mushroom cloud shadow that David Cronenberg never fully stepped out of, that of the aforementioned Milton. Having helped shape his son's creative urges with his own love of science fiction in particular and of reading and writing in general, his father's lingering death from leukemia had an equally devastating effect on the young writer-director.

"Later, when my father died, I did feel haunted. I really understood what haunting is all about. I would hear phrases and words that he would use and it felt that if I just turned around, he would be there. I would wake up in the morning and feel that I was him. I sat up in bed the way he did. It was very eerie. It was partly my attempt to deny he was dead, to become him." (4) It's difficult to imagine a starker example of self-identification with somebody else, an inspiration, a loved one, especially with regard to his writer side mentioning words and phrases his father would use, and the horrifying identity crisis confusion caused by their slow and painful death in front of you.

Milton's heart-breaking form of leukemia caused his bones to break if he rolled over in bed. I can't help feeling that the trauma of his healthy-minded, ruined body tearing itself apart must've influenced the body horror in his son's films, though to what degree is anybody's guess. The director's philosophy about loving cancerous mutations, the excitement of new bodies and new organs, seems to me a way to fuse his own conflicted feelings over fleshy ruination, love and death, examining them on film to create a grim and beautiful and scary form of art.

Disturbing musings on so-called 'creative' cancers tearing bodies apart and 'new flesh' sprouting in the human brain don't just come from nowhere.Another dark-minded, art-horror auteur, *Nekromantik* (1987) director Jörg Buttgereit, wove the early, painfully lingering deaths of his parents into his own no-holds-barred, notorious, flesh-loathing existential films for much the same reason.

In the right hands, from tragedy sometimes comes philosophical poetry, dark and distressing as it may be. And in those hands, it doesn't matter if the medium is film or paper; the medium is not always the message, to paraphrase another Cronenberg inspiration, Marshall McLuhan. And David Cronenberg can ultimately think himself lucky: he went on to imprint his unique worldview on not one medium, but two. And it's always better to become an obscure novelist later on, because starving artists often starve to death. Which was never to be this particular writer-director's artistic fate, thankfully.

(1) Cronenberg on Cronenberg, 1992, edited by Chris Rodley, P85.
(2) Cronenberg on Cronenberg, 1992, edited by Chris Rodley, P2.
(3) Cronenberg on Cronenberg, 1992, edited by Chris Rodley, P4.
(4) 'David Cronenberg's Consuming Obession,' September 2014, Geoff Pevere, Quillandquire.com.

Special thanks for research purposes go to:
Alan Zipkin, www.derringerbooks.com
Phil Stephensen-Payne, www.philsp.com
Rodrigo Baeza

CRIMES OF THE FUTURE

Brian Evenson

I.

I have been here for some time. I do not know how long they were following me but they did it with such deftness that by the time I realized they were there all I could do was increase my stride, walk faster across the lawn and then, when it became clear the three of them were on the verge of cornering me, break into a full-scale run. I had made it halfway over the wall when one of them, an Adrian Tripod by name, leapt high enough to grab my ankle. I tried my best to kick him off, managed to strike him in the face and send his glasses askew, but the fellow, despite his anemic, severe look, despite his delicate smoky glasses, had more strength than one would have supposed. A moment later one of the others, a bushy-haired man whose name either escapes me or which I was perhaps never given, had clambered onto the shoulders of the third and final man. Together, he and Tripod succeeded in pulling me down off the wall.

The strange thing was that they seemed to believe that they knew me. They did not know me—how could they, since I did not know them? *Antoine*, they kept on calling me, as they stroked my shoulders, stroked the top of my head, trying to soothe me, propelling me along. I cannot, it is true, remember what my name is, but I am certain it is not Antoine. *Monsieur Rouge* one of them called me, the one with the limp, but how he had the impression that I spoke French I cannot say. I do not speak French, I never have. All this was, I was sure, either a case of mistaken identity, or, more likely, a means of putting me off balance, a means of manipulating me.

They were at once forceful yet strangely solicitous, as if they wanted to hurt me a little bit but not too much, not permanently. Just enough to remind me of who was in charge. Mostly they wanted to bring me somewhere. But where? A place I had never seen before, or at least had no memory of seeing before.

By this time, Tripod had reaffixed his glasses properly. He proceeded before us with a strange jerky gait, his hands clasped behind his back, his coat billowing out around his legs. We followed behind the fellow, one man grasping my left arm so firmly that it began to ache, the other similarly grasping my right. Together they propelled me relentlessly, achingly forward.

"I am not supposed to be here," I claimed. "There has been a terrible mistake."

"No mistake, doctor," said Tripod without turning to look at me. "You belong with us."

"I'm a sick man, a very sick man," I said, though whether this was true or not, I could not in actuality say. It is enough to say that I felt it *could* be true as I spoke it.

This time he did turn. "We are all sick, doctor," he said. "Unto death," he said. "And perhaps well beyond." He smiled sadly, and then swiveled his head back around. He did not look my way again until after we had arrived.

II.

We passed along a gully constructed in concrete, and from there mounted a grassy verge to the side of a building. We sidled along a concrete ledge, stepping through a window into a building which seemed to have once belonged to a university. Perhaps it still did—if so neither the students nor faculty were in session. Everything was empty, deserted.

We were first in a room which seemed to be an office of some sort, though in disarray, papers scattered everywhere. I was told not to touch anything, that all was very carefully organized despite all appearance to the contrary. "Your work is not here, Doctor Rouge," suggested Tripod.

"I am *not* a doctor," I told him. "My name is not Rouge. I do not speak French."

"Ah, doctor," he said. "How soon we forget."

He led us in a careful line across the small room, through

the mounds of papers and out into the hallway proper. The hallway was concrete and brick, brutalist: the sort of building that ruthlessly asserted itself and made those who were forced to be inside feel oppressed. It made me anxious. Tripod either was not anxious himself or was so good at hiding his anxiety that I could not perceive it.

We walked farther down the hall than I thought it possible to walk in a building of even exceptional size. Abruptly, Tripod stopped before a door.

"Ah," said Tripod. "Here we are."

He reached out and placed his hand on the handle. But it proved locked. This did not deter Tripod. He extracted a key from his pocket and opened it.

"After you, doctor," he said, and bowed.

The men holding my arms propelled me forward and hurled me inside. I fell sprawling to the floor and by the time I managed to regain my feet the door had been closed again. As I reached for the handle, the key turned crisply in the lock.

I pounded on the door, demanding to be let out. This demand went unheeded.

"We've left you your notebook," said Tripod. "And a handful of pens. You'll find them on the third bookshelf from the right."

I looked around fully for the first time and realized I was in a large supply cabinet of some kind, the space lit by a pale exposed bulb, with a pull-string dangling beside it. Most of the shelves were empty, but a few were littered with scattered possessions: a red rubber ball, a shoe, a vial of milky fluid, a pair of lacy women's underwear. And there, on the third bookshelf from the right, was the notebook, just as Tripod had promised.

I picked up the notebook. "What am I to do with this?" I called through the door.

"Fill it," said Tripod. "Describe the event. Once you are done slide it under the door."

"What event?"

But he and the others were already gone.

III.

I paced back and forth. I canvassed the shelves for foodstuffs but found nothing. I pounded again on the door and asked to be let out. I was not let out.

After that, for many hours I simply lulled, did nothing at all. I slept.

When I became very hungry indeed, I began to write.

Or would have had the notebook not already been partly filled.

Instead, what I did was to read.

I read, on the first page, in all capital letters, *HOUSE OF SKIN*.

A few pages further on, I read, *To be released, I have been told I must describe the event. And yet how can one describe that which is by any measure beyond description?* Here, with the script hurried and easy, rather than stiff and artificial as it was with the all capitals, I felt there was something about the hand that I recognized. This hand was not, I would go so far as to say, unfamiliar to me.

I read, *My former difficult patient now welcomes me with open arms.* Perhaps this was the event that had been alluded to? Or perhaps not.

I read, *Provocative spheres: aquaria. Perverse multidimensional images.* I had no context for understanding these fragments, or if they were even meant to be understood.

And then, halfway through, the writing trailed off and ended. *My feet and legs are most unpredictable*, he had written, and then he had ended there, on the word unpredictable, the e trailing away. Those were the last of his words—though if I am being honest with myself I do not know for certain that the person who had filled the pages of the notebook was a *he*. I can only say that something about the handwriting made me think it was likely, but perhaps this is as much a function of my prejudice as it is an indication of anything actual.

I say it was the last of his words, but in saying this I am not being entirely truthful. Written inside the back cover with a different, smeary pen was the name *Antoine Rouge*.

I stared at the name. Did it ring a bell? If it did, this bell rang at such a distance that it could not be heard where I stood.

I was still staring when I heard a gentle tapping at the door.

"Doctor," said Tripod, his voice partly muffled by the wood so that it sounded as if it were coming from a great distance. "Doctor, we're waiting." I could see now the tips of his fingers pushing their way through the crack of the door, as if expecting to be handed the notebook. After a long moment they withdrew. Holding my breath, I heard his footsteps recede down the hall.

IV.

After much thought, I reluctantly determined there to be only one path forward. With deliberation, I tested each pen on the inside back cover of the notebook, drawing a series of lines, one below the other, all below the name Antoine Rouge. When I had found the pen whose line least resembled the line of the pen that had been used to write in the notebook proper, I decided this was the pen I would use.

I went to the last page, and after *My legs and feet are most unpredictable*, I added a period. I poised my pen, ready to write, but I hesitated. *What if,* I worried, *my handwriting was proved exactly the same as that which was already in the notebook?* That would, I knew, be terrible. But even more terrible still: what if it was different?

In the end, I pulled the string connected to the lightbulb and switched off the light. Just enough light comes from beneath the edge of the door for me to see the outline of the notebook, but not enough for me to be able to scrutinize the words in it, let alone determine the character of the handwriting. I have written all of this in just this way, in the dark, and have no intention of reading it.

In just a moment I will finish this page. Then I will close the notebook, place it on the floor, and slide it under the door. I will leave it to you to look at the handwriting and tell me: did the same man write everything in this book, or have you mistaken me for another? If the latter, I demand you allow me to leave this place. If the former, I beg you to tell me why can I not remember who I am?

And so in a moment, I will wait, my ear pressed to the door to see if I can hear the feathery turning of the pages as you read these words. I will hold my breath and wait for your verdict, wait for you to tell me who I am.

COMMUNICATION

(Film treatment)

Blake Butler

Film rolling inside a VHS tape

Room with mirror-lined walls, greatly over-lit, smoke in the room

Double or triple exposure of night sky, so that many moons appear to split out of 1

Black paint being poured over a person

Long hair

Shitloads of telephones

A front lawn on fire

A young boy looking into the mirror in a shabby room holding several knives

Pills, teeth

Windows

Mirror-lined room with one man standing in it shirtless, ratty pants, long hair, back to the camera, eventually raises up his arms

A body sleeping on a bed

Dirt

Mud

Maggots in food

A river flowing backwards

Clock hands backwards

Shitloads of dogs

Light bulbs shattering

A mouth with black lipstick eating ice cream while laughing

Flesh-colored putty

Hammers banging water

Flowers crushed under a machine

Wire being wrapped around a man's arm like a bracelet

Parking lot at the mall in broad day light

A person erasing a drawing of a young person, face first

More fire

A calendar with the year 2667 on it

Holes

Floating ash

Metal band holding their instrument but not playing, looking directly at camera

Melting cassette tapes

A U.S. flag being wrapped around a person's face

A black flag flying

A mirror burning

Screaming face without noise

A ton of people outside a church in the dark

Scalp being shaved up close

Up close on eyes

Mounds of ground beef

A pile of bodies on a bed

Milk with blood in it

Nails in the ground

Shaking sky

Shitloads of hands rubbing each other

Fruit against a belt sander

An empty movie theater playing no picture

Duct tape being forced across a female mouth

Mouth full of eggs

The moons again

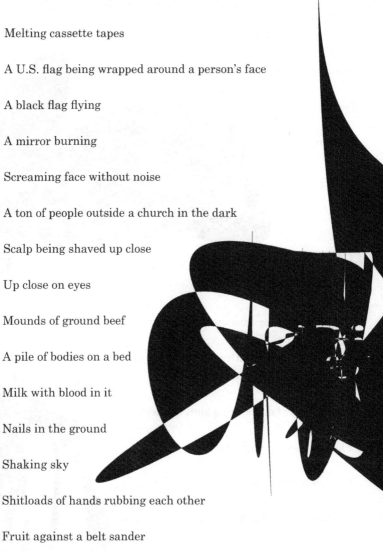

Smoke in the yard

Frantic sign language

Dozens of children

Pudding

Bodies

Pubes

Pigs

Too much light

Black cubes being arranged on a white table

Mirror-lined room with many people in it, many shirtless or naked, chaotic movement, smoke

Rapid shots of doors being shut and locked

Flowers covered with black paint

Ground beef burning

Metal band playing but no sound coming out

A pendulum

A grown man having his hair cut with shears

An orange sky upside-down

Melting chocolate creatures

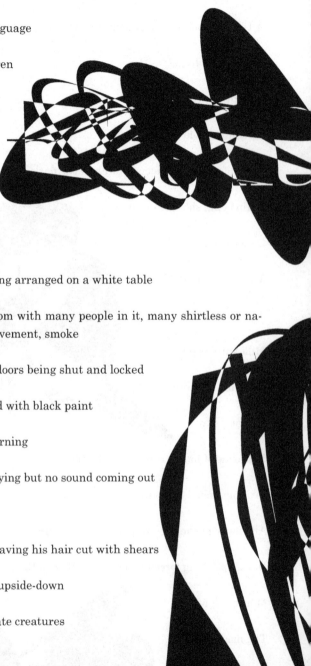

Burning books

Camera splitting a stairwell into many

Foam on a swimming pool or ocean

Someone underwater, bound

Black paint or blood poured on a carpet

A foaming mouth

Candles, crosses, telephones

Smoke over dark water

The many bodies in the mirror-lined room turn around to face the camera

Ice melting

Shaking color

A speaking mouth splitting to many mouths

An empty black room

Rain in reverse

An egg

A blood-colored dot

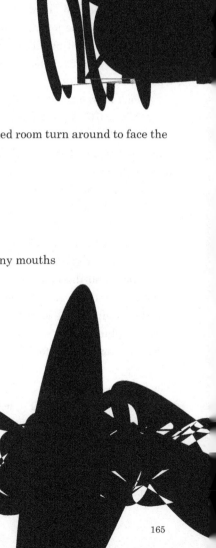

Heaven Help Us, Heaven Forgive Us

John Reed

His wife suggested they trade-in for a shorter fat man.

Of course, he'd already investigated that.

"What," she said, "now you're not talking to me?"

There would be a connection fee—the equivalent of about a year's worth of heating bills—and as it turned out, their fat man was only 5'4", not 5'6," and since 5'2" was the smallest model, the trade-in was pointless.

"Don't patronize me and I'll talk to you."

"Isn't he 5'6"? I think they come 5'2"."

J.T. didn't answer—walked into the kitchen and picked up an orange; citrus had been terrible for ten years, and all of a sudden, it was delicious.

His wife glared at him.

"I already investigated that," he managed.

"Well?"

"I don't want to explain myself."

After they argued, and he explained himself, she retracted her suggestion, and the problem of the fat man was once again unresolved, without even a notion of resolution, without even much chance of rising to the level of conversation. Like any young family—a daughter of two, a son of four—some conversation had to be foregone, some battles, forfeited.

The fat man had straight black hair, matted down in a Hitler bowl cut. J.T. attended the hairstyle himself. Twice a month, the serviceman dropped in to swab the fat man with a mild bleach solution. So the fat man was very, very pale.

J.T. brought him down a carton of pre-sliced white bread. Twelve loaves. On sale at the supermarket. The bread had no actual flour in it—mostly sugar and wood pulp—and some of the cartons were flattened, and others had been eaten into by mice. J.T. had taken the time to find a better carton, one in reasonably good condition, but when he got home he discovered there was a mouse hole in it after all.

The fat man reached into the box—pulled out a bag. With watery eyes and shaking hands, he unwound the tie. He spat on the slices and pressed the dough into fist-size balls, which he nibbled with his hands close to his face, as if by smallness he could diminish the problem.

Around his abdomen, the fat man's rolls had slackened into a single sheet. The fat man had cast aside his lap blanket, and J.T. was shocked at the sight of the fat man's legs—thin and atrophied, skin withered and unstretched, like an old balloon deflated.

"Oh my God," said J.T.. "Did your leg just move?"

Below the knee of one of the fat man's folded legs, J.T. had seen an ankle reposition itself, creased wet skin touching the air for the first time in—for the first time since J.T. and his family had moved in, four years before.

That flesh, pink and raw like an abrasion, had probably never touched air before. J.T. had always wondered if the serviceman swabbed the cracks.

"I just had an itch," said the fat man.

J.T. knew that was a bad sign. For the fat man to have any sensation at all in his epidermis—J.T. had read all about it. Not a good sign.

"You have nothing to worry about," said the fat man.

He hated that he had once played checkers with the fat man. He had once heard the fat man laugh.

J.T. didn't often vacation with his family.

Sitting on the porch, looking down into the misty valley, his children in the green grass, his wife at the bird feeder, doing something over there—all was right with the world. That the fat man was overheating the house—no cause for anxiety.

He, J.T., was a man. And the best thing about a man was his silence. His wife didn't understand: a man's work, a man's words, were his flesh.

All the effort, all the hours, day in day out, that the world sucked out of him. All that nature took in trade for a happy family, for checks with his name scrawled at the bottom. How could a woman, with all her cooing words of consolation for her children, ever understand that all a man really wanted was peace?

It wasn't like they'd said. The greenest grass was on his own side of the fence.

J.T. felt sick when he walked into the house—a perfect 68 degrees. Sick at his sternum, like he was simultaneously suffocating and throwing up.

The thermostat delivered the bad news; it had reset. From 45 degrees, the vacation setting, to 68 degrees, the "standard" setting. The fat man—for two weeks, the length of their vacation—had been subsisting on 2500 calories a day. Twenty-five hundred calories a day, at 45 degrees, was 1300 calories over the recommended allowance; J.T. had expected the fat man to put on seven to nine pounds. But at 68 degrees, the recommended allowance was well over 6000 calories; the fat man had lost close to 50,000 calories. J.T., grimacing like the bullet hit his groin, staggered to the basement door. Down the stairs—the steep wooden staircase—he held the rail and hoped.

And unbelievably, the fat man didn't look too bad.

The fat man lifted his head:

"I've been very inactive."

J.T. heard himself giggle—

"Good. Good."

J.T. heard his wife calling to him from the kitchen. She had the serious tone of voice that told him to ignore her.

Then, J.T. smelled pasta sauce—

"When did they start making marinara?" J.T. processed the data—open a can of tomatoes, cut up the basil, put the swill in the microwave, six minutes—there was no way all that had happened since they walked in the door.

"Oh that sauce was frozen," said the fat man. The frozen sauce J.T. remembered smelled like sage, not basil.

"That smells like puttanesca," said J.T..

The fat man shook his head no—

"Marinara."

"Jesus Christ," said J.T.. "You've been in the kitchen, haven't you?"

J.T. had always thought of the basement stairs as a last line of defense, but they had failed him.

"How the fuck did you get up the stairs?"

"I didn't walk." The fat man was pleading. "I crawled, I swear."

J.T.'s wife was calling him from the top of the stairs. She was asking about a second frozen tub of marinara.

"I'll be up in a minute," he said.

"I thought it's what you would have wanted," said the fat man. "I was ... I was wasting away."

J.T. called in the serviceman to see that the fat man had reconnected his vents properly.

"You've got an expensive problem," said the serviceman.

"Could I replace him with a dog?"

"Shoulda been a dog in the first place."

"Maybe I could pick up a unit and we could do something off the record."

"I'd like to help you out, but I can't do that."

"C'mon man, you see I got kids."

J.T. was reaching for his wallet.

"I'd like to help you out, but I'm not gonna take your money and do something that's not gonna work."

"You'd be a hero to me and my family."

"Listen, I'm being straight with you. A dog isn't gonna work. Not even a big dog. Their respiratory levels are just too low. All your vents, all your plumbing, it's way too big. You're not gonna have any pressure. You're just gonna have a warm basement."

"What about a woman?"

"Wish I could help ya, they don't come in females."

J.T. reached for the door handle; they still hadn't checked the fat man's valves.

"So we'd have to redo all the vents?"

"Yeah," said the serviceman. "I'll do it. Tear up the whole house, though."

J.T. opened the basement door, started in, but the serviceman kept standing there.

J.T. pulled five bills out of his wallet.

"There is maybe one thing I could do. I mean, I wish I could, but I can't risk my job."

J.T. peeled off three more bills. "You'd really be a hero."

J.T.

Every day, he walked, he drove, a piece of crap nobody cared about. At home, his wife talked to him about things he didn't want to talk about until, over the course of the week, he got so resentful she'd have to have sex with him.

J.T. and the serviceman knelt over the fat man. The serviceman held the syringe. He had pulled off the fat man's blanket and was holding the fat man's dimpled knee.

The serviceman had explained the "patch" to J.T.. The injection would destabilize any tissue within an inch of the tip of the needle. Bone, flesh, cartilage: to jelly.

"Oh my God, please, please," pleaded the fat man. "I won't walk again—I won't I never will I swear I swear to God."

The serviceman readied the syringe, plunged the needle into a vial and drew a viscous gray fluid into the barrel.

"Will I still be able to feel my legs? Not too far up the thigh, ok? Please. Please."

Like J.T., all the serviceman wanted was peace. His hand on the fat man's knee, he leaned forward and struck the needle into the fat man's temple. The tip of the needle sank in deep—into the middle of the fat man's brain. The fat man looked up with his watery eyes, his mouth parted, as the serviceman depressed the plunger.

"His expression will never change again," said the serviceman—

"It will just age."

Abstract Cruelty

David Roden

O'Blivion swivels impatiently in his baronial chair during Max's trite apology for erotic entertainment. The Already-Dead Professor wets his thin moustache.

Orange jumpsuits daub Rosa with an invitation camouflage of fish paste. The python's tail undulates to Bukkake rhythms as does the jungle girl/vore legend. Her soused head soon dangles from the eyeless abomination.

I watch all this in a public séance, glad to conform finally. We never watched ghost-porn at home, even after links were disseminated by worm.

You sat in an area of the theatre designated for the Cabal. This iconoclast bathes with us, interminably bored. Everything is operational and broken. With each transition, it became harder to acknowledge whatever we shared.

Narcissus hires surgeons to make him an art pâtisserie. He is superbly filleted for the injection of *crème anglaise*, sugar glazed into an adorable post-operative triumph!

You look rested—your whisper from the back row.

I see Rosa among his tasters, cream-filled mouth buzzing with knives.

I leave the theatre in an orderly ripple of souls. Behemoth's replacement is out there, assessing the threat weather. The driver sniffs and returns to the car.

Gulls remonstrate above the esplanade.

I too like to think that I am delicious. But then we heighten the sensation with the usual brand of magic (which I never claimed to understand).

Cut me. The scars waver in a thousand modal windows. She lifts the hair from her neck. *Cut me there, just a little.*

My parents became ludicrous meat products. I dab procreative ulcers while they honk and roll together. Later I stick lighted matches in my side. You can picture my relief.

Nicki, meanwhile, is concerned by the poor quality of the pirated tape but 'turned on' by its representation of a woman being flogged in a bare room with wet clay walls.

Early Blocs of code self-embed and later, self-assemble.

I love you to see me like this. Rosa lifts her hair above her neck. Max wants only what she wants. (This is how he paralyses his victims.)

Nicki lifts her hair. We never left that room. Yes, there is only one sexed wet room. I only want to touch you.

Nobody uses organs anymore.

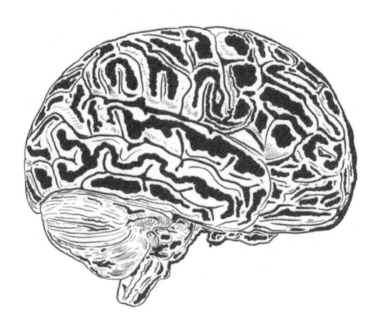

SECRET WEAPONS
(1972)
Starring: Charles Oberdorf, Lister Sinclair and Barbara O'Kelly

Kelso: While anthology drama appeared to have died an early death in the United States in the 1960s, Canada has continued to indulge and champion the medium to this very day. Unfortunately, its attitude towards its own broadcasting achievements remains muted and wilfully modest. Scripts and unlisted kinescopes from this period have been relegated to cardboard boxes in the dusty vaults of the CBC complex in Toronto. It's here that a number of interesting Cronenberg curios slumber unreleased. Almost deliberately erased.

Cronenberg remained busy in the 5-year spell between *Crimes of the Future* and *Shivers*, his next feature and first fulllength. One of his most significant efforts from this period was *Secret Weapons*, a short television movie for a CBC anthology series named *Programme X*, which featured experimental and low-budget work from rising talent in Canada. In this short, we see a young Cronenberg explore a burgeoning third space of existence: an alt-future, dystopian Canada. This liminal location allows Cronenberg to marry noir and arthouse cinema tropes, creating a landscape strewn with future drugs, quasi-psychoanalytical jargon and an opaque mythology surrounding a psychic war. The use of a liminal space leads us to believe that his intention was perhaps to create a sense of anomie in his characters (and indeed the viewer) by synthesising a post-industrial nightmare for them to occupy, a liminality that would be pivotal to later works.

In *Secret Weapons*, we see his imagination firing on all cylinders (well, almost)—the short runtime makes this feel like a halfbaked and underdeveloped concept, but it remains a mesmerising antique from the Baron of Blood nonetheless. We open to a reel of heady Moog-synth music[1] against a light-blasted forest. Fall,

---

[1] Music conducted by Canadian electronic band, Syrinx, active from 1970 to 1972. The group were considered pioneers of the national music scene musical owing to

1977 and North America toils in its 5th year of civil war. A fatalistic research scientist[2] has been summoned to the offices of General Pharmaceutics—an archetypal Cronenbergian conglomerate, stymieing insurgent factions who seek to question their righteous indomitability. The scientist previously helped develop a neuropsychopharmacological technique for depatterning a subject's brain and stimulating their desire for battle, reminiscent of the MKULTRA mind control experiments the CIA conducted before and during the Vietnam War.

The central conflict of the film is simple: will he relinquish the drug to his oppressive theocratic overlords or offer it over to the instruments of the uprising? But here he stands accused of sympathising with the insurgent faction as the imperious Mr Lee, played by early Cronenberg favourite, Ron Mlodzik, outlines the three stages of "hidden crime," engaging the protagonist in psychic judo.

"Do you believe in magic?"

"I believe in science, which is like magic."

The entire interrogation is being overviewed by an unseen figure who occasionally tickles Mr Lee lightly with a feather duster, as if to keep him on point, or to cast a deliberate and menacing shadow over both men. The research scientist is told he will be sent to an ominous retreat where he will turn over his research to the organisation. Our protagonist refuses and lights a filter from his deck of Lucky Strikes.

We discover that the Holy Police are masters of subtlety and persuasion… cue lots of incomprehensible mythologizing and arty wandering around warehouses, until the scientist hooks up with a motorcycle gang and eventually makes contact with the insurgent leader.

A film like *Secret Weapons* is interesting for several reasons. Let's think about the modern ailments of humanity—today's world is so utterly void of genuine jouissance that one is left almost to

their multi-genre inspirations.
2 Played by screenwriter, Norman Snider

curse their own damning surplus of consciousness. Of course, not everyone is awake to this terror. With the advent of mass communication systems, we are offered more opportunities for agential expression, yet this isolated state of existence is entirely manufactured to meet the whims of the mega-corps. This seems like an obvious observation, but it shows the resonant themes in Cronenberg's work and how astutely he utilised them throughout his career. Far from stimulating our mind for battle, as was the case in *Secret Weapons*, today's mass communication systems are intended as sedation. We are cocooned in a state of naïve realism, yet the objective remains the same—the conglomerate-led inertia of humanity.

The scientist in the film is reminiscent of an inverted-Oppenheimer. Having successfully created a weapon of total-destruction and relinquished his creation to the government, Oppenheimer was plunged into a state of regret and depression having played his part in the attrition of the species. The scientist in *Secret Weapons* refuses to relinquish his knowledge, no matter the consequence. He is the classic idealist hero.

Oppenheimer had to destroy the world before he about-turned and became an anti-atomic bomb activist—a move that by today's standards seems almost naïve in its sincerity. It's been decades since someone truly regretted having a negative impact on the world: such is the nihilism of digital-era capitalism.

Cronenberg was young and principled in 1972. He probably believed we would produce scientists like the one in *Secret Weapons* who would start-up their own conglomerates but with moral tenets and egalitarian underpinnings. Little did he know we remain doomed to occupy the contorted logic of a paradox, in which we'd come to believe we had no choice but to aid the shadow corps in the ongoing dismantling of our dignity.

Rice: Every Cronenberg film has proven prescient in its own way, but *Secret Weapons* is uniquely unnerving in its relevance to the maddened and maddening confluence of technology, Big Pharma, thought crime, and simmering rumors of civil war that we're dealing with today. The concept of drug companies merging with governments and purveyors of mind-altering technology to create a unified corporate state, against which a band of violent revolutionaries wages endless war, is the stuff of 70s science-fiction and, increasingly, 2020s reality. Never before in my lifetime has North America seemed as divided against itself as it does now, in an era where no communication travels without the intermediary of multi-billion-dollar companies that may or may not be government proxies, while one large chunk of the population views Big Pharma as our lone means of deliverance from a deadly pandemic, while another fears it's acting in league with the government and the mass media to propagate a Nazi-level program of medical experimentation and forced compliance. Add to this a rapidly spreading distrust of all traditional sources of cultural and moral legitimacy—not only science, media and government, but law, academia and mainstream entertainment as well—mix in a few hundred million guns, rampant inflation, psychotic profit motives in fanning every last flame within the discourse of a gigantic, lonely, and decentralized population, an accelerating loss of community and diminishing contact with anything resembling bedrock reality or trust in practical solutions to tangible problems, and a narrowing horizon of opportunity for all but the ultra-rich, and the stage does indeed appear set for a new civil war... even if, as one also suspects, this too is nothing but an elaborate psyop, yet another scam coughed up by a culture that values nothing above the inalienable right to scam everyone, all the time.

What's most provocative about this situation—as I write in early 2022—is the way in which, as in a Philip K. Dick story, time feels out of joint. The zeitgeist feels at once *post* and *pre*, as if we were living in the aftermath of an event that has not yet occurred. Every event that does occur feels like either a warning or an aftershock of something larger and more conclusive (an unrecorded psychic war, perhaps), which leads to a state of omnidirectional suspicion, as if everything and everyone were only a front for something else, either hiding a massive past event or promising a future "Big One" that will never arrive. This leads to the further suspicion that one's own thoughts cannot be treated as genuine, or even as necessarily *one's own*, a brand of paranoia that again syncs us up with the 70s, when *Secret Weapons*, along with so many other paranoid classics, such as *The Parallax View, The Conversation, All the President's Men,* and *Marathon Man*, emerged into the miasma that the Pentagon Papers and Watergate stirred up.

It must have seemed then, as it's again starting to seem now, that all mental activity was a property of the corporation, incepted through propaganda, drugs and the simple logic of saying and even thinking whatever it takes to avoid capture ("What are your opinions, or, shall we say, your beliefs about the work we do here?" asks the leader of the government program in *Secret Weapons*, to which our potential insurgent replies, "I believe whatever you do.") Indeed. If the 2020s are not the deranged reincarnation of the 1970s, then they are something even more sinister, about which I ought to stop writing before it's too late.

Category A

Michael Cisco

From out of the gloom and shade of the institute I climb back into the light of day, and presently onto busy streets filled with traffic and bustling pedestrians. I seem to be the only one without earbuds, or those comically large houseware headphones some people wear while they're out and about. Through the din of the cars and trucks, the blare of sirens and loudspeakers, acrid diesel exhaust, fried food...

I don't interact with anyone en route. I like it better that way. A silent driver. A smooth ride, adrift in the back of a huge black SUV, everything dim in the tinted windows, and then to the airport, the security checkpoint and the usual palaver there. The family car, the family helicopter, no insignia, but everyone gives you a wide berth. Everyone gets out of your way. We lurch into the sky. I watch a regular grid of streets jammed with all but motionless head and tail lights fall away and slide through space, before we roll out over an ocean of trees, dotted with concrete archipelagos ablaze with light.

There's ours.

With a curt nod and wave I disembark and walk through the cold toward the glass doors, rotor wind pummelling my back. The doors close behind me and all is silence, motionlessness, sterile freshness, tepid air. Something in me always expands to welcome institutional atmospheres. I warn myself against its relaxing influence; I'm not here to relax.

Nobody's around. I was told to expect that. Dr. Toland is their "keeper" and represents 25% of the permanent staff here, 18% of the total population. There's a groundskeeper-custodian named Boggs, Almanzar the nurse, Inoue the behaviorist die-hard who refuses to leave, and Toland. Now, with me here for the day, that's seven into one hundred is one and ten with three becomes thirty that's four with the one and how much left? Two? Twenty, nearly twenty-one which is three, so that makes me about 14.3% of the total population now. Here comes Toland. Together we'll make (stop) 28.6%.

She's not as impressive as I'd expected her to be. She's grizzled, tired, and walks with a swinging, stiff-legged gait.

I take the dry little hand she extends to me with a sigh.

"Mr. Pruit," she says, compressing her mouth. "I'm Dr. Toland."

"How're you doing," I say flatly.

"Could be worse," she says. Is that an attempt at raillery or is it that she doesn't care what I think? This would be the moment to ask me about my flight, my trip. She doesn't.

"Hang on," she says, pulling out her phone. She turns away for a moment.

"Yes this is Dr. Toland. I'm bringing a Mr. Pruit on site now. He's from Central."

A pause.

"To observe the administration of an experimental new drug for the A's. From Central. Yes, Pruit brought it himself ...?"

She turns to give me an interrogative look and I nod.

"Pruit brought it himself."

A moment later she rings off.

"All set. Shall we go?"

"No problem."

We wind through soothing concrete passageways beneath heavy panes of ghostly grey glass that show phantom trees silhouetted against a leaden sky. We pass one empty lab after another, all aglow with nice even fluorescent light, and fragrant with the smell of antiseptic, fresh stationery, the bone-dry dryness of the silky air. Dr. Toland leads me out through a side door into the wind and the cold, the thrashing pines.

"Storm coming," she says, scowling at the clouds.

"No doubt."

We round the back of the building and there's a ridiculous little cottage down below us, terraced into the slope, surrounded by bagged rose bushes and the remains of a garden battened down for the coming winter. A winding path takes us toward the tiny peaked roof with its toy chimney, and a shimmering pulse of alarm goes through me—they're *in there.*

Dr. Toland precedes me, her arms jolting awkwardly up around her. We approach the cottage from the side, and she takes me along a narrow concrete stairway, through an incongruous glass door with a red exit sign and into the basement. The lights flicker on, showing me rows of antique consoles, Eames chairs, dead cathode monitors with flat screens and laptops scattered on top of them.

"I've just made coffee," Dr. Toland says. "Want any?"

I take the cup she thrusts at me.

"From what you saw of Stringfellow, would you say he was crazy?" I ask her.

Her eyes might as well be painted on her face.

"Ask *them*," she says. "You have the medication?"

I take out the hard case, black and deadly-looking, opening it with a keycode and my thumbprint (a bit of theatre), extract the tube from its foam sheath and hand it to her. Two half-black, half-white capsules rattle inside. Without a word, Dr. Toland goes over to a laptop and taps it awake; the screen blinks on, showing several different colored lines tracking along a numbered grid. She sets the tube down carefully on the console and does a bit of typing, keying in the time of administration and so on. This project has been all hers now for three years; three years living out of her office, single-handedly keeping the Stringfellow telepathy experiment on life support. I wonder if she has anything better to do. All the same, she has everything just the way she wants it.

"Right," she says to the screen. She takes the tube and heads for the stairs.

As instructed, she will give them the capsules in my absence, although I can see her doing it on one of the active monitors. There they are—two vague figures blue in blue on the screen, sitting together—I can't look at them without that spasm of panic coming back again. I all but knew this was going to be bad and now I do know. It's bad. I take a deep breath and pull out my own little tin pill case, the one with the matchbox drawing of Kali on it, shake a couple of tranquilizers onto my palm and down them with some coffee.

For collegiality's sake, it was necessary to tell Dr. Toland that I was a reject from category A. My latent sensitivity means that sudden exposure is dangerous to me, and possibly for them as well, since their contact with strangers has been strictly minimized for decades. They're just not used to outsiders anymore, not ready. Stringfellow's whole approach had already been unpopular with some whose opinions mattered, and the suicides had been a pretext to shift resources and attention in other, more promising directions. The telepathic-monastic communes he envisioned lost all their appeal by the eighties; by then, on the contrary, all the real money was on a two-pronged anti-social approach emphasizing increased isolation coupled with resocialization to phantom communities centered around electronic media and then the internet. Drugs and direct conditioning, forced intimacy under incessant clinical scrutiny, all started to look crude and cumbersome in comparison.

The current approach is working, but some—myself included—wonder at the long-term viability of all this self-cancelling anarchy. Any scenario will be volatile, but surely there are more manageable, more predictable approaches. That's part of the reason I kept an eye on these old dinosaur projects; you never know when some of the old ways might come in handy, and I'd seen for myself just how much time and energy the social media crew wasted reinventing wheels that old creeps like Stringfellow had already worked out two generations ago. It's like anything written on a typewriter is indecipherable to them. Well, *I* can still read.

The main problem with the communes was that they produced entirely insular group individuals who were unintelligible to anyone but themselves. Some cracked, like the suicides, and maybe the schizophonetic female—but if anyone knows what became of her, they're keeping it under unusually tight wraps—but even the stable ones, like the two up above me right now, couldn't interact meaningfully with anyone else in the absence of Stringfellow's guidance. That was a key problem, hidden inside what should have been one of the most attractive features of the conditioning; the communes were all keyed to a control, a psychic pacemaker, but that meant they were instrumentalized elements of the control mind. This would have worked fine, even taking resistance into account, if the relationship between controller and controlled had paralleled an innate relationship of conflict and suppression between the ego and the id, but our research has shown time and again that this relationship is far more typically a cooperative one, with the active syntheses of the ego arising from and depending on the passive syntheses of the unconscious, rather than competing or conflicting with them. So Stringfellow himself also had to resist, because it was the relationship, and not his will, that was determinative, and he was dead set on being in control. This resistance was then communicated to the other subjects and the whole thing was just a fucking mess. That was enough to get further research along these lines booted to the bottom of the priorities list, unfairly, I think.

Dr. Toland clumps halfway down the stairs, bends forward to look at me, her face melting into the red safety light, and says, "OK."

I steady myself, take another deep breath. The tranquilizers are leeching tension out of me, relaxing me without my will. The handrail floats numbly into my hand, and I push myself up the narrow stairway and see them.

Now I'm in the cottage observation station. A room with more gear, most of it gathering dust, some chairs, and a two-way mirror, or one-way which is it again?, and them sitting there on the other side, next to each other on the sofa... withered old men with frail necks and skinny wrists and it's definitely *them*, from the films and photos, the one gazing into space and the other looking down at the floor through his knees. But I feel it and they feel it—they stir and look up, around—they know I'm here. The panic inside me batters against the tranquilizers in a painful, chemical struggle in my blood and brain; it's like feeling the dim stirrings of what wants to be a convulsion deep down in me, but balked and thwarted by this inexplicable, painful tranquilizer numbness that keeps it from growing, from coming, or happening. It's hard to resist the temptation to talk to myself, even though I know that's not how it works.

Not that I was ever graced with true telepathic contact, but we were all carefully instructed about it; there will be no sensory experience, and certainly no language. There's nothing in the mind for another mind to read. "You're not a book," my control said. "No one can read you." Instead there's something much, much worse. Direct contact. You're right up in them and they're right up in you, before words, before sounds, before sight or even touch, and there's nothing to know, which is somehow the worst part. So what I sense and think is all just what you would expect, with no foreign presence, but there's contact between me and those two old men sitting there on that shabby old-mod leather sofa staring into space with their hands in their laps. For an instant, perhaps, it's as though... as though part of my body were over there, sitting, looking, breathing, digesting, what? Feeling itself aware of... another? Across the glass that reflects them back at them?

"You all right?" Dr. Toland asks unsympathetically.

"I'm fine."

I walk over to stand by her side. Walk jerkily, it seems to me.

"You should have a seat," she says. "There's no telling how long this will take. You sure you're all right?"

"Thanks, I'll stand for now."

"You must have just missed category A," she says.

"I wouldn't know. Our records were kept from us."

"I saw your record," Dr. Toland says, her eyes on the two in there. "You didn't lack for sensitivity. They tossed you on aesthetic grounds."

"Why the hell would you say that to me?" I turn on her.

She seems startled.

"Maybe it's been a while since you had a normal conversation," I say.

The flush of anger here is good, very good, a real gift. I can use this. Get into it. It steadies me, that is, against the... against...

"Do I go around insulting you?"

"Sorry!" she says, "Forget I said it, jeez. You don't have to blow up at me."

"Yeah, well you don't have to talk shit."

Dizziness wells up out of my core and I have to press my hand to the glass and steady myself.

"Sit down," Dr. Toland says.

"I'm all right—watch them!"

I'm angry at her, angry for her providential rudeness, her stupid obliviousness... Keep the focus there. Eyes inside, look, stray over mine unseen in the glass, and then one of them, the clean shaven one, suddenly stands and walks over to the glass, right to me, skinny legs in baggy stockings, a velvet caftan swings loose around his knees, and presses his hand directly over mine, eyes searching. I'm hyperventilating now but I can keep it together—

"Mr. Pruit!"

—silvery, icy, electric, gossamer, traverse the flesh, leave minute and delicate arabesques of nameless non-pain, non-pleasure attention... exposure... burning into you and being obediently absorbed, folded in to the tissue.

It's bad, it's bad, it's like I never took anything at all, the tranquilizers are already fried, my protection is melting away. This gentleness, and acceptance, this godlike, serene attention, is going to break me.

The eyes right in front of mine roll back in their sockets and he falls. The duress on me lifts in an instant, so immediately that I shout. Dr. Toland darts past behind me and through the door, into the room. The first subject is limp and heavy. Dr. Toland kneels, gathering him up, shouting incoherent orders to me, calling on me to help. I'm riveting my attention on the other one, the one who must have received the weaker dose of the two—I've got to watch him. Bald, a fringe of long hair spread over spare shoulders, a wispy moustache over a drooping mouth, now rolling his head around and around on his shoulders, palpitating his own body with knuckly, arthritic fingers that stab out in my direction.

No good, though, no good. I'm sensitive, I'm one.

One of you, one with you, right? Danger—poison—fatal poison—what do you do?

The one on the floor is dying, the one on the sofa is dying his death with him.

The one on the floor is dead.

"Pruit!" Dr. Toland howls. She slaps the dead man, tries CPR, then stiffens. She claps her hands to her own chest as if she were going to resuscitate herself. The man on the sofa is dead.

I hear something snap inside Dr. Toland. She stares at me, invisible, the other side of her own reflection. Blood spurts from her nose, gushing down her chin. She collapses. She slumps forward, draped stiffly over the corpse of the first subject.

Three dead bodies in there. A few minutes ago, all were alive. Now, all gone.

I feel the rushing departure of the mental presence. Still. How long has it been? I pass into the room. Three twisted corpses. All ice cold. It's been some time, then. Not that anyone would notice. My legs hurt, badly. I guess I've been zoned out, standing.

So, have a seat.

Thank you, Dr. Toland.

So quiet here. I gaze out from the sofa, a dead man slouching next to me. Lavender. Some abstracts on the walls. No TV, of course. A picture window with a view of the woods rolling away forever. I'm sitting where he sat. The first one.

It's done.

Whatever happens now, this much is done. I'm not sure I have it in me to do the rest, to burn them. A fire in the house... seems like a pretty shabby bit of theatrics now. I rub my head.

My mind is so stretched out and empty that it aches. Not my brain or my head but my mind. The sadness that comes next is worse, much worse. The tears burst from my face. I sob and the noises I'm making bounce back to me across the dead bodies crumpled all around me, return to me from the walls. Everything, the whole thing, a waste, especially me.

187

"I *had* to."

Over and over I say it. At the moment one of a telepathic commune dies, other members of the commune will experience that death as well. It's too powerful to shut out or to defend against. During communion-formation, all the bindings that constitute an individual are rebound to the group, and when someone dies, all those bindings come unbound and threaten the bindings of the partners. You have to rebind, reconstruct, after a death, but first you have to deal with innate self-defense mechanisms which are rebound from individual to group. The group needs to protect itself from the chaos that a death causes.

All stuff Stringfellow was already worrying about when he died, but the thing is, as you study his notes, you come to realize that telepathists might protect themselves by projecting the shared death experience *out* of the group.

And now I've proven it. I poisoned them both, one with an instantly fatal dose and the other with slightly less, so one would definitely die before the other. The survivor instinctively projected the death profile outward; not on me, because, as a sensitive, I registered as part of the greater psychic organism to which he belonged, so I'm not outside the commune.

My apologies, Dr. Toland. But you do have to admit that, in death, you have made a profoundly significant contribution to science. Probably your greatest. As it happens, you were also the only witness. You were outside, and you were certainly not sensitive. The sudden establishment of contact between a telepathist and a non-telepathist can be quite a shock, and when that contact involves the unbinding power of death...

My unauthorized experiment is a success. As I sit here looking at dusk deepening over a forest that's communicating the distant storm's presence to me, now I really have to make up my mind. I have a little kit here with me, in my coat pocket. Spray them with phosphorus and destroy the bodies, nothing to autopsy or examine. No trace of poison left, and I'm long gone before they're found. Sit and look out the window, feeling helpless, barely able to move, tears pouring down my cheeks, sobbing, and all the power to change the world right here and now.

Destroy everything and disappear, or die, the point is that I will have plucked this power out from under their noses and tossed it into nothingness. What could they do with this, now that at last someone, some shitty little human asshole, had figured out how to weaponize grief? So do I give it to them and get my plaque, or do I torch the place and walk away?

"I *had* to."

Sure, they'll find me. They'll figure out something. But they won't know what happened, the grief that can kill. Over and over I say it to the dead bodies lying all around me.

"I *had* to."

I've killed the last telepaths. Me.

Contiguity to Annihilation

Chris Kelso

- *'This is my El Dorado. Everything I need is in this place, Ivan'*
- *' Then fucking go. What do you need my blessing for? What do you need me for?' - As he stared into her electrically excitable cells, that possessed the power to sooth his tired limbs and elevate his soul, Ivan knew he had lost her.*
- *'That's not what I meant.' – She lied.*

You can see from this exchange with her boyfriend and bandmate, Ivan, that Marina had left Germany for this place—just off Briarson & Fuller—in the full knowledge of the cosmic threat confined within this innocuous little American town. And she knew deep in that elemental vacuum which sucked at the coil of her soul that these were more than mere rumours designed to terrify tourists. Scientists and spelunkers alike, some even from Berlin, had returned as deaf and wounded shadow-people with seemingly evidential reports of malignant entities—photographs and murky infrasound recordings of wandering monsters who lurked in the obscured folds of space and time. Overheard voices that begged for sacrifice in an alien language. And the transmission tower which hung over the town like a latticework wicker man begged to be explored as a source. So, Marina had to go, didn't she? She was compelled by her art. Her insatiable creative spirit. Ivan may have hated her for leaving, and there was no guarantee Berlin would have her back when this was all said and done, but the promise of a new annihilation sweetened her fear. Her soul was waiting to lose its petals in a wind-blown cascade. Flowers of orange.

AMBIENCE MAGAZINE: Marina, Evan, hi. In the '90s, your music had this kind of dialectical affiliation with rave culture. Do you miss that?

EVAN: Yes and no. It's all merged into this global Internet world and we have to adjust. But I don't miss anything really. Not even Marina.

MARINA: That's just globalization. Everyone knows everything about everything. The holy grail for a music fan, I think, is to hear music from another planet

And the little American town seemed relatively normal at first—'normal' being the most suitable adjective since 'normal' usually meant, sub-textually, that there was a concerted desire and effort to conceal malignant truth behind a veneer of flimsy props and stage-furniture. And this little American town—the one just off Briarson Fuller—stank of artificiality. A complex stage design of charming wooden town houses lined the main street, more Germanic in style than American. The museum and adjoining public library sat like perfect sentinels of upright academic pursuit, not dissimilar to the Kunstbibliothek across from her and Ivan's old apartment in Matthäikirchplatz. Then there was the CIVIC-TV transmission tower pulsing the power lines with powerful, low-level biomusic. She noted this into her recording device and cursed her stupid sentimental longing. She was only two days away from Ivan. Homesickness at this stage was a sign of weakness.

DOUBLE-NEGATIVE MAGAZINE: Do you miss Berlin when you're on tour? Do you get homesick?

EVAN: NO.

MARINA: No.

DOUBLE-NEGATIVE MAGAZINE: I need to be honest; I can't understand a word of dialogue in your latest EP.

MARINA: That's the intention. It's just another way of withholding certain details for yourself. Because you don't know what someone's saying, whereas I do. I know every syllable on that EP. Not that I would expect anyone to care, but it's a way of keeping my privacy.

DOUBLE-NEGATIVE MAGAZINE: I put one phrase into software and reversed it, because I thought that it had been reversed, but that just made it sound... more reversed.

MARINA: Well, I was doing that. We're both German, and it always sounds backwards when we talk. It's probably what attracts me most to working with other Germans. It's one of the few reasons Evan and I are still together.

Quaint family-owned businesses adorned every available corner; the town was unsullied by the empty and aggressive commerce of the neighbouring cities. The townspeople appeared pleasant and quiet, even the young people conducted themselves with admirable reserve. And she noted that the weather was pleasingly warm for spring and the smell of autumn-blooming native plants desired to fill the senses with freshness and hope for a merciful winter. Marina observed all of this with a keen eye but was not fooled. The town structure was nothing but elaborate cardboard scenery in a complex theatrical ruse. But who was behind it? What was the purpose? She had no answers to these questions but knew that behind every well-behaved mask lay the silent but thickly-present promise of a black hole, albeit masterfully contained. It was here that the music hid dormant but restless, ready to explode in a fit of electromagnetic mellifluence. She and Ivan were performers of some renown in circles where ambient music is held in regard, and it was her search for a field-recording of the unheard pitch, the tunings of evil, that had brought her here. To this town. Forcing herself to face the dead eyes of the townspeople in an effort to extract the sonic source of their ugly spirits. And these raw materials interested her, oh yes. Even if it meant literally *killing* one of them and surgically removing it by hand, she would get her sound. Even without words, the biophany of the town was deafening. What a shame, she thought, that Ivan had lacked her commitment. Lacked her courage.

> **SHRIKE MAGAZINE**: Your music has always been cutting-edge, courageous, and there's no doubting your commitment to the exploration of new sounds. In most of your newer music, there's a lot of detuned sounds and these very shuddery, in-between sorts of harmonies. Do you remember when you first discovered those sounds?
>
> **EVAN**: I don't know when I did, but I've always liked and enjoyed weird scales and tunings. I've been using my own scales for quite a long time now.
>
> **MARINA**: *Your* scales?

An old man who resembled a decaying Brian Eno stood by the roadside observing Marina over the rim of his bifocals as she herself observed the town. He was wearing an apron and slip-resistant work shoes and leaned against the wall waiting for Marina to look in his direction. Eventually their eyes met and a cold fear instantly struck the girl in the pit of her chest. The old man told her to approach without using words. The locked stare brought Marina into involuntary motion. She crossed the road and followed the old man into the alleyway behind the fishmongers named 'Al's Cod'. She assumed this was Al.

'I'm Al'—he said with words. So, she was right.

'Marina'—the girl replied, still transfixed by the intensity of his gaze. The old man emerged half from the shadow of the alley and Marina could tell already that he was not human. Although his skin draped tightly over a human skull and his body was the shape of a standard bipedal mammal, and while he spoke English well and by all accounts resembled an elderly anthropoid... he simply was *not* human. Nor was he necessarily malignant. If it's possible for a being to possess an atonality then Al would have embodied this concept fittingly. Al blinked and raised a palm to Marina's cheek. In the spirit of seeking new experiences, she allowed him to do this.

Marina saw in Al's eyes pistils containing nanoscopic glimmers of hope that caught the defeated and dead children buried in her own long-neglected tombs of memory. And reflected back to her from the transmission tower antenna—perfect diffracted holograms of precious nostalgia. This energy knew her. Intrinsically. In that moment she decided to trust Al implicitly.

'You do not belong here. I can see who you really are. It's dangerous to come here so nakedly.'

'Nakedly?'

'Without camouflage.'

'Well...I'm...here...so...'—Marina tried to speak in coherent sentences but her voice was failing her. Her distraction was too extreme. She knew she was talking to something not human and she couldn't stop thinking about it.

'Why are you here?'—it asked.

'I'm an artist...'

'Painting?'

'No...'

'No?'

'Music'—she eventually let out. The ringlets around the old man's eyes were like hypnosis wheels and it was clear Al had power beyond fixing fish.

'German?'

Marina nodded.

'You need to pass through to the next town right away. Do you understand?'

'No...I *can't...*'

'You come here looking for a truth beneath the surface. This is not a truth you want to discover. These masks we wear are designed to protect people like you from seeing what really lies beyond.'

'Annihilation...'

'Yes'

'You are not ready. Your type are proponents of the pastoral psychology and of magical thinking. You seek a proximity to god while indulging death drives and the pleasure principle. We don't have the answers you want or need.'

'Please...do you think...do you think...'

ROLLING STONE MAGAZINE: Do you think technological developments affect the way we create and interact with music and sound art?

MARINA: Oh yes, we can also look at the ways in which alien sounds in ambient music tend to 'conceal' found sounds of far-off spaces. I've heard it compared to bringing a souvenir back from your holidays. Then there's the emergence of ASMR composition, which has begun populating YouTube and creating more accessible ambient therapy. But I'm really concerned with bringing back that souvenir. We need to locate and explore alien worlds first. I think NASA and their space programs should use music as their motivation for terraforming. It doesn't have to be about rebuilding society, it could be about just finding new music instead.

ROLLING STONE MAGAZINE: Who is speaking in your last EP?

MARINA: Just Evan and I because we are the only people who exist in our world. We're just back from a tour with House of Skin, Annalaura Alifuoco and Silvia Battista, and Steve Davismoon but we were always alone. We are all always alone. Evan and I have tried to focus on the social and political implications of the last EP, why not use it to speculate what an alien world sounds like for the next full-length album? Unfortunately, that will just be speculation.

ROLLING STONE MAGAZINE: You are certainly committed...

MARINA: We have a good producer in Nicki Brand. What would be the point in compromising with our music? Even if we are just... speculators.

Sensing Marina would not compromise or reconsider, Al decided to give her what she wanted in the hope that a glimpse of the secret horror would send her fleeing in the opposite direction. But he knew there could be no microdosing tactic. Once she saw and heard what lay beneath she would be changed, warped forever into something new and broken. He sighed, lifting both hands to his cheeks, flattening the loose flesh at either side, before peeling his fingers around his jowls and prizing away the face like a biscuit tin lid.

It made a *pop* noise.

The first thing that struck Marina was the smell—an ethereal mildew. But the black gaping maw soon stole the edge of her attention. A deep dark hole that extended beyond the dimensions of Al's skull burned itself on the girl's mind, on her soul, and most interestingly, on to her auditory faculties. A drum noise scuttled out of an invisible analogue machine at around 120bpm and joined a tuneless synth in a psychoacoustic ostinato. Marina tried to press the RECORD button on her device but her brain would not obey the demands of her mind. Children screamed from all corners of her psyche as slime-covered beasts ate her dreams and eventually consumed her dream-parents. In memory, men and women Marina had loved wailed so hopelessly that they vomited-retrograde into their own memory-souls.

'Can you feel it getting closer? Is this what you want? The truth?'

Marina fell to her knees. When the sound ended she knew Al had reapplied his face lid. Everything was now silent. All noise had been sucked into Al's face and she heard the world for what it really was. Silent. And Marina knew her auditory faculties had been stolen, never to return. Was it all for nothing, this loss of hearing? She thought she was ready. Her hand held the recording device limply with her broken thumb stabbing the PAUSE button into the metal frame around the plastic.

So, it was all for nothing.

No evidence.

Only the loss of music and conversation from her life.

She would never hear her mother's voice again.

Never hear David Bowie or Massive Attack.

No more Aphex Twin or KLF.

She would never hear Ivan curse her or say 'I love you' again.

They existed only as vague stereo-spread audio-memory.

Placozoa.

Sickened by this loss, Marina fell silently to all-fours by Al's slip-resistant shoes.

'You are just a young girl. You were not ready'—a voice spoke to Marina from within her own mind. An alien voice, not her own.

'Spermarche, menarche. IDs with swim wings on. And you, Marina, rely on adults with dead children in their eyes to guide you. A parallax. A wreath. Say goodnight into my void, will you?'

Marina felt the organic glue that held her flesh mask in place start to loosen and tear free from the seams. She tried to scream but the voice was lost. She felt her face fall into her palms, landing like a wet glob of gelatine, and looked up with a new voiceless void.

'Goodnight'—she thought.

> **AMBIENCE MAGAZINE**: 'Goodnight' by Soul Tragedy is one of the albums you've independently produced—do you think the band will continue without your partner of 20 years? Will Max Nicki Brand continue to oversee production?
>
> **EVAN**: Without a doubt. Marina's silence has spoken volumes. I know she's out there and as long as she found what she's looking for then I have no ill-will towards her. Well, maybe a little...

ART**GOD**

Elle Nash

in the umbilical cord,
my blood drives

wrapped in Her hands, supplicating

and i feel—squeezing shut—
Her fist, bottlenecking

my toes graze the revolting flesh.
Her fist is a veiny organ.

lust pumps, i guess, in a
backward direction.

the simplest word for it
is *beg*. there is no
better word.

in its speaking,
it does exactly what
She wants: opens my mouth,

so She can slip herself between my lips.

THE LIE CHAIR
(1976)

Starring: Amelia Hall, Susan Hogan, Richard Monette and Doris Petrie

Kelso: *The Lie Chair* is often unfairly dismissed as predictably scripted and operating without the usual preoccupations of Cronenberg's grand oeuvre. There are no cold characters contemplating new mutations or disfigurements. No abnormal genitalia or armpit phalli. No sinister conglomerates engineering global body horror via subliminal or overt means. But it would be too simplistic to dismiss it as Cronenberg filler. And while it doesn't demonstrate his trademark iconography, it does delve into several of his future fascinations as an artist and filmmaker.

Having thrust the Canadian film industry into the limelight with the profitable and controversial *Shivers*, a fledgling Cronenberg was asked by newly appointed CBC director, John Hirsch, to direct a teleplay of *Peep Show*—a moderately popular anthology show in the spirit of a BBC Sunday-Night play[1]. *Peep Show* was a series that gave emerging Canadian actors and directors a platform to showcase their talents[2]. With *Shivers* under his belt and some newly acquired experience of shooting in 2-inch video, Cronenberg was ready to flex his new muscles. Like all great auteurs, he spent his time as a 'working director' sensibly, taking odd-jobs so he could use his accumulated pay to fund passion projects with more substance. *The Lie Chair* also serves as a reminder of his versatility as a filmmaker.

Scripted by David Cole,[3] *The Lie Chair* is a somewhat stock but solid example of 70's multi-camera television. Originally airing on 12 February 1976, we open on a rainy night. Obligatory thunder claps and haunted house vibes. The acting is naturalistic and some of the dialogue is memorable (*'Carole, I love you. Now*

---

[1] Although *Peep Show* actually predates the likes of Tales of the Unexpected

[2] Peep Show also gave early opportunism to Martin Short, Clark Mackey, and Martin Lavut

[3] Cole would go on to become a regular writer on the relatively tame and largely uninteresting Canadian hit, Due South

shut up'). Soon we will discover a series of characters who are slaves to their automatic processes, who are either stuck in a kind of proactive coping mechanism or find themselves facilitating this delusion. But we'll come to that. For now we have a couple, Carole and Neil, seeking shelter in a nearby home after their car has broken down. A maid called Mildred, a wild-eyed clockwork-orange-type who has learned 'never to feel', answers the door and the couple are immediately requested to adopt the personas of another elderly tenant's (Mrs Rogers) grandchildren. So begins an interesting and familiar paranoid-narrative.

"For tonight, your name is Sylvia."

And so the old woman, supposedly senile and habitually soused on Cheri, believes the couple are her absent grandchildren—however she seemingly breaks from this fugue state at will and returns to self-awareness quickly. Already we see the themes of identity, self-deception, and estrangement rear their head, and actually remain prevalent throughout—explored in depth long before Cronenberg scripted his own similar theses with *Dead Ringers, Spider, History of Violence* or even his take on Burroughs' *Naked Lunch.* Two uncritical believers who actively ignore the ontological distinction between reality and imagination, we discover that Neil and Carole are simply two spiralling dream souls. On the surface, Neil is your standard 70's fop—garbed in tweed jacket and French-collared shirt. Carole is all Karen Carpenter in her poncho and bellbottoms.

In the episode's climax, Neil sits on the titular Lie Chair and Mildred engages in the obligatory expository dialogue. What's interesting is the depth of the self-deception at play, levels of which are only later seen in the likes of *M. Butterfly*. Although this was a pay check gig, Cronenberg didn't shirk on the preparatory legwork, delving into early investigations of self-deception. It was probably established early on that Robert's character would engage with a strategic paradox and Cronenberg's research would have shown that a kind of cognitive load occurs when people feel they must preserve two separate forms of content in their working memory—consciously mediated reception: where factual content is suppressed and false information is propagated. An entirely real-life phenomenon. It's this commitment to realism that gives the episode its muscle. In *The Lie Chair*, Robert's deception has replaced the truth in conscious memory by reporting the misinformation via retrieval-induced forgetting. On some level, conscious or subconscious, this character knows they are lying and the consequences of being caught means the deception becomes deeply rooted. Lies require important departures from reality and those who practice deception take their practice literally, rehearsing their lies until conscious awareness is dimmed. Pure survival. We see Neil, Carole, and Mrs Rodger break character. Memory is a virus, something to be ignored, paved over and run away from. While Cronenberg didn't write this, and there is little of his stylistic flair, it does open up ideas which would remain omnipresent throughout his repertoire. Neil realises he is a dream persona manifested by Robert's childhood fantasy. 'Lies to make a happier truth'. A young boy trapped in the body of a man. Arrested development of the soul. Creating an interior world where one might escape death and the reality of adulthood. It's a relatable fantasy. Cronenberg enjoys the relationship between the mind and the body, the vessel and the sentient mist within—but *The Lie Chair* surveys the mind's relationship with itself. Parts of the mind can be the foreign body and a wild and fertile imagination is the foreign body engaging in parasitic union with waking reality.

"Choose the lie chair over the imperfect world of man" is reminiscent of the philosophy of *eXistenZ*, where a games developer designs a simulation which is so immersive and limitless that it consumes the reality of its user. In the end, Robert embraces Mildred and Carole flees into the night like a PG-13 Final Girl. She gets to her car, tears open the passenger's seat to reveal the limp, slumped corpses of their respective doppelgangers. Robert and Sylvia's dream-cadavers—Neil and Sylvia. The remains of their imagination.

Cronenberg does a good objective workmanlike job in *The Lie Chair*. He essentially removes himself to serve the script. But I do not believe he is merely motivated by financial gain in taking on this project. No doubt the central question—to what extent do self-deception and delusion intercept?—would have interested him. Cronenberg can take even the most standard script and express his understanding that both self-deception and delusion can be understood in folk-psychological terms. The creation of elaborate escapist scenarios as avoidance-orientated coping mechanism.

Callum McSorely, himself a self-proclaimed techno-fetishist and owner of a rare Mantle Retractor, has been writing short fiction and collecting various national awards since he was 23-years-old. He is considered something of a national treasure in the emergent mainline literary culture in Scotland. He has previously extolled praise on the later work of David Cronenberg, but I wanted to hear his take on something a little removed from the usual tropes of Cronenbergia. What better place to start than *The Lie Chair*? Callum and I watched the film in a dilapidated hotel room in the East-End of Glasgow. The floor is strewn with tubing and surgical clamps. A single television projects a transmission from a dead channel. Amid the clutter of gynaecological tools we watch streams of nebulous static clear and the opening credits emerge…

CK: This might seem like a stretch but to me the codes of post-humanism are present in *The Lie Chair*—perception and agency, information coding through multiple levels of knowing—but what do you think? Do you see any themes/preoccupations that crop up in later Cronenberg movies?

CM: Well, first of all I'd say it's an enjoyable slice of short horror like a *Twilight Zone* episode or a *Future Shocks* script. It has lots of elements that seem campy now and, if done today, would be seen as pastiche.

CK: It does have a kind of hokey premise.

CM: Honestly, one of the first things I thought about when Mildred opened the door to the Crofts at the beginning of the film was that line from *Friends*: "Betsy's been dead for ten years" (said in spooky old lady voice). As such, it's a little hard not enjoy it in an at least partly ironic manner—there's certainly plenty of lines delivered in a dramatic, enigmatic style worthy of Joey's Big Break: "For tonight, your name is Sylvia... I share this house with memories now.... I thought this old house had swallowed you up..."

CK: Does it still feel like a Cronenberg movie to you? I think it seems smarter than your average low-budget anthology episode.

CM: Through the filter of 2021 and Garth Marenghi, it has a cosiness that probably wasn't present when it was made in the mid-70s ("Carol, I love you, shut up," might have been a line written by the author, dream weaver, visionary, plus actor himself)...

CK: I love that line.

CM: ...yet it's hard not to immediately notice that old horror trope where the woman of the couple is adamant—and correct—that there's weird shit going on while the man tries to convince her she's being oversensitive because exiting the scary situation would be a hassle for some reason, but that said, the concept of *The Lie Chair* is genuinely spooky and the twist still works for me. (Trope-wise you've also got a decrepit old house in the middle of nowhere, a big storm, car trouble... enough to make a bingo game out of.)

CK: And the ending?

CM: I think the ending, where the Crofts are subsumed by the lie is fitting for Cronenberg—his characters rarely get out of scrapes clean, they either get swallowed up or must undergo some kind of transformation, they never just end up back where they started with everything going back to normal. You could also look at the way Carol and Neil become their assumed roles of Sylvia and Richard as a kind of body swap/mind swap, certainly a transformation. So I do feel there is something that links this film with his oeuvre and his recurring themes. Style-wise though it's very 70s, everything is brown: the clothes, the wallpaper, the carpets, the furniture. It lacks the visual wizardry he's often known for—I'm thinking of the big head sculpture in *Scanners* [Am I tripping or is there a bit where they hide inside a big head?]. The whole thing looks low key and nothing physically gross happens (*what!?*). The Cronenberg stamp certainly isn't so clear in this respect.

CK: Do you have any unique interpretation of *The Lie Chair*? Is it worth deeper interpretation? Do you think it's saying anything profound about the power of imagination/self-deception/delusion—or is this just a solid BBC-afternoon-drama-style piece of television?

CM: It's both a solid bit of enjoyable, slightly schlocky drama *and* has something to say about self-deception, although ultimately maybe nothing particularly original in that respect. We're brought up to believe a painful truth is better than a pretty lie and *The Lie Chair* reinforces that message, albeit through the horror form—so the Crofts are swallowed by the lie and fall into their imaginary roles but because it's horror, we're supposed to be scared by this, and it *is* a scary idea that we could lose ourselves, lose our memories, even the ones that aren't so pleasant. It's a reality that's hard to face that as we get older this could actually happen to us that we could forget.

CK: That's interesting...

CM: But this made me think: Often people with dementia, such as my gran, tend to believe themselves to be much younger than they are, living, in their mind, somewhere in their twenties or maybe even earlier. My gran talks about her husband, my granda, who passed a few years ago, and her son, my father, who died a long time ago, as if they are still here and it is agreed among family and the care home staff to just play along with her because there's no point upsetting her with the truth when she's happy in her own world, and she is often happy now she's past the point where her forgetfulness worries her. It would be an unkindness to keep trying to remind her over and over of when and where she is or putting her through fresh grief over traumatic things she doesn't remember.

I'm starting to lose my thread here, but I think what I wanted to get at is that maybe a more interesting thing for *The Lie*

Chair to have done is to paint this transformation, this self-deception, this extreme power of imagination, in a positive light. For all its pretensions to transgression, horror—and particularly older works of horror—often just reaffirms commonly held prejudices, beliefs, and political ideologies of its time and place. I'm thinking here of the way monsters are often used to symbolise certain groups of people deemed undesirable, or the anti-communist alien invader stories from Cold War America.

CK: So there is a message about self-delusion, you think?

CM: *The Lie Chair* certainly has its message about delusion, for sure, but it's not a particularly unique one. Nor is there much discussion around it within the film—it has picked a side and settles there firmly. While the madam does voice that "Even the illusion of happiness should not be dismissed out of hand", it is musically underscored by a sledgehammer/nail bit of spooky piano work. Same for when Mildred describes the stories told in the lie chair not as evil or deceitful but "Lies to make a happier truth… Nothing was ever lost, no one ever died, no one went away, there was nothing that could not be accepted…"—her expression and the musical accompaniment tell us this is not to be trusted, that there is something bad and, as Carol says earlier, unhealthy about it.

This isn't to say I didn't enjoy the film as it is though, there's this brilliant moment near the end where Herbert the missing mechanic is mentioned and there's a wobble, like everything is about to come tumbling down and be stripped away again, but then it passes and instead we're left with the family opening the rosewood box with the fairy wing inside, but the audience can't get a look in and I'm left with a big smile on my face.

The Lie Chair

Matthew Mark Bartlett

The house stood stolid against the cold, punishing rain, bracketed by unkempt shrubs, hemmed in by barren trees, frequent lightning spotlighting the edifice against the black-clouded sky. By contrast, the soft light in its lace-curtained windows promised warmth and comfort, perhaps the aroma of bubbling stew or freshly brewed tea. A frantic, four-legged thing under a broad raincoat ran up the driveway, shoes splashing in the puddles. Thunder chuckled darkly at the creature's plight as it climbed the stairs to the covered porch, and there it sloughed off its coat, revealing a youngish couple, gasping and shivering.

"Honey," Carol Croft said, "Don't you think you're more into the *idea* of settling down than actually doing it? What do you know about the country?"

Neil ignored her and rapped on the door. She scanned the area. Dismal. No houses in view, no other lit-up windows, not even in the distance. No cars whooshing by. Just drenched, drooping trees, the half-flooded desolate road. "This place, it's just so isolated…"

"Carol, I love you, but shut up for a second. Where *are* they?"

The door opened, just a crack, and an older woman's face filled the gap, a maid, Neil guessed from the white apron and the coronet cap over her pulled-back silver hair.

"We had some car trouble," said Neil. "May we use your phone to call a garage?"

"We have no telephone here," she said brusquely.

"Who is it, Mildred?" a strained voice called from inside. "They must be drenched! Bring them in!"

Mildred, with obvious reluctance, opened the door and bade them enter.

"Well, you made it!"

The source of the voice was an elderly woman, clad in a

sweater-dress and pearls, seated in a cushioned rocking chair in a living room as warm and cozy as its light had promised, if a little cluttered and run down.

"We'd almost given up on you! Sylvia, sit here. Robert, I know you prefer the armchair! Mildred, some sherry for our dear guests!"

Neil and Carol shot sideways glances at one another.

"I'm sure they'd like to freshen up first," said Mildred. "This way..."

They followed her through a short hallway into the adjacent kitchen, where an icebox and a narrow stove vied for space with a double-sink and stacks of moldering newspapers.

Neil said, "I think you'd better tell her we're not who she thinks we are."

"Mrs. Rogers thinks you're her grandchildren," she explained. "She was expecting them for dinner."

Neil looked at her for a moment. "Okay..." he said, "But what about our car?"

"Well, Herbert is at the village. He's good with cars..." She dismissed the thought. "Listen... Mrs. Rogers was so excited about Robert and Sylvia. If you could stay for dinner, and afterwards..."

"Who's Herbert"

"He does work here."

"We might as well stay," Neil said.

Carol shrugged. "This is Neil. I'm Carol."

"Sylvia," Mildred confirmed, smiling warmly.

"Pardon?"

"For tonight, your name is Sylvia."

—

"A toast! To Robert and Sylvia."

Carol squeezed Neil's hand under the table. "Croft," she said.

"What?"

"We're Neil and Carol Croft. We're not your grandchildren."

"Yes, of course. What you must think. I get a little lost in memories here in this old house."

"We understand," Carol said.

Mrs. Rogers turned her attention to Neil. "What do you do, Mr. Croft?"

"I'm a reporter for the newspaper in Halifax. We're looking for a place in the country."

Mr. Rogers brightened. "I can remember when the quickest way to Halifax was by sea, and that took over three hours! My Thomas would go there for work, and he'd come back with such stories! It seemed like the other side of the world then. But our world was always here."

Mildred came in with a tray of biscuits. She placed it gingerly on the table.

"*Your* world was always Thomas's den, wasn't it, Robert? It's as you left it. The safe is still there, and the chair." She affected a husky, deep voice. "'Open up the safe if you know what's good for you.' Such a dear child you were, Robert. Such an imagination!"

Mildred shook her head and exited the room.

"Mrs. Rogers," Carol said carefully. "Are you okay?"

"I'm fine, my dear hat was for Mildred's benefit. The poor soul... Mr. Croft, could you please fetch my shawl?" She gestured. "You'll find it there, in the dining room."

"I'll go with you," Carol said, and they rose and walked out together.

"Let's get out of here," Carol whispered.

"Where to, exactly? Let's just wait for Herbert." He plucked the shawl from the top of one of the dining room chairs.

"One or both of them is crazy!" Her eyes narrowed. "Did they say Herbert was coming back for dinner?"

"Why?"

"There's only four places set."

"So...maybe Herbert eats in the kitchen."

Mildred entered the room. "Are you looking for something, Robert?"

"It's *Neil*. Mildred... is everything okay? Maybe I can help."

"I don't expect your help," she said. Her eyes went strange. "I expect nothing I feel nothing. I've learned never to hope. And now you... you are here."

She put her hands to her face and fled the room.

Mrs. Rogers called from the living room: "Have you found my shawl?"

—

"I thought this old house had swallowed you up."

"Mrs. Rogers," Neil said. "About Mildred..."

"Mildred's been with us here since she lost her family in the Halifax explosion. She's a good friend."

Carol said, "But, there is a Robert...?"

"My daughter's son. He was born on Mildred's birthday. And when my daughter died shortly after the birth, Mildred took it as a sign. She raised Robert singlehandedly. Now... she can't accept that he's dead. And I... well. Even the illusion of happiness shouldn't be dismissed out of hand."

"How did Robert die?"

A bell sounded from the dining room. "Mildred is ready for us," said Mrs. Rogers.

—

"How is your chicken, Robert and Sylvia?" said Mildred.

Neil said, "Fine, thank you. Tender." Carol nodded her assent.

"For dessert, we have vanilla ice cream. That's your favorite, isn't it, Robert?"

Neil smiled and with genuine fondness in his voice said, "Yes, Grandmother."

Carol gasped. And then, just as Mildred left the room, there came the unmistakable ring of a telephone.

Carol looked at Mrs. Rogers. "Mildred said you didn't have a telephone!"

"Perhaps you misunderstood, my dear."

"Mrs. Rogers, I don't like this charade—it's not doing anyone any good."

Mildred returned, carrying a tray with four small ice cream bowls. "Who called?" said Mrs. Rogers, obviously glad for the distraction.

"Herbert. His wipers aren't working. He'll stay in the village until the storm lets up." She looked at Neil. "I told him about your car, Robert. The garage is closed 'til morning. Nothing to do but enjoy our ice cream."

When they'd finished, Mrs. Rogers wiped at her mouth with the napkin. "I'm sure you'll be comfortable here," she said. "And we've got the game to think of, Robert! We'll be partners again! I think beforehand, I shall have a nice nap. Mildred, will you help me, please?"

—

Mildred stood by Mrs. Rogers's bed. "Newspaper reporter," the latter scoffed. "I remember when it was *safecracker*. *Game designer*. And *Chinese restaurant waiter*. Why can't he be himself and face reality? And Sylvia caters to him. She's whatever he wants her to be."

"You know why," Mildred said. "Life is so sheltered for them here. Like a fairy tale. They've never seen the real world."

Mrs. Rogers sighed, put her delicate hand to her cheek. "Thomas and I so loved our family. Breakfasts in the sunroom, the teacups, the blue China jardinières. The ferns and the copper statues—Thomas would catch the sunlight on the edge of his knife, and dance the reflection around the room. Tinkerbell! They would try and catch Tinkerbell!"

—

"Neil, I don't want to stay here tonight."

"Neither do I, but what could happen? They're weird, but they're just old ladies."

"The phone! Call the garage!"

And suddenly Mildred was there, as though summoned. "The phone doesn't work. The lines must be down somewhere. It's late, and I'm tired. Mrs. Rogers is surely asleep by now. Let me show you to your room."

"What game was she talking about?" said Neil, as they followed Mildred up a set of carpeted stairs.

"There hasn't been a game in this house in years. She says that every night. She'll sleep through 'til morning."

—

The storm battered the bedroom windows, the wind whining around the eaves. The rain was loud on the roof above. Carol looked worriedly out the window. Neil sat on the bed, bounced a little, a childlike grin on his face.

"Neil... how do you feel about... about this Herbert? Do you think he exists? He's supposed to do the work around here, but the yard and the house are so run down."

"Maybe he's out there right now," Neil said, still grinning mischievously. "Creeping through the underbrush with an axe."

"Robert, stop it."

"I'm sorry." He walked over to the door and locked it. "There. Okay?"

Carol nodded.

"Honey, there's nothing we can do but get into bed, snuggle up. Next thing you know, it'll be morning."

"I suppose."

"You know what would be nice?" Robert said. "Pajamas would be nice."

"Middle drawer," said Carol, pointing to the dresser. "Left-hand side."

Now it was Neil's turn to gasp. "What did you say?"

Carol's face was ashen. "I don't know... it just came out."

"We should take a look."

"Robert, no!"

"The worst thing that could happen is I find pajamas." He opened the drawer. Looked. Shook his head. Lifted out a tan-striped pajama shirt and held it to his chest, his eyes wide, but still, that childlike grin.

"Robert... I can't stay here."

"Oh, it's just a coincidence." He walked over and embraced her. "Listen, I was just talking to Herbert on the phone. D'ya know what he said? First thing in the morning, a guy from the garage is gonna come with his truck. He won't even charge us to tow it! Told ya! Everything's gonna be fine!"

Carol pulled away, whipped open the door, and fled down the hall. Neil groaned and ran after her. He caught up with her on the landing, grasped her shoulder. She spun around. "Why did you say that? Why would you lie?"

"I wasn't lying. I thought I'd make it better for you..."

Then a man's laughter from downstairs. Raucous, rough. Affecting a rough Nova Scotian accent, the man cried out: "...and I yelled, *come on, ye heathens, it's Captain Tommy Rogers from Nova Scotia's waiting for ye! And my mate, Robbie, too!* And with that, the savages threw down their spears and made tracks!"

A child's laughter, free and wild. "I saw 'em too, Grandpa! Wild natives in the village by the store! I love you, Grandpa!"

"I love you too, Robbie. Here in the ol' Lie Chair, we got things well in hand, don't we."

"The den!" Neil cried. He took Carol by the hand and ran downstairs through the dining room to the den door. Neil pushed the door open and they stepped in. A fire crackled in the fireplace. Ancient tomes lined two walls, the third spanned by a fringed tapestry depicting a troupe of helmeted horsemen with lances and hunting dogs. A Victorian Parlor Safe, gilded gold, adorned with intricate designs and fronted with dial and cast-iron handle, stood adjacent to a Captain's swivel chair, facing away from them. In the chair sat someone with unkempt silver hair. The chair spun around. It was Mildred, her bun undone, her expression avid.

"Where's Herbert?" cried Neil.

"In the village."

"I heard a man. And a boy!"

"There's no one here."

"I *heard* them!"

"Sit *down*," Mildred commanded. And like obedient children, they promptly sat.

"I'm going to tell you about a boy who grew up in a fairy tale," said Mildred. "A boy who didn't know that life is cruel, that people are beaten down for chasing dreams. For him, everything was a gift. And if it wasn't suitable, it was exchanged. This house? A castle. In this castle, in this room... was the Lie Chair. The boy would sit with his grandfather in that chair, and they would tell each other lies. Not evil nor deceitful... but lies to make a happier truth. Nothing was ever lost. No one ever died. No one went away. Everything was perfectly acceptable. And when the grandfather died, and the boy became a man, and he found that everything was not perfect, he chose the Lie Chair over mankind's imperfect world."

"What happened to him?" asked Carol, transfixed.

"To Robert?" Mildred laughed merrily. "He died. He and his cousin, Sylvia. They climbed into his automobile and suffocated themselves. How everybody cried. What a waste, they said. But Robert's life will never be wasted."

Neil smiled, fell to his knees, embraced Mildred. Carol backed away, then fled from the room, from the house, out into the storm. To the grove. The broken-down car loomed before her. She opened the door. There she was, dead, in the passenger seat.

—

Late afternoon light shone through the dormer windows, painting the church pews gold, intensifying the reds and yellows and greens of the tall, stained-glass windows. Game designer extraordinaire Allegra Gellar gazed proudly upon the raised stage where her latest focus group, four students from the nearby college, awakened, blinking, adjusting their game pods, scratching carefully at their ports, reacclimating themselves to reality. "So," she said. "How did you like *The Lie Chair?*"

Millie Allen blinked, examined her young-again hands. "Phenomenal," she said. "It's a terrific game! The old country house, the storm, such effects, such a great space. I particularly liked my closing monologue. It just rolled off my tongue, like I was coming up with the words myself. I... I just wish the gameplay had been a little longer, maybe had a variety of settings to explore?"

"Well," Allegra cautioned, "at this point it's not so much a game as what we call a 'playable teaser.' When you fill out your forms, you'll be assisting Antenna Research, and me, in really fleshing it out into a truly special eXistenZ module."

"I loved it," said Neal Adamson. "I didn't know *who* I was!"

Katie, Neal's girlfriend, squeezed his hand, grinning widely. "We were ghosts. How fun!"

"And my character, Mrs. Rogers," said Rochelle Thomas. "I... *she*... was so cheesy. 'Fetch my shawl.' What an old biddy!"

"I wish I could take full credit for the specific game data and characters," said Allegra, "but this game and its new modules are the result of our recent innovation, retrofitting game pods with reproductive systems, and, well, letting nature take its course. Which has resulted in variations even we can't foresee. Now, we haven't yet released this information to the press, so you're the first to hear it."

—

In the vestibule, just beyond the walk-through metal detector, a man in grease-stained overalls with a white patch on his breast reading Herbert, listened to the applause from inside. The sound served only to intensify his rage and his resolve. On the floor beside him lay the security guard, blood pouring from the gaping wound in her throat. Herbert tightened his grip on the handle of an axe made of bone and sinew, and with his other hand he reached for the door handle.

IDENTITY AND FREE WILL IN *THE LIE CHAIR* AND BEYOND OR: *THERE WAS NOTHING THAT COULD NOT BE ACCEPTED, BECAUSE EVERYTHING WAS PERFECTLY ACCEPTABLE*

Matt Neil Hill

I wonder how many people who, like me, went in cold to *The Lie Chair,* sat waiting for Mrs. Rogers to plunge a salad fork into Neil's eye, or for Mildred's oesophagus to explode in a shower of twitching meat and vestigial teeth?

Well, we were in for a disappointment.

Barely a footnote in his filmography, of all the early work used as inspiration for this anthology, *The Lie Chair* (written by David Cole) is the least obviously *Cronenbergian.* A TV directing gig for the short-lived Canadian weekly showcase *Peep Show*—sandwiched between the shooting and release of *Shivers*—if his name wasn't attached, you'd struggle to figure out Cronenberg was involved. But, despite the lack of body horror and traumatic enucleation, there are ghostlike echoes of the director's style as well his themes of identity and free will.

A young couple's car breaks down on a storm-wracked night and they seek refuge in the nearest house. The lies begin early. From the very beginning, Carol is sceptical about Neil's desire to move out to the sticks, and he is dismissive of her concerns while optimistic about his plans. Mildred the housekeeper answers the door and lets them in only when the off-screen voice of Mrs. Rogers tells her to. It's actually only in Mildred's first and subsequent appearances that there's any hint of Cronenberg's directorial style, with lingering close-ups and uncomfortable pauses that enhance the foreboding of the scene. Mrs. Rogers mistakes the couple for her grandchildren Robert and Sylvia, and Mildred asks them to play along. When alone with them, Mrs. Rogers concedes that she knows they're not Robert and Sylvia—

> *"I share this house with memories now. They fill every room."*

—but reverts to the charade when Mildred returns. Mrs. Rogers' daughter died in childbirth and Mildred, who she and her husband had taken in when she became an orphan herself, *"raised Robert single-handedly, and now she cannot accept the fact that he is dead. And I... well... even the illusion of happiness should not be dismissed out of hand."*

The memories the house contains are pervasive. Invasive. *Parasitic.* Neil is the most readily infected by them, although Carol is not immune. The memories have voices that both of them can hear, and the Lie Chair is revealed. Mildred tells them the fairy tale of Robert and his grandfather and explains the function of the Lie Chair:

> *"They would tell each other lies. Not lies as evil or lies as deceit... but lies to make a happier truth. If anything began unhappily it was brought to the Lie Chair, and a new truth was forged for it. Nothing was ever lost, no one ever died, no one went away... there was nothing that could not be accepted, because everything was perfectly acceptable. And when the grandfather died, and the boy became a man, and he found that everything was not perfect, he chose the lie chair over the imperfect world of men."*

And yet Robert eventually also chose suicide, alongside his cousin Sylvia—and there is potential darkness in their role-playing as husband and wife that fits well with some of the director's other material—but Mildred refuses to believe it, the implication being that even the Lie Chair couldn't overcome the endless weight of the real world in the end. And such is her refusal to believe that Neil becomes Robert with little resistance.

I'm still not 100% sure of the twist. Are Neil and Carol really geographically lost innocents who have their lives rewritten by two sinister elderly women whose grief transcends reality? Or are they metaphysically lost ghosts trying to escape their deaths by reinventing themselves as living people? Whichever is true, a transformation takes place that wipes away what came before.

Part of the reason *The Lie Chair* feels so distant from Cronenberg's other work is the supernatural element strongly to the fore. There is no ethereal hand at work in his films, only the influence of meat and bone and paranoia and derangement. There may be clandestine organisations of ill intent in the shadows but there are no spectres, and the only inkling of an afterlife comes on an extinct videotape format, or maybe—just *maybe*—in the form of (the) new flesh. But when I began rewatching his back catalogue, it seemed that the themes of *The Lie Chair* were everywhere.

Throughout the early films and later work, one of Cronenberg's key themes is that of identity, or more accurately how people's identity can be subsumed, altered, or erased by forces beyond their control. More sinister than this though, is the existence of an agenda that completely refutes or ignores people's right to remain who they were. In Cronenberg's world, humanity is broken and can only be fixed by passing through the bloody gates of the next stage in its evolution. Admittedly, there is no blood spilled in *The Lie Chair,* no deviant sexuality drawing the characters into their new paradise, but there is a sense that Mildred and Mrs. Rogers have decided that Neil and Carol have little choice in what will become of them. And this exchange is key in defining the reality that exists within the house:

Mrs. Rogers: *"Why can't he be himself, and face things as they are? And Sylvia, she caters to him! She's whatever he wants her to be."*

Mildred: *"You know why. Life is so sheltered for them here—like a fairy tale. They have never seen the real world."*

And if the hapless travellers of *The Lie Chair* are collateral damage to their host's plan for the world, then this indifference is writ large in Cronenberg's later work.

One thing that leapt out at me when viewing select examples of his work through the filter of *The Lie Chair* was how often his male protagonists seemed like little boys, how excited and increasingly out of their depth they become in pursuit of the new world they're compelled to envisage because the "world of men" is not complete or nourishing enough for them. Max Renn, Seth Brundle, Elliot and Beverly Mantle, James Ballard: all of them exhibit a naiveté that invariably dooms them.

Videodrome's protagonist Max is oddly squeamish about real-life sexuality for a relentless seeker of hardcore filth. Alarmed when Nicki Brand exhibits some minor fetishized self-harm, he's a voyeur who rapidly becomes a participant; a man-child with visible weaknesses ripe for exploitation. And by the time he figures that out, he's too far in to do anything but embrace it. There's a symbiosis between his relationship with Nicki and his increasing immersion in the one-room snuff porn universe of Videodrome, each acting as gateway drug to the other in a spiral of escalating desire and need.

In terms of free will, Cronenberg said of characters like Max and Seth that:

> *"They cannot turn the mind off; and the mind undercuts, interprets, puts into context. To allow themselves to go totally into the emotional reality of what's happening to them is to be destroyed completely. They're still trying to salvage something out of the situation: 'Maybe this isn't a disease at all. Maybe it's a transformation.'"*[4]

In *The Fly,* Seth's boyishness plays to the stereotype of the child-genius grown up: a little kid still in awe of his first chemistry set but also a man willing to devote himself entirely to changing a world that doesn't work for him. If refusing to accept reality can be seen as a kind of lie—either lying to oneself or fabricating

---
4 Chris Rodley (ed.), *Cronenberg on Cronenberg – revised edition* (London: Faber and Faber, 1997), 115.

a lie so detailed that it actually alters reality—then Seth fulfils the Lie Chair's function perfectly. And then pays for it. But *The Lie Chair* is open to interpretation in a way *The Fly* is not. When the experiment ends there is no second chance for Seth: even if his unborn child were allowed to come to term, his consciousness would be neither there, nor there to be erased. Another striking difference is that Seth's mind and personality are broadly retained while his flesh changes catastrophically, whereas Neil and Carol retain their outward appearance but have become entirely different people. The similarity lies in the fact that neither is who they were at the start.

Dead Ringers actually shows us the Mantle twins as young boys. The world—of women in this case—makes no sense to them in the way they are directly able to encounter it. This personality type is seen in many of the films I mention, and as Cronenberg says of the Mantles:

> *"They want to understand femaleness in a clinical way by dissection and analysis, not by experience, emotion or intuition. 'Can we dissect out the essence of femaleness? We're afraid of the emotional immediacy of womanness, but we're drawn to it. How can we come to terms with it? Let's dissect it.'"*[5]

As the Mantles' disintegration unfolds, they plumb greater extremes to maintain the lie. Beverly dismantles their own retractor design when it proves inadequate for the way the world of women has mutated in his eyes, necessitating the commissioning of terrifying and unique surgical instruments. Elliot destroys their symbiotic career further through drug regime synchronisation, so strong is his identification with the story of the original conjoined twins Chang and Eng.

Whether *The Lie Chair* is about a man being erased by the ghost of a boy or a ghost trying to escape its fate by pretending to be a man, it resonates with the complicated identity games of

---

5 Rodley (ed.), *Cronenberg on Cronenberg*, 145.

Dead Ringers. The Mantle twins could be seen as one boy split in two, and the fear of either complete separation or reassimilation of the two halves is palpable, while their near-perfect impersonation of each other adds to their unravelling because it is unsustainable once the parameters of their relationships with women are altered. And a male character is not the only one wanting to change an imperfect world. As Claire Niveau says:

> *"I'll never get pregnant. I'll never have children. When I'm dead... I'll just be dead. I'll really never have been a woman at all. Just a girl. A little girl."*

And this loss borne by maternal figures also hangs heavy on the world of *The Lie Chair,* so keenly felt that the very fabric of reality is altered by it. The death of a child—or the death-like state of a wished-for child never conceived—is an event that leaves a black hole in the space-time continuum that sucks all other matter into itself.

There's a black hole at the centre of *Crash* as well, but it isn't maternal loss. Although it does still revolve around the twin drives of sex and death. In James Ballard and Vaughan exists both attraction and separation; two satellites at different points in their elliptical orbit of the collapsing star of the twentieth century, destined to collide. Twins born years apart, conjoined briefly before being ripped apart—the surviving twin driving dangerously towards extinction.

But it's in the two climactic scenes between Ballard and Vaughan that I found the closest thematic link between *Crash* and *The Lie Chair.* In the first, Vaughan is shown as sexually submissive to Ballard, very much at odds with how he's presented previously. And it clearly doesn't sit well with him, as immediately afterwards he rams his car into the junkyard wreck Ballard shelters in to reassert his alpha sexuality, then strands him there. Their final encounter comes when Vaughan tries to ersatz fuck Ballard and his wife in his JFK death car; crashing, burning, and taking a crowded airport bus out in the process. Both scenes are perfect examples of the lack of concern exhibited by the controlling forces—Mildred and Mrs. Rogers just as much as Vaughan or any of the other manipulators in Cronenberg's work—for the agency of the bystanders caught up in the world they're remaking.

In one interview, Cronenberg talked about resisting the desire of some distributors to make the Ballards more wholesome at the outset of the film, before they are corrupted by Vaughan:

> *"I said, 'That isn't right, because there's something wrong with them right now. That's why they're vulnerable to going even further.'"*[6]

This also applies to Neil and Carol in subtle ways. They're seeking an escape from their lives (or afterlives) to the country, away from the crowded world of men. So the matriarchal world they enter (or re-enter), where the male inhabitants are already dead of old age or suicide and the void of loss is *so* great, has a bearing on their fate. And the Ballards' refrain at the opening and closing of the film—

> *"Maybe the next one, darling. Maybe the next one."*

—expresses hope for a new state of being; a lie that works for *them*.

And where do *we* sit, as writers, if not in the Lie Chair? We are surely its most promiscuous visitors—remaking a world that makes no sense to us, or makes perfect sense but remains unacceptable. Heedless of the trials we put our characters through, though not unaffected by them: *there is nothing that cannot be accepted, because everything is perfectly acceptable.* The movies *Naked Lunch* and *eXistenZ* focus on writers as protagonists; characters adept at manipulating reality, however lost they might be in the new worlds they've created.

Cronenberg's *Naked Lunch* is replete with quotes and di-

---

6 Rodley (ed.), *Cronenberg on Cronenberg,* 194.

alogue that mirror the preoccupations of *The Lie Chair*. In the opening credits alone, the following quote from Hassan-i Sabbah is used—

> *"Nothing is True; everything is permitted"*

—which feels like a perfect summation of Mildred's monologue. And then the Burroughs quote from the source novel—

> *"Hustlers of the world, there is one Mark you cannot beat; the Mark inside"*

—seems like it could easily be applied to Neil and Robert as they battle with their chosen identity as it conflicts with the world around them. And the Kerouac cypher Hank's early advice—

> *"So you can't rewrite... 'cause to rewrite is to deceive and lie... and you betray your own thoughts"*

—resonates with both the shifting identity of Neil and Robert and Mr. Rogers' and Mildred's agenda.

Naked Lunch focuses much more on the protagonist-as-willing-pawn aspect of identity than the movies previously referenced. When the bug typewriter Clark Nova explains to William Lee that he was programmed to murder his wife as part of the conspiracy propelling him towards Interzone, Lee shrugs and continues to allow his own manipulation—partly because of his addictions, but partly because he wants to see how the story turns out. Of one conversation with William S. Burroughs, Cronenberg writes—

> *"I said, 'Do you believe in the afterlife? Because I can feel that from your writings. And does that mean you are not afraid of death?' He said, 'No, no. Death is very frightening, because if you do it wrong you might end up in the wrong company. You might be setting yourself up because*

> *of what you write; because of what you reveal; because of what you create."*[7]

—suggesting that the lies told to past selves come full circle to affect future incarnations. And *Naked Lunch* itself is a story within a story, a semi-lucid, auto-cannibalistic blending of source material, real life, and interpretations of that life and source material. Like *The Lie Chair,* both *Naked Lunch* and *eXistenZ* play with concepts of free will and its absence, and the lack of conscience exhibited by its manipulators:

Lee: *"And it didn't matter that I didn't know anything about it?"*

Clark Nova—*"An unconscious agent is an effective agent, Bill. The situation does generate some ethical paradoxes at times. I'm the first to admit that."*

Mildred and Mrs. Rogers appear to view themselves in much the same way Clark Nova and every other shady player in *Naked Lunch* do: as an essentially benign force operating for the greater good, prepared to sacrifice a little free will—and a life or two along the way—if the desired result is achieved. And the end of the movie hints at an infinite loop of Joans being killed by Lee in order to open the portal to the next phase of reality, ushered in by authority figures with the same faces: something not dissimilar to what takes place in *The Lie Chair,* if it is indeed about ghosts returning under different guises to continue a life of lies.

eXistenZ plays with the same fluid understanding of identity and free will. Relatively unusual for Cronenberg in having a female main character calling the shots in Allegra Geller, *eXistenZ* is perhaps closest to *The Lie Chair* in this regard, although we do have the boyish Ted Pikul along for the ride. As Allegra says:

> *"You won't be able to stop yourself. You might as well enjoy it."*

Pikul: *"Free will is obviously not a factor in this little world*

---
[7] Rodley (ed.), *Cronenberg on Cronenberg,* 165.

of ours."

Allegra—*"It's like real life. There's just enough to make it interesting."*

And this is vital in *The Lie Chair:* Robert and Sylvia made the choice to take their own lives, but Mildred and Mrs. Rogers cannot—*will* not—accept this, controlling the fabric of reality to bring them back. Robert's childhood game became an addiction, one that couldn't beat the system. And so he chose to stop. But his elderly relatives demand that he keeps playing. Whether just once or multiple times, Robert is respawned... yet appears to be the one without the knowledge of this reincarnation. The difference in *eXistenZ*—at least on the surface—is that the characters are *eager* pawns in what transpires. Cronenberg said the appeal of the game is—

> *"...to find yourself questioning what reality is, to what extent do we create our own reality, to what extent are we all characters in our own game? And as you get older, you realise that it becomes a very strongly evident and palpable thing that people define their own characters almost as though they've written the movie; you decide what things appeal to you, about how you project yourself in society... and we do all play certain roles"*[8]

—and this rings true for the characters in *The Lie Chair*. There are various points in *eXistenZ* where the people are seen conspicuously running their hands along furniture and other environmental objects as if evaluating their authenticity, and others where they feel compelled to follow through with actions that feel alien to them, both amplified by forced and chosen exits from the game:

Allegra—*"So how does it feel?"*
Pikul: *"What?"*
Allegra—*"Your real life. The one you came back for."*
Pikul: *"It feels completely unreal."*

---
8 Video interview with David Cronenberg (crew uncredited) included as extra content on the Blu ray release of *eXistenZ* (101 Films, 2018).

Allegra—*"You're stuck now, aren't you? You wanna go back... because there's nothing happening here. We're safe. It's boring."*

Pikul: *"It's worse than that. I'm not sure. I'm not sure here, where we are, is real at all. And you, you're beginning to feel a bit like a game character."*

I felt the past echoes of this in the scene in *The Lie Chair* where Neil and Carol are preparing to stay the night and know things about the room they've been given that they shouldn't. Carol is unnerved but convinced by Neil to rationalise the experience—after all, he's been the one most susceptible to engaging himself fully in the game from the very beginning. The shifting sense of identity and purpose in both films makes sense of the idea that the fantasy world is both the one to be escaped from and the world that people escape to, the boundaries between truth and lie blurring with each immersion.

It feels fitting to conclude by viewing *Shivers* through the lens of *The Lie Chair*. Cronenberg's debut feature is chronologically the closest to his TV work, though couldn't be more different—although it's also the film where I found myself thinking about the physical spaces involved as much as about identity. There is a powerful sense of claustrophobia in both stories—different in scale, but with commonality in the setting of a home that becomes a prison, and of that imprisonment being transformative. In both instances that transformation ostensibly leads to a happier, more care-free existence—the bleaker aspect of this being that the new, more contented life is not sought out by the protagonists and comes at a steep price. But *does* it? Once the transformation is complete—whether by arcane means or symbiosis with a venereal parasite—none of the characters appear to pine for their previous existence, however hard they once fought for it.

Distinct from the cosy country house of *The Lie Chair,* the locations in *Shivers*—individual apartments, the *Starliner* apartment complex, the secluded island—are all equally inescapable, at least in the characters' original incarnations. Lines of communication to the outside world are unreliable or cut off altogether. There is a sense in both films of a trap being laid, and discovered too late to avoid. The protagonists can run, but to where? Once the threshold has been crossed, that is the only world they will ever be allowed to live in. And they won't *mind*. Cronenberg said that the characters in *Shivers*—

> *"...experience horror because they are still standard, straightforward members of the middle-class high-rise generation. I identify with them after they're infected. I identify with the parasites, basically. Of course they're going to react with horror on a conscious level. They're bound to resist. They're going to be dragged kicking and screaming into this new experience. But, underneath, there is something else, and that's what we see at the end of the film. They look beautiful at the end. They don't look diseased or awful."*[9]

—and those words could easily be applied to the characters in *The Lie Chair*. Once their transformation is complete, Neil and Carol—or rather, Robert and Sylvia—seem blissfully, naively happy, and if Mildred and Mrs. Rogers can be seen as parasitic in their interactions with them, then it is with a happier future in mind, protecting them from a hurtful world. The implication is that when the endless grind and hustle and morality of regular life are wiped away, we can be who we were *meant* to be—we just won't remember who we *were*.

And this is how Dr. Hobbes views his test subjects in the film. His work is geared to returning humanity to its sexually aggressive roots, to reset the world to a time before weary moral conventions took hold. Like *The Lie Chair's* Robert, here is another man who cannot accept reality and feels validated in his coping mechanisms—yet who kills himself rather than face that reality. But Hobbes' primary surviving patient, Nick Tudor, appears to be *exactly* what he was aiming for: amoral, sexually charged, and irretrievably connected to the parasites he carries.

And with Nick and others, free will rears its head again, as

---

[9] Rodley (ed.), *Cronenberg on Cronenberg*, 82.

does the strength of an individual's identity. Nick shows no signs of being repulsed by his condition—quite the opposite in fact. Separation from his parasites causes him both physical and emotional pain. He *wants* this altered world that has been thrust upon him. And he is able to control his new (or ancient) urges better than the majority of the other residents. But not *all*—there are notable exceptions to the orgiastic zombies roaming the apartment complex: Nurse Forsythe, Betts (Janine Tudor's confidante) and Merrick (the building manager) are all successfully able to project their pre-infection demeanour at least long enough to lure in new victims. No explanation is given as to why this occurs, but maybe it's a question of strength of will. Carol is able to resist her remaking in *The Lie Chair* till the end, while Nick accepts it with visible relief—but then he was always the one who most enthusiastically played the game. Whatever the reason, the outcome is invariably the same: *no one* is to be spared in the new world.

Or is *everybody* being spared from the old one?

DEATH AND DECEIT IN *THE LIE CHAIR*

Charlene Elsby

In 1975, David Cronenberg directed *The Lie Chair*, an episode of *Peep Show*, which was a production of the Canadian Broadcasting Corporation. The episode was written by David Cole. *The Lie Chair* has since been packaged with *The Italian Machine* and released on DVD as "David Cronenberg Shorts." In what follows, I argue that the short film accurately portrays humanity's distaste for reality, our preference for deceit and ultimately death, and how the villains we (humans) aim to overcome are time and space themselves.

Existence is Terrible

What is so disappointing about reality is that it is real. And while Nietzsche attempted to redeem reality, identifying Socrates as the villain who had robbed us of it (replacing reality with the abstract forms to such an extent that reality was to become unreal and the abstract to become the real real), the sickness which has led humanity to prefer the abstract has not yet been cured.

The Lie Chair provides us with a case study of that sickness.

Neil and Carol Croft arrive at Mrs. Rogers's doorstep, hoping to use the phone to call a mechanic. Mildred informs them that there's no such phone and attempts to send them away, but Mrs. Rogers overhears and insists the couple come inside. Now Neil and Carol become Robert and Sylvia, Mrs. Rogers's grandchildren, whom Mildred claims she was expecting for dinner. When left alone with the couple, both Mildred and Mrs. Rogers acknowledge the identities of Neil and Carol, but insist on keeping up the charade for the sake of the other; Mrs. Rogers explains that Mildred cannot accept that Robert is dead, and that, "Even the illusion of happiness should not be dismissed out of hand."

Neil tells Mrs. Rogers how they're moving to Toronto for a job as a reporter, and confusing Neil with Robert, Mrs. Rogers says to Mildred in the hallway: "Newspaper reporter... I can remember when it was safecracker, then doctor, cowboy, pirate. Why? Why can't he be himself and face things as they are? Sylvia, she caters to him; she's whatever he wants her to be."

To which Mildred responds, "You know why. Life is so sheltered for them here, like a fairytale. They have never seen the real world."

Of course if we're talking metaphysics, Mrs. Rogers's estate is very much the real world. It's constituted of material, exists in time, and in no way escapes the finite, spatio-temporal reality to which we are all condemned. What Mildred means to say is that Robert always preferred to imagine another reality, of the same metaphysical constitution, but differing in its details.

Now we may be tempted to conclude that what Robert imagined is some objectively better reality, the same way in which we all imagine in what ways we could improve our circumstances to become happier, better thriving humans. Some people believe that honours will bring happiness, or wealth, or power. There's always some better circumstance to be imagined. But Plato, with the sickness that Nietzsche ascribed to Socrates, would insist that the only reality we could imagine that's any better for us than that in which we find ourselves is a reality rid of materiality all together—and the only way to achieve that circumstance is death. (The theme of how philosophy and philosophers have always aimed toward death is featured prominently in the *Phaedo*.)

Simone Weil, who was intimately familiar with the Greek texts and their integration into contemporary Christianity takes the argument one step further, and this is the point I wish to emphasize: that the imagined reality isn't better because what is imagined is better. What makes the imagined reality superior is that it is not real. She identifies, as does Plato, death with eternity and our escape from reality as the renunciation of time. Imagining a better future becomes a coping mechanism for having to live in the present, only to the extent that what is imagined never becomes real. When what is imagined comes to be, it acquires a quality (actuality) that renders it no longer desirable. When what is anticipated comes to be, it takes on the distasteful modification of being real. She writes, in *Gravity and Grace*:

> When we are disappointed by a pleasure which we have been expecting and which comes, the disappointment is because we were expecting the future, and as soon as it is there it is present. We want the future to be there without ceasing to be future. This is an absurdity of which eternity alone is the cure. (Weil, *Gravity and Grace*, 20)

The phenomenon is intuitively verified by those who self-reflect on major life events and accomplishments which, we have been told, are fulfilling. We (humans) have these contradictory tendencies to (1) believe that something in the future is the key to our impending happiness; and (2) failing to achieve any such fulfillment when what is anticipated becomes actualized. We believe that marriage, children, a degree, a position may increase our base level of happiness and pursue these ends. However, when we imagine these things, we do not account for the fact that were these things to happen, they would happen in reality—that is to say, in moments that we still have to live through, and it's living through them that robs them of their desirability, i.e., the fact that what was once imagined is present. An imagined experience does not have the same temporal and spatial grounding as an actual experience, and that temporal and spatial grounding ruins it. A dream job is not a dream job when, every day, it must be worked.

Subjecting this situation to a reduction, looking for the premises that must be true in order for this to be the case, we can discern some necessary preconditions for the above two truths: (1) we are never fulfilled; (2) we are always hopeful (desirous) of what does not exist; (3) the existence of something renders it undesirable, i.e., present and therefore not future (whereas desire lives for the future).

And ultimately, the present is the problem, for at least the past has the decency not to exist anymore. Mrs. Rogers, remembering the antics of her husband Thomas, takes refuge in the past precisely because it has no longer any threat of existing.

Hic et nunc

The quality of something's being "here and now" is what Edith Stein refers to as "primordiality" in *On the Problem of Empathy*. The distinction between the times of the past and future (for we do remember things happening at some time, and we expect other things to happen at some other time) is that the time at which the thing occurs is not primordial.

Ultimately, the here and now aspects of reality are what make it undesirable, and here is where deception also comes into play. For deception brings us closer to uniting an unreal reality with our present situation than does either memory or expectation (or imagination, where imagination refers exclusively to the future). Thoughts of the past and future are always separated in time from the present situation, in such a way that what is imagined, remembered, or anticipated, is immediately excluded from the possible existence in the present reality by the implied separation of time.

That is to say, if we want to retreat from reality, we don't want temporal separation getting in the way. The best sort of reality avoidance should take on the primordial character of the present. The past and the future are too easy. We can imagine that anything happened when it didn't, and we can imagine that anything will happen, when it won't. But whenever we do so, we implicitly acknowledge that the temporal distance between our circumstance and that of the content of our imagination is what allows for these manipulations of reality. If you want someone to believe that something absurd has occurred, you tell them that it happened long in the past (cf. Hume on miracles). And if you want your audience to suspend disbelief in an imagined circumstance that deviates from reality in significant ways, then you place the story in the future (where anything is possible). But the past and the future are always experienced from within the confines of the present.

And thus the present itself is our nemesis, that which must be denied. Better than wallowing in the past or imagining a better future, a false present rids our lived experience of its reality and satisfies our longing to negate it. Beyond asserting that that which is not, is (which is just the definition of a fiction), the willful adoption of a deception appeals to our hatred of reality by assuring us that that which is, is not.

In *The Lie Chair*, we learn that while ultimately Robert preferred death to reality, a stopgap measure on the way to suicide was the imagination of a present that wasn't. When Neil lies to Carol, saying that someone would be there in the morning with a truck to tow their vehicle, she knows he's lying and confronts him. "Why did you say that? Why did you lie?" Neil responds, "I wasn't lying. I thought I'd make it better for you. I don't know. I don't know."

An analysis of actual experience reveals that the consciousness of something "not real" is accepted with the same authority as something that is real—until the deception is revealed. Husserl gives the example of a wax figure in *Logical Investigations*. Aware that such a thing is a wax figure, we approach it with a representational mode of consciousness—with the attendant acknowledgement that the thing we perceive is a representation of something else. However, unaware, we might approach it as any other perception—we see a woman across the room and never become aware that she is a wax woman, a representation of some other thing within reality, something with a higher ontological status due to its not being a representation, a deception, or a fake. We either bump into a woman, turn to apologize and realize she was made of wax all along, or we bump into a woman, never turn to apologize, never become aware that we were deceived, and carry on. (What is "false" integrates seamlessly with reality.)

The premise of *The Lie Chair* is explained by Mildred, who

tells of how Robert died, because he (like all humans who've contracted Socrates's illness) averred reality.

Mildred: "I'm going to tell you about a boy who grew up in a fairy land, who didn't know that life is hard and cruel, that people are beaten down for chasing even the smallest of dreams. For him, everything was a gift tied with a ribbon, and if it was not suitable it was exchanged. The house he lived in was a castle. Peopled only by the family and those who served them. In that castle was a room and in that room, was the lie chair. The boy would sit with his grandfather in that chair and they would tell each other lies. Not lies as evil or lies as deceit but lies to make a happier truth. If anything began unhappily, it was brought to the lie chair, and a new truth was forged for it. Nothing was ever lost. No one ever died. No one went away. There was nothing that could not be accepted, because everything was perfectly acceptable. And when the grandfather died, and the boy became a man, and he found that everything was not perfect, he chose the lie chair over the imperfect world of men."

Carol: "What happened to him?"

Mildred: "To Robert? He died, they say. He and his cousin Sylvia. They climbed into his automobile and suffocated themselves. Oh, how everybody cried and went on. Such a waste, they said. But Robert's life will never be wasted."

(At this point, Carol runs outside to find herself and Neil dead in the car.)

Death as Lie

What is interesting about the "here" and the "now" is that of all the ontological categories, these two are meant to distinguish between individuals. We may share substance, quality, quantity, relation, action, passion with other individuals, but an individual's time and place define its perspective in contradistinction to other individuals. That is to say, universality becomes individual when its "when" and "where" are specified, such that the here and now are definitive of subjectivity. And here I mean nothing other than that spatiotemporal existence corresponds to particularity.

At the same time, we are so attached to living, and to our own identities. If death is the elimination of spatio-temporality (i.e., finitude, subjectivity), then what we are afraid of losing is precisely a "here" and a "now." And not just any here and now, but our particular here and now. For there is a here and now in relation to each individual that distinguishes one from the other—a zero-point of orientation from which the world is experienced, which is not transferrable to any other individual. I am attached to my very own perspective, and none other will do.

Neil and Carol do not want to be Robert and Sylvia, because they are individuals who do not want to be somebody else. We find this comprehensible, because we are all irrationally attached to our own identities. (Rationality is for the domain of the universal, whereas particularity defies rationality by refusing generalization.) The point I am making here, is that there is a significant parallel to be drawn between choosing death and choosing deceit; the purpose is to eliminate the here and now from one's consciousness. Robert and Sylvia's suicides naturally follow as the logical conclusion of the rejection of reality established throughout their lives and represented in the form of a chair of lies.

In the case of deceit, the here and now is replaced by another plausible here and now, which suffices to negate an actual existence which we find abhorrent. In the case of death, the here and now is eliminated with the death of the body, responsible for tethering the individual to the material world of particulars. Adopting deceit as a way of life, The *Lie Chair* ends happily, with the characters focused on trivial concerns which make up human life.

We may wonder if Neil and Carol ever existed: whether they were the fictions of Robert and Sylvia, dead in the car, trying to get back inside the house, unsatisfied even with death. Or perhaps Neil and Carol are two separate people who happened also to die on the property and, when faced with the loss of themselves, were happy to take on any identity whatever, if only to retain some individuality in face of the elimination of all particularity. (A "here" and a "now", even if not mine, may be preferable to dissipation, into either universality, or perhaps nothingness.)

Wouldn't it be nice, though, if instead of deliberating our means of escape, we were to achieve the Nietzschean ideal of achieving a positive relation with reality. That is to say, wouldn't it be nice if reality didn't stimulate repulsion, with the accompanying desire to flee.

The Italian Machine
(1976)
Starring: Gary McKeehan, Frank Moore, and Hardee T. Lineham

Kelso: Cronenberg has never hidden his affinity for motor vehicles. We see them dotted throughout his filmography as straightforward fetishised race cars in *Fast Company*, limousine-cum-offices for slick indifferent yuppies in *Cosmopolis*, or as venues for aberrant sexual practices in *Crash*. Cronenberg's appreciation for the aesthetics of a good-looking piece of machinery has always been evident. But *The Italian Machine* is more than just a dalliance into the joys of fast cars and boy-toy-masturbation. It is subtly complex.

Written and directed by Cronenberg for the Canadian series *Teleplay*, *The Italian Machine* combines two of Cronenberg's most prominent loves—technology and art. This 23-minute episode tells the story of 3 gearheads desperate to unshackle a priceless Ducati 900 Desmo SuperSport[1] from the neophyte clutches of a creepy techno-art enthusiast. The premise is simple and the execution is assured and effective.

We open on a dingy repair shop, a grey cube potted in the middle of some Canadian elbow-crook. Commentary for the 1958 Isle of Man TT plays over the protagonist as they go about their business. Cronenberg favourite Gary McKeehan plays Lionel—a bonafide vintage bike fetishist—who is conducting an engine teardown while Fred—the straight-character played by Frank Moore[2]—quietly eats some cereal. And then Bug appears (Hardee Lineham) with news. It seems he has caught whiff of the titular Italian Machine at Reinhardt Psycho World Limited. Reinhardt is a sleazy showroom owner played to slimy perfection by Canadian TV mainstay, Chuck Shamata.

The men embark on a journey to retrieve it, a mission they

---

[1] *Interestingly the structural model for Seth Brundle's Telepods was inspired by the engine cylinder of Cronenberg's own Ducati 450 Desmo.*

[2] *Moore arrived on set fresh from receiving his Canadian Film Award for Best Supporting Actor in 1976 for the film The Far Shore*

believe they are undertaking on behalf of the whole bike community. They are disgusted to find that the man who bought the Supersport is not a bike enthusiast at all, but rather a collector of technological sculptures. He simply wants to display the motorcycle in his living room.

Cut to Lionel back at the garage, curled in the foetal-position. He is hugging a detached handlebar and slipping gradually into abject mania at the loss of such a prized vehicular artefact. This climaxes in a hilarious scene where an enraged Lionel leaps atop a table and starts jumping up and down until the legs break beneath him. Of course his fellow gearheads are forced to subdue him in the only rational way they can think of—by first restraining him in a draughtsman chair and then playing loud revving on the record player. The growl of high speed racing brings Lionel into an almost orgasmic state of calm.

After some digging Fred discovers the collector's name to be Edgar Mouette. A heist (of sorts) ensures when the men decide to finesse Mouette into relinquishing the bike by masquerading as staff members from Techno-Art magazine. The Ducatti is being housed at his neo-organic condo. As well as the bike another piece stands out as a particularly decadent and disturbing addition to Edgar Mouette's collection—a human being named Ricardo. Ricardo is not formally introduced because in this house 'he is not a person.' He's more of a pet or a living, breathing sculpture. We see familiar themes of dehumanisation, and the idea of machinery-as-sculpture foreshadows the likes of *Dead Ringers*. The cold bug-eyed art collector is also classic Cronenberg. Here he is played by British actor Louis Negin, but it is not hard to imagine Robert Silverman taking on the role to great effect.

Rice: This finally feels like a fully-fledged Cronenberg film in miniature, without the gore perhaps, but definitely suffused with the ironic and ambivalent attitude about the interpenetration of humanity and technology that fuels his greatest work. What I find most compelling about *The Italian Machine* is the main characters' animal panic at the prospect of a beautiful Italian motorcycle being held as a static art object, rather than set free to tear up the roads. A more conventional director might have worked with this same concept, but stopped at the *idea* that these motorcycle fanatics want to free a motorcycle from a life of stasis in a rich man's collection. What sets Cronenberg apart is his insight into the raging animal *need* that motivates people's relation to technology, far deeper than any sober interest or want—so deep that it touches on the basic necessities of bodily survival. For Cronenberg, machines are not toys or trophies; they're as essential to human life as hearts, lungs, and genitals. Viewers would have to wait a few years for *Videodrome* and *Crash* to express this relationship in its absolute fullest form, but *The Italian Machine* is still a major step forward in the director's process of questioning where flesh ends and chrome begins, and how the two are connected by libidinal needs as strong as (if not stronger than) the need to reproduce.

As a key step in the development of this worldview, the film is suffused with anxiety about where human and machine existence coincide, and also where machines become art, and art becomes a machine. Historically understood as a vessel for expressing the innermost contours of the human spirit (and perhaps accessing the point where that spirit merges with the divine), art here is on the cusp of transformation, taking on an autonomous, anti-humanistic function, a process that appears to work in two directions at once: the motorcycle seethes with its own form of imprisoned life, while a handsome male cokehead is rendered nearly inanimate by an arrangement in which he too becomes a kind of sculpture, consigned to the same collection as the motorcycle.

And yet, here at the start of Cronenberg's mature phase, it would be an oversimplification to lament the mechanization of art and the dehumanization of the people associated with it. He's too nuanced a thinker to simply balk at this seemingly anti-humanistic turn, as, indeed, he came into his own as an artist by exploring these anxieties from many angles at once, not all of them negative. On the one hand, mechanical (and, now, digital) art may be automating human emotions and forcing us to comply with its own secret will, and yet, at the same time, machines (themselves the progeny of human ingenuity) are drawing new emotions out of us, and perhaps thereby allowing us to *become human* in ways that were never before possible—the motorcycle fetishists' profound admiration for the Italian machine certainly seems like an emotion they've never felt for themselves or for other people.

Even without any explicit body horror, *The Italian Machine* takes us substantially deeper into Cronenberg's most fertile territory, wherein the processes of life and death, automatism and bodily autonomy swarm and seep together, creating reactions that may be chemical in nature, and yet, as human psychology itself came to be understood as a chemical process, also manifest as profoundly representative of core emotions like lust, greed, love, hate and, most significantly, the throbbing allure of vitality in a world where it's no longer possible to tell what is and isn't alive.

By crafting these anxieties into physical objects and then imbuing them with motion, Cronenberg's cinema has its cake and eats it too, creating an environment where people are both sculptures and autonomous beings at the same time, while machines are both overpriced toys and living gods, barely contained within their metal bodies. "One must live with a sculpture for some time before one understands it," simpers the collector, to which one of the fetishists replies, in a line that Cronenberg must've relished writing, "I think this is one sculpture you're never gonna understand."

Artrevs and Cokeheads

Graham Rae

"We declare that the splendour of the world has been enriched by a new beauty: the beauty of speed. A racing automobile with its bonnet adorned with great tubes like serpents with explosive breath... a roaring motor car which seems to run on machine-gun fire, is more beautiful than the Victory of Samothrace."

—Filippo Tommaso Marinetti, *The Futurist Manifesto*

David Cronenberg has a secret, rarely-seen side. Away from when he's exploding heads, or making externalised internal organs stand up and salute their recently-vacated hosts, the audience-shocking auteur likes to hang out in a very, very different world.

It's one of noise and stink and pluming exhaust fumes and oil and grease and engine calibrations and roars and accelerators and brakes and stuttering speedometers, of catcalls and whistles and shouts and lip-dangling cigarettes and joints, of sweaty ragged denim clothing and nude calendars and randomly-slugged half-warm beers, a whole other chopshop universe celebrating torque and ever-spinning wheels and rust-shining mechanical craftsmanship.

That's right: David Cronenberg, holder of the Order of Canada, and the Order of Ontario, Baron of Blood, King of Venereal Horror, is also a total gearhead, be the speedfreak medium in question cars or motorbikes.

If you think about it from zero to sixty seconds, sidestepping his usual viscerally and psychologically perverse subject matter makes perfect sense. The Canadian brainiac has always had an overarching interest in how things fit together (and come apart, for that matter), be they physical or mental or emotional. So why not add technology into that heady bruising brew?

After all, it's all just cinematic experimentation with the clockworks and mechanics of the interaction of the brain and body, and the breech-births of new species of techno-flesh. Think of the semi-insectual Seth Brundle trailing pipes and viscera and suicidal thoughts in *The Fly* (1986) and you're not far off from the ultimate flesh-and-steel fusion objective under the itchy larval skin of some of Cronenberg's strongest work.

It's counter-intuitive to take a step back and think of the grisly body horror-pimping Canuck intellectual as somebody who could be obsessed with something so material and earthy, so down-and-dirty as racing cars and bikes. It's a far cry from his usual nerdy chin-scratcher musings and quasi-futuristic ideologies.

But the evidence of this seldom-acknowledged facet has always been there. When he was a kid, he used to film car races on 8mm film. Getting older, he was an amateur race car driver himself. He once managed to wipe out an expensive 1952 Ferrari short-wheelbase Berlinetta, running it into a wall. The name of the *Videodrome* protagonist Max Renn is a transposition of Rennmax, a sports car brand. In the aforementioned *The Fly*, the director showed production designer Carol Spier his vintage Ducati (more on which later) bike. The telepod in the film ended up being partly based on the mean machine's cylinder and cylinder-head, merely turned upside down.

Those in the audience more attentive to the director's career arc will have also noted that he directed the drag racing B-movie *Fast Company* in 1979. Whilst not an original script of his, he did modify the screenplay during shooting to include some of the energetic slanguage of the drag racers after it excited the writer in him, drawing himself and the audience deeper into their dangerous-driving world.

And if you think about it, Cronenberg's 1996 anti-epic *Crash*, based on J.G. Ballard's notorious semen-and-petrol-and-blood-spilling 1973 techno-sex novel, can be regarded as a demolition derby coda to *Fast Company*, bringing the race he started sixteen years earlier to a juddering, terminal, burst-tyres halt.

Cronenberg noted that when he was growing up, the guys from the neighbourhood who got cars first had the first sex, having a mobile bedroom to take girls to secluded areas to do things to them. So clearly the mass arrival of the automobile in the mid-20th century had a huge effect on the psyche and developing libido of the young director, being partly a catalyst for some of his thoughts on auto-eroticism.

The fusion of flesh and steel often dreamed of by Cronenberg protagonists never quite happened in the wreck of the film of *Crash*, though it was not for want of trying.

Sometimes you really do just get the feeling that the director would love to be some sort of H.R. Giger-like chrome-ribbed slimeborg; for any real bike or car enthusiast, being part of the machine that excites them so much is not an entirely novel or outlandish concept.

Not that fly-telepod-guy Seth Brundle would much recommend it, mind you.

One gearhead who would instantly understand the wailing-sirensong allure of being part-man and part-machine, however, would be obsessive motorbike enthusiast Lionel, the main manic mechanic protagonist of a 70s short film that Cronenberg made.

Whilst the director was waiting to start filming *Rabid*, he directed *The Italian Machine* (1976) for the Canadian Broadcasting Company, a government-funded TV and radio broadcaster. The 16mm film, which premiered on December 2nd of that year, was made as part of the *Teleplay* series. Running from 1970-1977, this was a Montreal-produced series of dramas, made for new writers to try out their televisual skills, through independent stories without common links.

The Italian Machine introduces us to a grungy motorcycle workshop populated by dodgy subterranean biker characters Lionel (Gary McKeehan; *Rabid*, *The Brood*), Fred (Frank Moore; *Rabid*) and Bug (Hardee Lineham; *The Dead Zone*). They're the kind of wheeler-dealer freaks who sit round reading bike mags instead of porn mags, listening to vintage 1958 bike race broadcasts from the Isle of Man instead of the usual rock fare that would be blaring round the average repair shop.

These slightly off-kilter details are a nice way of introducing us to the self-enclosed obsessive world contained in the film, where motorbikes are central and everything else is off the characters' radar. Another thing: the way the characters are brought in introduces us to the element of bawdy, raucous, unsubtle humour running throughout. This is a rare element in a Cronenberg film, though not entirely missing in his other work, and the man is frequently very funny in interviews. It's interesting to see this different side to his normally sober, sombre existential oeuvre. The frequency of outrageous laughs would not really be repeated, except in spots, in any of his future films.

As Lionel tinkers round with a screwdriver and Fred 'reads the articles' in a bike mag, an agitated Bug brings in some troubling-but-exciting news from the unimportant external world: there has been a sighting of a Ducati 900 Desmo SuperSport ("The greatest motorcycle the world has ever known") in their parochial greaser neck of the woods. This bellissimo titular Italian crotch rocket, limited to a mere 40 worldwide, is a soggy dream vehicle for our antagonised protagonists.

Lionel is agonised to find out that the bike was spied at the salesroom of his nemesis, bike salesman Reinhardt (Chuck Shamata; *Death Weekend*), and our three biker buddies motorvate across to Reinhardt's place to find out what happened to the Ducati.

"Boy oh boy, you've really got the hots for this machine, huh?" Reinhardt teases an increasingly animated Lionel. "Okay, yes, I got the hots," he admits. The biker constantly dabs at his nose, and it seems that his excitement is more than just bike-related. His cokehead agitation is exacerbated when he finds out that the Ducati has been sold to a rich art collector. To add insult to injury, the nameless knucklehead buyer, not even a member of the bike community, has procured the superbike merely to put in his living room and use as a sculpture-like objet d'art.

Back at the workshop, a heartbroken Lionel, cradling a piece of bike handlebars as a comfort blanket-cum-fetish-sex-toy, rages about liberating the SuperSport from the hoser holding it hostage. "A guy like that makes me want to kill! How can he look at it and not wanna make it go? I don't understand it!" Lionel howls in mortally offended, wounded-libido animal rage. The Ducati's living room exhibition fate is a crime against motorbikes, as far as he is concerned.

The uneasy rider starts jumping around screaming like a spoiled, coked-up child with no cut-off switch, jumping round on a table, smashing the place up. Bug and Fred counter steer the blockhead to a chair and clamp headphones over his head, playing the record of the loud engines of the Isle of Man racing bikes to act as a hilarious sonic pacifier to the tantrum-throwing man. They clearly know how to deal with what are obviously not infrequent journeys into his coke-stoked chaos. Three cheers for the electroconvulsive therapeutic qualities of garage-furniture-saving high fidelity.

On a recon mission to some local sculptors Fred knows, he finds out that the bike has been bought by a high roller and swinger named Edgar Moutte (Louis Negin; *Rabid*). Our intrepid biker trio pretend to be from a nonexistent mag named Techno-Art World, making an appointment to visit Mouette in his futuristic-looking house to supposedly photograph the Ducati as a work of art. As this is exactly the sort of preening exhibitionist exposure the poser bought the bike for, he gladly allows them access to his newest acquisition.

Mouette introduces his swinger wife Lana (Toby Tarnow; *Howdy Doody Show*) and the suave lounge lizard of their home, Lana's lover Ricardo (Geza Kovacs; *The Dead Zone*). He is kept around the house to service Lana, but also primarily as another Warholian living art piece for Mouette to enjoy. There then follows some slightly stilted musing on machines and human beings as art, and the corporate commodification of art in the modern age. "The art world just becomes another branch of Canadian Tire," shrugs Ricardo.

The pretentious aphorisms being lightly mocked here, contrasted with the roughness of the bikers, are the sort of thing that J.G. Ballard would often come up with. They're the sort of highbrow concepts that Cronenberg would explore in many other films. With a longer running time than *The Italian Machine* has (more on which later), Cronenberg would have had the chance to flesh out and explore some of this stuff to interesting effect. Here he's just trying to jam in too much, to both satirise and provoke thought, in the rush to move the plot along.

For his distracted part, Lionel doesn't even notice introductions being made, or musings on sex and art and commerce. Prostrate on his knees before his own personal deity, he is hyperventilating over the Ducati in the centre of the living room. He has eyes only for one inhuman beauty, swooning in beyond-ecstatic reverie at the sight of his heart-betrothed bike. He reels off its technical specifications like another man would liplick over a woman's bodily measurements.

Lionel gets overly excited, as usual, when he finds out that Mouette, innocent of any concept of bike maintenance, has neglected to fill Lionel's lover's oil sump, not wanting it "to drip oil on the carpeting." Lionel is mortally offended by this whole situation because, at his core, he and Mouette are far more alike than he would even care to admit.

His half-sexual admiration of the Italian machine as a work of art far surpasses the rich man's. His jealousy and despair at the bike belonging to the wrong person are like a man walking in on his woman with somebody else, or being jealous of somebody else's partner.

The barely-veiled techno-libidinal elements of Lionel's bike obsession, the wistful whispered enumerating of its vroom-vroom va-va-voom curves and bodily fluids, and a half-buried desire to merge with the machine, all echo what Cronenberg would penetrate and explore in a far deeper sense in *Crash*, two decades later.

Lionel starts to rant at the philistine Mouette and is dragged away for a pep talk by Fred. He has noticed a weakness for the old Bolivian marching powder in Ricardo, and thinks he has a plan to wrest the bike from Mouette's scandalously bike-vandalising clutches. Lionel persuades the art-stud to petition his owner to sell the bike in supply for two months' supply of cocaine, which the bikers get wholesale.

The devious, coke-addicted Ricardo can't really afford to turn the offer down. He corners Mouette and says he wants to buy the bike cheaply for himself. His masterstroke is to appeal to Mouette's pretentious avant-garde sensibility and ego: Ricardo says it would be like one objet d'art buying another for the first time in human history.

Mouette loves the self-aggrandising idea, which can be photographed and documented for New York art magazines. He agrees to sell the bike for one dollar. "To keep one's name before the public is almost an art form in itself," he sighs wearily. All roads lead back to Mouette. Being a trendsetter is such a time-consuming bore.

Never underestimate the ego of a shallow, affluent show-off prick, though. Ricardo learns this to his cost, on finding out he has been replaced in the art collector's fickle, affected affections by a new male art model—and a much uglier one at that. It's the hard knock life for a peacock cokehead layabout, and that's a tragic eternal human truth.

Zoom over to the happy ending. The biker boys, and Lana, await Lionel's return to the garage after his first tarmac-hugging consummation with his new gutsy revving bride. "It's a very serious machine," Lionel sighs in satisfaction, when he returns. "You're starting to treat the machine just the way Edgar did. It's for riding, no?" notes Ricardo philosophically.

The film closes with the three motorcycle musketeers bombing along the Canadian highways and byways, zipping around each other, the Ducati finally getting the good hard riding Lionel has been wanting to give it for the whole short running time. What a relief.

Interestingly, the end of the film could be seen as a precursor to the start of Cronenberg's next feature. At the end of *The Italian Machine*, Fred, played by Frank Moore, is driving along the highway with Bug and Lionel, as noted above. At the very start of 1977's *Rabid*, which Moore plays a major role in, his character has a motorcycle crash that injures the main star of the film, Marilyn Chambers, who is the bike's passenger, prefiguring all the hydrophobic horrors that follow.

Whether or not Moore was on a bike in Cronenberg's subconscious at the end of the 1976 short, carrying over into the 1977 film, is anybody's guess. It's just a passing talking point, is all. And, of course, there are several other actors from the CBC short film in *Rabid*, too. Also interestingly, the now-deceased Gary McKeehan ended up writing some Hells Angels novels. Perhaps he was inspired by Cronenberg and/or *The Italian Machine* as well. We'll never know.

Despite all the quasi-futuristic trappings and arty-farty mumbo-jumbo musings in *The Italian Machine*, it's actually a relatively autobiographical film in some ways for Cronenberg. The opening credit sequence is only the name of the film, followed by Cronenberg's name appearing over an exterior shot of the film's garage. This immediately locates us in the headspace we can view the film in, if we know enough about it.

And why do I say this, and assert that the film is somewhat autobiographical? Well, the Lionel character was loosely based on a real-life friend of Cronenberg's from his youth, a now-deceased man same-first-named Lionel Douglas. The director and his Jewish friend were best bike buddies for a while round Cronenberg's college years.

A talented writer, photographer and poet, the bike-obsessed Douglas was also a small-time drug dealer, which perhaps informs some of the drug material in *The Italian Machine*. Whatever the truth, the two men were very close for a while, twin bike obsessives. Douglas sadly died in 1979 at a mere 35 years of age, ironically—if perhaps fittingly—in an accident on a bike he was testing. So the short film could be seen partly as a fictionalised homage to Cronenberg's one-time close friend, which is perhaps why there is more humour and slapstick camaraderie material in it than is usual for the director.

A couple of closing thoughts about the film. The performances and directing are uniformly fine. However, any observant viewer will notice several jarring jump-cuts, often in the middle of dialogue scenes. Anybody attributing this to bad editing would be wrong. The depressing reason is that the original film ran for a full hour, but CBC took Cronenberg off the final edit for some reason and hacked it down to a mere 23:37, a horrendous act of cultural butchery.

It makes even less sense when the running time for most other episodes in the series run bang on half an hour, so, even in cutting the film down for broadcast, there doesn't seem to be any real reason for not leaving a couple of the conversational cuts in to add a few more minutes.

The Italian Machine really starts to fall apart slightly towards its close. We don't get to see Lionel's reaction to being told the bike is going to be sold to Ricardo. More importantly, we don't even get to see Lionel mounting the vehicle for the first time, to go for the ride he comes back from near the end of the film, which is utterly ridiculous in context: the whole film before this has been leading up to that pivotal plot point.

We don't know why Lana is at the garage at the end, or why she is hitting on Fred, when Ricardo is right there with them, unless it's just for another swinger's kick. The hackwork editing really makes a pig's ear of some of the material. We are left to wonder if the hour-long version still languishes in some CBC vault or other. However, that being said, the existing disjointed version never gets totally lost, and is relatively efficient in what it presents us: we are never totally thrown out of the film, just slightly disorientated sometimes.

The 16mm cinematography gives the film a grainy, grimy grindhouse aesthetic, but with some highbrow ideas, which is pretty much the usual early Cronenberg aesthetic mix anyway. So whilst what ultimately remains is a slightly mutilated beast, the hacked-edges remnants of the film are well worth watching. They present us with a warm, funny, personal, personable Cronenberg film of rare vintage, with the seeds of some major themes and threads he would explore over the coming decades. It's still a film any fan of the man's work will love, and it's easily available on Youtube and elsewhere on the net. Next move's yours.

Special thanks for the photograph of Lionel Douglas go to his son Max. More details on Lionel's extraordinary life, along with samples of his excellent poetry, photography, and writing, can be found at Max's great memorial site for his father: www.spiltink.org/

Thanks also to Fraser Philip for helping rescue this article due to a PC meltdown.

RE: Queen of Ashes

David Leo Rice

Before either of us became who we are today, we wrote our dissertations side-by-side in an unfurnished flat two streets over from the street where the rest of our cohort—mental midgets one and all—had taken up residence, and our distance from them, intellectually and geographically, has only increased in the fateful decades since. The book-length studies we each produced in that flat established the fundamental principles of the body of work that has come to be known as the *Scorched Earth Topography of Petra Mance,* cementing her status as the world's greatest and, some would say, *only* living artist.

Some would go on to say, and neither of us would beg to differ here, that we put Mance on the map by first drawing that map, defining a space that had never before been filled and then facilitating the process by which she alone came to fill it. What is a society perennially at war, we induced our legions of readers to ask themselves, without the clock ticking down toward the next Mance opening, in which the suppurating fallout, the ruined cities, and the clacking skeleton children feeding like beakless birds on corpses piled up to and then somehow *through* the sky, will all be gathered into the durable expanse of her vision, reified and catalogued for us to behold at the time and place of her choosing, provided we've secured timed tickets long enough in advance?

What, indeed, *is* war if not simply a layman's term for the sum total of Petra Mance's achievement? From where does it issue, if not from the images she has awakened from what might otherwise have been their eternal slumber, in a realm all can intuit yet none before her could access? My conclusion is simpler by far: *there is no war*. There never has been, and, provided we recognize this truth with a few seconds left on the proverbial clock, there never will be. To a degree verging on the tautological, *there never can be*, since any evidence to the contrary is bound to dissolve into the already-almost-infinite imaginarium that Mance has built around herself, and, by extension, around all of us as well.

We are, instead, condemned to a purgatory of nearly unbearable peace, with which all of art—certainly all of Mance's art—has been an attempt, on a planetary scale, to cope. It has been the great tragedy of my life so far that I've been unable to convince my brother, my twin, of this simple fact, upon which, if only it were acknowledged, an entirely cogent worldview could be founded. Every text I've ever produced on the Mance-conspiracy, from my dissertation to my first bestseller, *Dreams of Ruin: Yearning for an End That Will Not Come* (which, though I try not to gloat more than a little, was responsible in no small measure for procuring the elegant cottage we've shared, all these years, deep in the Black Forest), all the way to my recent *Trapped in the Mancescape: Dispatches From an Imagined Front*, has been, at root, an attempt to disabuse my brother of his increasingly deranged conviction that Petra Mance has dedicated her considerable genius—this much I do not dispute—to helping humanity orient its thinking around a new world war which will, he's convinced, sooner or later grind our global experiment in billionfold cohabitation to a permanent halt, leaving only—what else?—Mance's masterpieces as relics, for whatever beings come after us, should any come, which my brother, naturally, is convinced they must, if only to regard Mance's work with the slavish devotion he's certain it will always deserve.

If a person won't see it willingly, they cannot be forced to. The limits of force, in psychic as well as bodily terms, are clear enough, as Mance herself takes pains to show in piece after piece after piece, often constructing entire ruined cities to demonstrate in no uncertain terms—for those of us iron-stomached enough to meet with our gaze that which she has offered up to it—what it looks like when the limits of force, as humanly understood, break through to something altogether beyond the human scale, or, to quote my younger self, the author of the bestselling *Mance: A Primer for Facing Humanity's End* (a tome that is currently taught, I'm told, in two hundred secondary schools in Germany alone, with another fifty-eight in Austria and Switzerland, the result being that its outsize earnings, year after year, have almost singlehandedly kept my feckless brother and me housed in fine Bavarian style, with no end to the crisp white wine he consumes at a rate even beyond my own, which, I'm not too proud to admit, is already well in excess of what any respectable mitteleuropean doctor would recommend for men of our age), when "the limits of human control overcome themselves from within, thus appearing to show us from without, in cascading sprays of ash, smoke, and boiled viscera, what we've been made of all along."

If that's not as real as it gets, what is? This, if he and I were still speaking, is the precise question I'd put to my brother, who, though he sits beside me typing away at an identical console, might as well be drafting the charter of a pygmy kingdom in the New Guinea of some nineteenth century children's tale, for all the common ground we share at this late stage in our illustrious careers—or, at any rate, in *my* illustrious career and his at best highly questionable and at worst actively specious one.

As we sit at our consoles, typing along in fear of what I can only describe as "the ringing of the bell," although it's a purely internal deadline, and one that seems to come earlier and earlier in the day, until, soon enough, we'll find that dusk precedes dawn (as, ha-ha, it surely does already, and always has!), I watch myself type, "But at what point does the fear that Mance's art *must describe reality* become a self-fulfilling prophecy? At what point do we begin to commit the atrocities she represents *after the fact*, if only to obviate the otherwise unbearable dissonance of witnessing images of events that seem as though they *must be real*, and yet aren't? And who's to say this point hasn't arrived already, perhaps long ago, so that Mance's art does indeed describe an extant war, one that, even as we speak, might well be considered *the single motive force of human history itself...*"

I gag, remove my hands from the keyboard, drag my buzzing fingertips across my forehead and into what's left of my hair, and then, swallowing bitter jelly, delete this line. A harbinger of the bell's imminence, I've found, as if, at day's end, my conviction that I'm myself and not my brother was scheduled to fade, in anticipation of the moment where we're at last allowed, or compelled, to recede into our static-bath, dreaming that the rift between us had been healed long ago, or had never been opened in the first place.

"Still, it cannot be entirely discounted that something in us—in Mance's most committed admirers particularly—*yearns to believe* in the war, to imagine that death is grandiose rather than banal, that corpses pile by the thousands in the streets of Antwerp, Rotterdam, Dresden, and Leipzig, melting together into an otherworldly waxwork, rather than wasting away between sheets scoured with mass-produced bleaches, hooked to useless machines in rooms whose very normalcy conjures a horror far more profound than that of any hooded firing squad or mass grave in a birch forest bubbling with quicklime."

I sigh, delete this line, glance furtively at my brother, who's likewise sighing and deleting, and decide to knock off work on my new and likely greatest study, tentatively entitled, *Against the Tide of Anti-Mancism: 1,933 Reasons Why the War is Realer Now than Ever*. I'm not unaware that we've been knocking off a little earlier each day, a trend whose longterm impact is easy enough to predict, but still, when my energy leaves me, it's gone. No energy remains to oppose the loss of purpose that comes over me at moments like this. I try not to dwell on the possibility that some terminal sequence has thus been initiated, so that my brother and I, despite how much more we (or, at least, *I*) have left to say, are already facing a finale that will turn out to have come not so much *too soon* as, grimly, *right on time*, making fools of us both in the end.

If I were to dwell on this possibility, I would be unable to resist the conclusion that we are—or, again, *I am*—being silenced by the same forces that have elected Petra Mance as their supreme earthly avatar, and thus have a deeply vested interest in her colossal propaganda campaign never being identified as such. Indeed, I might go on to speculate that some force so large it can be grasped only in its dimmest emanations has conjured both my brother and myself to consecrate our lives to the tragicomic pursuit of elucidating not only *who* but also *what* Petra Mance really is, a fool's errand whose very foolishness takes on the transcendent quality of prayer.

Before I close my console, I glance over to confirm that my brother's distracted, as he always seems to be while the last of our energy steams through what have come to feel like holes in the backs of our heads, fontanelles open to a world beyond this one. Then, as quickly as I'm able, I access my sent email folder. This ritual has grounded me ever since I was quite a young man, when I began to reread the missive I sent to Mance upon the completion of my doctorate, asking, simply, for proof that the war whose representation she'd staked her career upon was indeed underway.

"Queen of Ashes," was the subject line. The text, after an honest if perfunctory preamble about the impact her work had had on me as a student and a sheepish link to the university archive where my (jejune, I'm at last able to admit) dissertation had been published, read, simply, "Where are the bodies? Not the bodies you sculpted, but the bodies you sculpted your bodies *for*… or, if you'd rather, *of*. The bodies whose agony your paradigm-shifting works ostensibly shifted the paradigm in order to commemorate. Please show me. I would love to see them, outside the context of the MoMA, the Tate, the Whitney, the Prado, the Louvre, the Venice Biennale, the Hamburger Bahnhof, or any of the new venues continually arising in Miami… I will meet you anywhere else. I will also give you my address, very near the geographic center of the Black Forest, in a cottage that will one day be famous for having been the site of the composition of the most lucid studies ever produced about your epoch-defining artwork. This cottage will also…"

But here, even back then, even before my brother and I lived in the cottage I'd already begun to claim as our own, I cut myself off before saying what I believe I'd already begun to intuit: *this cottage will also be famous as the site where your true self, greater than that of a human being, was conceived, gestated, and birthed upon a floor of ancient oak, in air redolent of virgin pine, by two fathers made motherly through some force capable of achieving this inversion without the slightest pressure to reveal itself, nor even to admit its presence in the background of all things, even now, when such notions are said to have been banished to the deepest of the deep woods, inaccessible to the human foot and the human mind alike… so that you are our daughter, much as we are, in no uncertain terms, your sons, imprisoned in the cottage we have perhaps been imprisoned in for all time, despite having dreamt of a youth and young adulthood at the university, in an unfurnished flat on the…*

Now, as then, I cut myself off before discovering what I actually believe the case to be. I would never admit that I consider certain notions best left unexplored, though I am well aware that my behavior indicates how fervently I do.

—

We gave up eating long ago, nourished since earliest middle age on our respective nighttime broadcasts alone, but we have not yet given up our early evening bottle of wine. We sit at our simple, though by no means inexpensive oak table in the gathering shadow of another dusk in what must be nearly the end of summer, and we say nothing as we bathe in the natural light—how salubrious this light will soon come to seem—and refill our glasses again and again, each of us surely noting that the other drinks more, and taking what solace we can from this fact.

When the bottle is empty and the sun has burned out in the depths of the underbrush, once again rendering the Black Forest genuinely *black*, we stand from our oak table and shuffle toward the innermost part of the cottage, where our twin television sets, pushed into the east and west corners of the room, await.

Here a kind of magic trick or physical impossibility occurs, as each of us helps the other into his handcuffs. Even, or perhaps especially, after the course of a lifetime spent in this exact nightly position, neither of us has generated a convincing hypothesis to explain how this is possible. Of course we have each, at one time or another, posited the intercession of a *third presence*, a stage manager or caretaker assigned to our case, but no evidence, other than the handcuff conundrum itself, has emerged to attest to this caretaker's reality—so that he or she, as I sometimes think while locking my brother's hands behind his back and pushing his head as deep as it will go into the warm bowl of static that boils out from the screen to receive it, becomes a miniature version of the larger Mance conundrum, insofar as her work attests to the near-certainty that the *war to end all wars* is raging through the night—this night, as every night—and yet what evidence, *other than her work*, exists?

Does all logic come to rest in this same graveyard of tautology, yielding only the premises it began with?

And what's more, I think, as I in turn help my brother into his handcuffs and ease his head into its screen with a kind of tenderness that would make me blush were he able to see it, who's to say that, if any evidence did emerge, it too wouldn't *become part of her work* by the time it reached us? What principle, indeed, could possibly limit the scope of Mance's project, and, if the answer is none, then what principle is there to say that Mance's project exists at all?

Are my brother and I alone in the world in believing that Petra Mance exists? I wonder, as the warm, sticky static flows first through the hole in the back of my head and then through my thinning hair and across my scalp, massaging my skull and seeming to *remove its outer layer* so as to play across the scrim of mucus housing my brain, soft as the shell of a softshell crab. It ripples over and then inside this scrim, penetrating it without breaking the surface, so that now my brain and the static are made of the same material, buzzing and frying together, as, from within this fry, her voice emerges.

Not only will I not answer your question, she hisses, *but I won't even admit that it is a question. You will fulfill your purpose. None can do otherwise.*

The static shimmers, breathes, and resolves into a panorama of soldiers in chrome masks spraying poison through the smashed windows of a housing estate. It resolves into country roads blocked with rusting tanks and butchered horses, and a woman in a shredded dress running from a farmhouse while a dozen sharpshooters turn her neck into a sponge. It resolves into fighter jets reducing dense forests to shivering spindles and giants herding children and livestock into barricaded churches while werewolves in leather trench coats douse them in kerosene and breathe them alight, and eyeless ogres hack apart gypsies with scimitars so long they vanish from the frame, and somber old men clad only in medals dine on the kidneys and bladders of screaming priests.

The fry is endless, working its way down our necks, along our spines, and into our bellies, liver, and groin, filling us up as, behind the endless proliferation of imagery—so familiar that it serves as a kind of blanket—Mance's face comes slowly into focus. It rises behind the flattened bunkers and rivers of lead, gazing down at the submarines rotting on beaches and the mushroom clouds that swallow the sky. She smiles, serene as she surveys the extent of her achievement, and nods as the shipping departments of the world's great museums, to say nothing of the acquisitions staffs of the many princes hidden away in castles throughout the Black Forest, arrive with their forklifts and flatbeds to collect what is theirs.

Our heads swell with static and heat as this final image—it is dawn in the scene, much as, surely, it is dawn outside the cottage—plays out, the slow, proud departure of the many flatbeds, each carrying its own battlefield and its own archive of teeth, its own mass rape and its own wedding party massacre, as they disperse into the wall of pines.

We are left to imagine them as they unload their cargo in the subterranean receiving department of one princely estate or another or another, their names so rarified as to hover above or burrow beneath whatever boilerplate passes for recorded history, altogether unknown to the credulous masses who will, in their own turn, wait for hours outside the great museums of Paris and Vienna and Rome and Saint Petersburg for their own pitiful chance to see, staring over the heads of their fellows, the latest in the seemingly endless series of masterworks by the incomparable Petra Mance, a being to whom, it now seems undeniable, all of human evolution has been leading.

—

We fall out of our TVs and into the light of day, our handcuffs suddenly released, our heads so swollen they prop our bodies at forty-five-degree angles when we try to lie flat on the floor. We lie—though one could equally well say *we stand*—like this for most of an hour as our heads slowly deflate, hemorrhaging static so that something like a skull can regrow around them, hard enough, save for in one place, to block our awareness that this crude bone shell will be melted down again at dusk.

As soon as the static drains from our eyes, deliquescing as tears on our cheeks, we look to one another and recoil from the sight of the smudged, nearly expressionless face looking back, like a mirror covered in petroleum jelly. Blurrier every day, we think, more pocked with dim whorls of black and white, as if some force were melting us down and fading us out, turning our once-taut skin to pulpy fat.

We grimace, force the image out of mind, and replace it with our longstanding enmity. Time to refute my brother's nonsense once again, we each think. For the good of mankind. This thought, canned as it's come to seem beneath the watery membranes that now pass for our skulls, is all we have left to set the workday in motion, coffee having lost its effect in the late 90s, if not before.

"The horror of what is currently afoot in every cranny of Europe," I write, "from the southernmost reaches of the Algarve to the northernmost fjords of Norway, from the west coast of Ireland to the bogs of Novosibirsk, is nothing short of the death rattle of humanity, a moral crisis that, without the divine gift of Petra Mance's nation-sized installation pieces, we would be forced either to behold in raw incomprehension, or to turn from in a kind of brute denial that would, in the final reckoning, be synonymous with suicide."

"Indeed," I continue, "if the art world, in league with the narrative management wings of a dozen Western governments, to say nothing of the UN and its many silent partners, persists in propagating the claim that Mance is *responding to* rather than *seeking to cause* a new world war, I fear that such a war will indeed *begin in earnest*, if only to relieve the otherwise unbearable pressure that this charade has caused in the minds of all thinking people. This, I maintain here, as I've maintained throughout a body of work that, in a less corrupt society, would've earned me the Nobel long ago, is the single gravest threat facing humanity in our lifetimes."

The day is off to a good start. I work hard for several hours, though never as many as I would like. Before long—earlier and earlier, it seems, a suspicion that I've perhaps voiced before—a kind of mental deadening comes over me, as it clearly comes over my brother as well, so that now we're at our simple, though by no means inexpensive oak table in what is no longer the *fading light of day*, but rather what we might more honestly term *the orange-yellow simmer of mid-afternoon,* our heads full of static even before we affix our handcuffs and ease into our static baths, as if the ritual of burying our heads and feeling our new skulls dissolve once again were merely cover for a transformation that's already occurred.

As if, I picture writing, *this too, all of it, were a Mance installation, a metaphor for a reality that can only be known through metaphor, and can thus, in truth, never be known at all.*

—

We're back on the floor in the morning, waiting for our heads to deflate. Then we're typing again, then popping a new bottle of white wine. Then we're back in our handcuffs, back in the static, synagogues burning, mosques burning, crosses burning, icons burning, records burning, train tracks burning, gas billowing down from spigots hidden in the ceilings of orphanages and ballet schools, bodies crushed together so tightly the dead stand straighter than the living.

All is rote, until, in the distance, the fry hardens into a phalanx marching toward us, along a country road made also of static—the surrounding wheat is static, the Atlantic coast, choked with antiaircraft guns, is static, the Flemish sky is so roiled with static it looks like a million black birds seething against a grayish white matte.

When the phalanx arrives, it consists of row after row of soldiers in teal uniforms with armbands sporting an impressionistic insignia, an artist's poetic or confused conflation of a swastika, a star, a triangle, and an infinity sign, while, at the head of the phalanx, a general in a darker, more regal version of the same uniform strides up to my brother and me, both of us likewise made of static, and hands us a buzzing notarized envelope.

It shocks our fingers when we accept it, but we do not flinch. We tear open the wax static seal, which bears the same insignia, and pull out the pulsing and breathing letter inside, which reads, in peppery text atop a salty crinkled sheet:

RE: Queen of Ashes

Hello. I've received your missive and am now ready to respond. Thank you, if it's what you want to hear, for making me what I am today. If it's any consolation, please know that the same forces that have turned me into this, have turned you into what you have become, or will soon become. There is, in the final calculus, only one force in the universe, though it works through many intercessors. Many avatars, many emanations, many metaphors. There is no saying what would have happened had you not written what you wrote, just as there is no saying what would have happened had I not made what I made. There is no saying, of course, because there is no future other than the future that there is, if you'll pardon the tautology, or allow me to call it fate.

We will proceed now to my studio, as the two of you are finally soft enough to work with.

The letter boils away as two officers shackle us, each in our handcuffs again. They march us through a ruined munitions depot and into the outskirts of an unknown city, beyond the train station, half-submerged in a crater, and out to a warehouse surrounded by tanks, helicopters, and row after row of guard towers, each protected by two barbed wire fences, between which sleek black dogs paw at frost-hardened thistles.

Beyond all this, we are, at last, buzzed into the studio. Inside, the phalanx disperses and no one emerges to take their place. The *Mance-spirit* is palpable everywhere, pungent as boiling fat, but there's no sign of Petra in person, and we know better than to cast about looking for her. We proceed across the tremendous empty space, trying not to shiver as the echoes of our footsteps disappear.

The space is wider than seems possible inside a building, wider than any field or pasture we've ever crossed, wider than the Black Forest itself, but, with patience, its width begins to dwindle and the familiar sight of our cottage comes distantly into view. Home at last, we think. We're nearly home at last. We picture our simple though by no means inexpensive oak table by the window, and how nice it will be, especially after the day we've had, to relax in our usual seats with our usual bottle of white wine, before we are compelled to handcuff one another yet again.

Home from the war, we think. We've made it home from the war, after days and weeks and years abroad, uncertain if this moment would ever come.

We let ourselves in through the front door and enact the table-and-wine-ritual we'd pictured a moment ago, sighing with relief as warmth and comfort return.

When the bottle is empty, we proceed to the room where we've slept our lives away, no longer attempting to type even for an hour at our consoles. We slip into our familiar positions, hands cuffed behind our backs and faces in the static, skulls already beginning to soften.

Now, at last, you face each other, says the voice which has so often denied that our question is a question at all. *Here, I'll show you,* it continues, as the static boils and churns before stabilizing on the image of the two of us with our hands cuffed behind our backs and our faces pressed up against one another inside a single TV set, nose to nose, mouth to mouth, eye to eye, no longer in our opposite corners, inside our separate sets. We boil back and forth like we're made of soft licorice, sometimes fusing together, sometimes pulling apart with ropes of blood and sinew dangling between us. *You will tour the world in this state,* the voice continues, its syllables soft yet totally self-assured, *from the MoMA to the Tate to the Prado to the Broad, from one end of Miami to the other and on to Las Vegas, until you arrive in the vault of a prince whose name will never be committed to paper. The Twins Who Saw It Coming, I'll call it, and my voice as you hear it now will play over and over in the room where you're stored, along with a reading of all the texts you've ever produced, arguing with yourselves unto eternity; the split fate of the world-spirit, known only to you two, and, as such, unknowable, by whatever measure you failed to know yourselves—this is what the piece will seem to stand for, in the minds of the many who saw it once.*

Your two faces, nearly melted by now, will melt the rest of the way together, so that neither will describe an extant person, nor even a parody thereof, but rather only the meeting point, the thin line of contact where nose flows into nose and mouth flows into mouth. This point will stand as the single locus of truth, the infinitesimally narrow line between one heresy and another, between nonsense and its double...

She laughs loud enough that the tableau, which we can see from outside even as we remain within it, shakes and groans, as if held together by nails already beginning to rust.

Now, relax. In a moment, the entity you long ago named Petra Mance, back in that unfurnished flat you shared at the start of what you each rightly foresaw as a world-historical career—or the flat you dreamt you once shared, from deep within the cottage where all of this was set in motion—will emerge with her welding kit and her teeming coterie of assistants, and your final transformation will begin. Take this moment to decide upon the thoughts that will recur in perpetuity inside your conjoined head, once Petra and her assistants have fused your separate softened skulls

*together. Whatever is in there then will be in there for all time...
...in the vault in the heart of the prince's castle in the heart of the Black Forest, before the war ravages even this estimable redoubt, and you are lost in the frenzy of looting and displacement, never to be found until that story, like all stories, finds its way back into Mance's project, so that, long into the future, you will be recast as a tiny piece of an immense tableau entitled* The Raid on Prince X's Secret Holdings, *a piece that, even on such a scale, will at some point itself fall victim to yet another war, which will then, in turn, find its own place in an even larger tableau in the...*

Something shorts out. It flickers, burns, and begins to smoke as the tableau's capacity to know itself fries its circuits and, in the silence at the very back of the screen, an emptied mind thinks, if only through force of habit, *the day's last light is coming through the window, long after the war to end all wars is over... spilling across our simple yet by no means inexpensive oak table, where the two of us are sharing a bottle of cold white wine in the dimming glow of another day's work well done, in silence together with all of our books arrayed neatly on the shelves behind us and nothing but a good night's sleep up ahead, handcuffed side by side as we prepare, in dreams, to enter that sacred space reserved in the universe for twins alone.*

Unless otherwise noted in the End Credits, all interviews were conducted jointly by David Leo Rice and Chris Kelso.

Communications

"OH SHIT, HERE COMES THE FUCKING WRITER"

Notes on the Making of Spider

Patrick McGrath

In 2002, David Cronenberg released a moody, introspective adaptation of Patrick McGrath's 1990 gothic novel Spider, *a contemporary classic of alienation, paranoia and the extremes of unreliable narration. Here, McGrath recalls how the collaboration came about.*

I'd already written the script, at the prompting of the producer, Catherine Bailey, a friend of my wife's, and someone showed it to David in Toronto. As far as I remember, he and his wife were on the next plane to London, where I was spending the summer. My wife and I gave them dinner and it was a very warm and friendly meeting. I don't think we talked much about the script then.

After this, we had to bring him and Ralph Fiennes, who was considering the role of Spider, together. They'd never met. We had no idea if they'd hit it off or not. The whole thing hinged on that relationship, and we could not be sure they'd commit to each other, no guarantee at all, and if there was any reluctance on either side, all bets were off. I remember we got out of their way (it was in a hotel lobby in London), and after about two minutes the pair of them were laughing. Phew!

Spider's dad was played by Gabriel Byrne. He told David he could never be sure if a line in the script was a true memory of Spider's or a false memory of Spider's, or a total hallucination, or what. That's how weird Spider's mind was. So David came to me and asked me to please mark up the script so as to make clear what realm of reality each scene was playing out in. So I did, and

Gabriel was much relieved.

Once we got down to work, he had one note only: get rid of the voiceovers.

All of them? I said.

All of them.

How will we know what Spider's thinking?

Cronenberg: We leave that to Ralph.

Me: Okay.

It took about an hour to delete all the voiceovers, perhaps less. And that was that.

So the process of literary adaptation was, in my case: take the script as it was, get rid of the voiceovers, and hand it off.

On set, we had no problem working together—in fact he knew exactly how he wanted to do it, and needed no further input from me. Whenever I showed up, he'd say, "Oh shit, here comes the fucking writer." (I like to believe this was a joke.)

I can't remember any difficulties or differences in our respective perspectives on the film. Basically I knew his work, I admired it, I trusted him. He had the script he wanted. He conferred at great length before shooting each scene, not with me but with his cinematographer, David Suschitzky, and with his actors, Ralph in particular.

I expected Cronenberg to inject a lot of body horror, as the character, Spider, has a great many somatic delusions. To my surprise, David did no body horror at all, and remained focused on Spider's very sick mind. I thought this restraint did the film a great service.

David and many of his support team had that easy going geniality that I associate with Canadians, as I'd lived in Canada for many years when I was younger. We shot all the interiors in Toronto (exterior shots all in London), and David of course enjoyed enormous respect and affection from his team, with whom he worked on practically all his movies. No friction at all. All went very smoothly apart from the production running out of money early in the shooting, and the crew having to take our producer's word for it that she'd find the money even if she had to sell her house. The backers, a group of bankers, had suddenly backed out, when we were already in production. David didn't interfere in any of this. He said to me, "You make an independent movie, the work is a joy and the money is hell. You work in Hollywood, it's the other way round."

Filip Jan Rymsza

While Filip Jan Rymsza will argue that any direct influence from David Cronenberg on his 2021 film *Mosquito State* is purely ascribed or assumed, there's no denying that Rymsza's stimulus is evidently Cronenbergian.

Set on the precipice of the 2008 stock market crash, we are thrust into the reclusive life of social leper and wunderkind designer of high-frequency trading models, Richard Boca. Boca anticipates the collapse and after his obnoxious yuppie colleagues refuse to pay heed, he goes about serving himself up as the human blood-meal for a hoard of home-invading bloodsuckers. Rymsza offers us a wonderfully unique mood poem of urban isolation, but it has the complexion of a modern film-maker experiencing his medium through the lens of ideologies and principles put in place by auteurs of the past—with Cronenberg unmistakably among them.

Q – What was your central motivation when making *Mosquito State*? How did the idea of a man succumbing to a tornado of bloodsucking insects come about?

A – Simply, I wanted to make something contained. The inspiration came from real-life—an infestation endured by my co-writer, Mario Zermeno. Then we developed the character to serve the premise. I wanted Richard to not merely "succumb" to the mosquitos, but to commune with them. For that to work, I needed their union to function both as a drug addiction—because, as the mosquitos multiply, so does the potency of the "hits"—and as a sex act—sublimating his sexual desires and becoming an abstract means of reproduction. In the end, his affection for the mosquitos needed to be paternal.

Q – There is a beauty to the swarm. Their lifecycle is presented in forensic close-up, but aside from the disfiguring welts they leave on our protagonist, the mosquito is never treated as an antagonist. Could Robert Boca be so disconnected from the rest of human society that he eventually sees the purpose and beauty in offering himself up as a living blood-meal?

A – Yes, he's that disconnected. He feels closer to his algorithm than to any of his co-workers, so it made sense that he'd develop a similarly protective affinity for his mosquitos. He creates an environment in which the mosquitos can thrive (a "mosquito state") and understands his place in this closed ecosystem. It's also important to note that, while his allegiance is with his algorithm and not with the market, away from work, it's with his brood of mosquitos, not with humanity.

Richard sees beauty and meaning in the mosquitos, so I wanted the swarms to suggest a certain consciousness, and, individually, I found a genus of mosquito that looked the least threatening, so that when "Mother" dies and is entombed, she looks almost angelic.

Q – Is it purely coincidental that this film was released in the midst of a pandemic or did it play a direct part in the impetus and overall shaping of the 'message' behind film?

A – Pure coincidence. Yet another black swan.

Q – The film is unique and shot with a singular artistic eye, but was the spectre of David Cronenberg ever hovering over this piece, simply by virtue of its modern body horror themes? How would you say he has impacted on your artistic sensibility, and that of your peers?

A – Not consciously. For whatever reason, I was exposed to Cronenberg a bit later than Buñuel, Roeg, or Lynch—if I can lump them all in together—so there's some Joseph Merrick in Richard's movements, but I don't recall drawing from Cronenberg, although

I can see why people would think that and I take those comparisons as praise.

I remember reading about *Crash* in *Film Comment*. This must've been during my junior year of high school and that sent me on a quest to find an uncut, NC-17 version of the film. That was my introduction to Cronenberg. Then, I saw *eXistenZ* and *Spider* during their theatrical runs... but everything else was on VHS. *Scanners*, *Videodrome*, *The Fly*... until *Dead Ringers* and *Naked Lunch* came out on Criterion. Those were the days! When each Criterion release was cause for celebration. It's really hard to assess Cronenberg's impact, but I'm sure his films shaped me in an unconscious way and became a part of my artistic makeup.

Q – We wanted to ask you as well about portents, the idea of making a film today set on the eve of the 2008 crash, and how that ominous atmosphere resonates now. What was your thinking along these lines as you developed the film? Also, how does this tie in to the various ways that Cronenberg anticipated the future, or worked with future-fear and hope? If Cronenberg's heyday was the 80s and 90s, anticipating the disturbances of the new millennium, what epochal disturbances are you thinking about or trying to evoke today, and how does 2008 figure into that?

A – The idea to set the film in 2007 started with Michael Lewis' book *Flash Boys*. I became fascinated by the "Golden Goose" and dark pools, so I decided to set the film in that world and modeled Richard after one of those quants. The screenplay predated Trump, but, once we got into production, I felt his noxious presence. We were all asking ourselves "how the fuck did we get here?" so this persistent dread factored in.

During prep, I watched *HyperNormalization* and that helped contextualize some of the things I was seeing and feeling. Not that I agree with everything Adam Curtis is saying, but, looking back at 2007 with a decade's hindsight, his notion of a "fake world" really resonated with me. We were living with present-fear, but the rot started back then, in the mid-aughts, so, in an attempt to find the causes, I decided to chronicle a week in August just before it all came crashing down.

Cronenberg's fascination with the flesh (and the New Flesh, in all its many forms) is somewhat different. Richard doesn't transform into a mosquito. His metamorphosis is mental and his relationship with the mosquitos is symbiotic, until the mosquitos multiply beyond his ability to sustain them.

Q – Thinking of mosquitos as a kind of technology, a living system that works very efficiently to produce certain outcomes, what do they have to tell us about finance, politics, and culture? Are they antithetical to human commerce, or a microcosm of the same forces? What central understanding can a study of mosquitos, such as you've undertaken here, help us to arrive at?

A – I was more interested in them as a would-be plague, like with the many Biblical plagues. To me, they're a harbinger. Pestilence, disease. On the other end of the spectrum, we have the honey bees, which are disappearing and no one knows why. So, I took Richard's prior obsession, the honey bee—ordered and productive—and replaced it with the mosquito, the single, deadliest threat to human life. This felt like a fitting juxtaposition.

Q – Given that a central theme of this book is Cronenberg's early work, and thus the notion of early work in general, how do you see *Mosquito State,* as your feature directorial debut, fitting into your career? Where would you like to go from here, and how might that either build upon or depart from what you've done so far?

A – You'll have to ask me in 15 to 20 years. What I'm doing next feels connected. Maybe not so much thematically, but its manner of storytelling feels related. While *Mosquito State* glanced back, *Object Permanence* looks forward... and I'm sure the Cronenberg comparisons will follow.

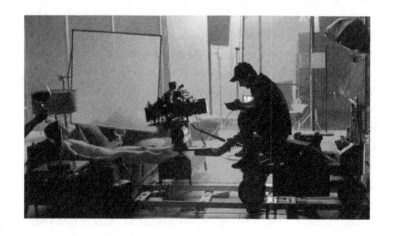

BRUCE WAGNER

Bruce Wagner is one of the most subversive, hilarious, and humane authors ever to examine the nexus of shame and dignity, often through the lens of Hollywood in novels such as *I'm Losing You, Force Majeure, Dead Stars,* and *The Marvel Universe: Origin Stories*. In 2014, Cronenberg directed *Maps to the Stars*, starring Robert Pattinson, Mia Wasikowska, and Julianne Moore, from Wagner's screenplay. Here, he discusses how that collaboration came together, and what Cronenberg's work and friendship have meant to him over the years.

Q – What is your earliest memory of contact with Cronenberg's work? I know you were active in the horror movie scene in the 80s as well, with Wes Craven and others—how did Cronenberg's films strike you then, and which ones were particularly impactful? Were they seen as instant classics, or did they take time to catch on in the US?

A – I worked with and loved Wes [Craven] yet unlike Wes' films, David's remain unclassifiable. Personally, the two men share/d a kindness; a scrupulous, easy tenderness, but that's where the similarities end. David's films are an admixture of visceral horror and cerebralism. And *stylish*. They go to unknown, unconscious places and are dangerous that way—you're dared to follow. To become a *Cronenburgundian* aficionado means to join the Illuminati of the Body of his work. So many of them struck deep chords. I always love when there's a clinic in his films; I love the names he gives to corporations and clinics. *Videodrome* stands out, with its cogent satirical dissection of entertainment and the zeitgeist. *Dead Ringers* brought me home. It had all the themes that captivate me and inform my own work: the double, incest, mutilation.

Q – How did you and Cronenberg first meet, and how did you begin to collaborate on what would become *Maps to the Stars*? What was it like collaborating with him, and what insights did he bring to the process of working in your narrative wheelhouse?

A – Years ago, David and I shared the same agent. My memory—which may be flawed—is that our agent told me that Cronenberg had read some of my work and was a fan. I immediately set in motion a plan to visit him in Toronto, under the auspices of my adapting a section of my first novel, *Force Majeure:* "The Holocaust Museum." That was the beginning of a long friendship.

I had written *Maps*—this was 30 years ago!—the way one would make a dream diary. I knew it would never be made. But it was cathartic because for years I did Hollywood hack work. This was something I could call my own and could never be poisoned. I showed it to David not as something he should direct because I knew he didn't work that way. You can't "pitch" him something. It would have been too crude. (Again, my memory may be flawed.) Things come to him in the ether—though mostly an ether of his own. I showed it to him and can't remember getting much of a response. Ten years later, he called just as I was leaving a movie theater—I can't remember which movie—and said he wanted to direct it. I was shocked, in the best way, of course. Because I knew he wouldn't make that sort of call casually. *I knew he was ready to go.* So that added a frisson. He flew to New York and met with Julianne Moore, who immediately signed on. As it turned out, it wouldn't be made for many more years, nearly another decade. A large part of the reason was because he wanted to shoot it entirely in Los Angeles. (Another thing that shocked me.) But the cost of that was prohibitive and the project fell by the wayside. He must have made four or five films after that; when each came out, it was bittersweet. *I could have been a contender.* Then he called again, when in Cannes for *Cosmopolis*. He said that Robert Pattinson had agreed to be in it. We were off to the races.

David's a writer but didn't change a word. He may wish he had! I was on the set for the shoot, along for the ride. Watching him work was like the twins in *Dead Ringers* but without the pathology and the kinks. Absolutely surgical, stylish, fearless.

Though he'll probably have a resentment about my saying without the kinks. So let's put it back in.

Q – Much of Cronenberg's success, in terms of making movies as subversive as his on a large scale, has been attributed to his resisting Hollywood and remaining in Canada, where of course the funding structures for movies are very different—in that way, he belongs to a small category of "major underground filmmakers," which almost seems like an oxymoron. Given your own extremely incisive take on the soul-sucking nature of the Hollywood machine, what was it like to work with Cronenberg on a film about the very machine that he'd spent so long avoiding? How was his perspective on Hollywood, as an outsider, different from your own, as an insider? What do you think would have become of him had he gone to Hollywood earlier in his career, and was *Maps* a reckoning of sorts for him?

A – I don't think he's anti-Hollywood at all. It's too easy a target. And Hollywood is quite capable of making art. Hollywood, inadvertently or deliberately, has made astonishing art. Both of us have said in interviews that *Maps* is *not* a satire. I see it as a tone poem and a tragic comedy. My inspiration was Strindberg—a "chamber play" called *The Pelican*—and not *The Player*. My novels aren't *about* Hollywood. Many are set there but in the end exhume the monstrous and sacred aspects of us all. The Human Tragicomedy. I was never interested in making *The Player* and neither was David. Why?

Q – People don't often think of Cronenberg's work as funny, but I've always found a streak of Jewish gallows humor running throughout it, harkening back to Kafka and Pinter, in its take on the paradoxes and absurdities of human life, especially within modern society. Your work, of course, has an extremely rich and powerful satirical aspect as well, mixed in with its horror. How does this kind of humor dovetail with horror, and do you find this to be an important aspect of understanding Cronenberg's work and worldview?

A – I would argue that people *do* think his work is funny. He's so funny that your head explodes. The Jews just can't escape that sort of humor. David and Leonard Cohen have the same radically mordant sense of humor. What respectable Jew doesn't? It's the punchline in the Void, the "laughter in the Dark." If you can't laugh through the horror, you're finished. Laugh as the Woke Police cart you away; laugh all the way to your cell; laugh when the steel door locks behind you; laugh as you're drugged, spayed, and erased. That'll show 'em.

Q – Many people in this book have written about the relation of literature to film in Cronenberg's upbringing and career. He's the son of a journalist, began his studies wanting to be an "obscure novelist," as he put it, has directed numerous literary adaptations, and eventually published his own novel, *Consumed*. You have also worked in both media, while focusing more on the literary side. How do these two art forms relate, and how do they differ, specifically within the career of someone doing both? How has literature itself been affected by cinema, and what can each art form express, in terms of the dark side of the soul that both you and Cronenberg plumb, that the other art form cannot? What does Cronenberg uniquely bring to the table when adapting someone else's novel?

A – Those questions are panoramically above my pay grade. What David "brings" is unique to the mysterious characteristics, attributes and proclivities of that unique sentient being called David Cronenberg. It's possible for an illiterate film director to make the most faithful adaption of an imposing, iconic literary work; so could a "literary" one. It's irrelevant.

Q – Why have his films from the 80s and 90s aged so well, whereas many other great filmmakers of that time seem more dated by comparison? What do these films have to tell us about the 2020s that still resonates, and can films of equal power still be made today or has some door slammed shut?

A – They age well because they come from a timeless core. They're not dependent on current fashions and idiosyncrasies, all of which are transient. He's alchemical; a potion is a potion is a potion.

Q – Which novel should Cronenberg adapt next and why?

A – "The Holocaust Museum" section of *Force Majeure*! I'm kidding. I'll go back to Leonard Cohen. When Dylan won the Nobel Prize, Cohen said something like, "To me, giving him the Nobel is like pinning a medal on Mount Everest for being the highest mountain." A mountain's going to do what a mountain does regardless of the medals and novels and theories we try to pin on it. And will outlive us all.

MICK GARRIS

A fresh-faced, soft-spoken Mick Garris first interviewed David Cronenberg 40 years ago for the Los Angeles based *Z-Channel*. The show was called Take One: *Fear on Film*. Garris played plucky mediator, as he often does to this day, to a roundtable of horror movie genii—John Carpenter, John Landis, and David Cronenberg. A mere seven years later Garris would pen the controversial sequel to *The Fly*.

Q – Do you remember David Cronenberg during his formative years? Do you recall your first encounter with the man, with his work—and did his sensibilities seem established even as a fledgling artist?

A – The first time I saw his work was when I saw *Rabid* and *They Came From Within* (*Shivers*) on a double bill at a suburban cinema in the San Fernando Valley. I was working as a receptionist, answering phones and operating the R2-D2 robot at personal appearances, at the Star Wars Corp., and I was so blown away that I actually wrote him a fan letter on Star Wars letterhead. I was dumbfounded to find that, when we met up when I was working at Avco Embassy a few years later, he had remembered that note, and that it had come at a trying time in his life. The very first time I took note of him was on my first ever trip to England, where there was an enormous billboard for *Shivers* posted in Picadilly Circus. I didn't see the film then, not until that fateful evening in the valley cinema, but when I did, I knew from the beginning that this was a very important and iconic voice genre cinema already.

Q – When discussing the merit of his early output (*Transfer*, *Stereo*, and the like), which is your favourite and why? Cronenberg himself is dismissive of his early work. He once told Serge Grünberg: 'My very first film, the one before it, which I've completely forgot the name of... *Transfer*!'

A – I confess that I still haven't seen *Transfer*, *Stereo*, or *Crimes of the Future*. I'm sure I'm the poorer for that blank space in my cinema education.

Q – Obviously Cronenberg is an artist you have due respect for, and you've been vocal about your admiration throughout the years: when you wrote your sequel to Cronenberg's *The Fly* did his looming image ever threaten your sense of creative freedom, or did you find you were able to proceed with the writing process with complete license and benediction?

A – I was completely intimidated by writing the sequel to one of the—if not the *very*—best monster movies of all time. But he was very supportive. The original script I wrote made every attempt to approach it in as adult a way as Cronenberg had. Stuart Cornfeld and Mel Brooks, himself, were very supportive of the approach that I had taken, but the powers that be at Fox were convinced that they wanted a teenage monster movie. But the shadow of David Cronenberg is a long one, and anyone trying to sequelize his work is a fool not to recognize that. I ended up leaving the process after a few drafts, and left it in the control of the studio so that I could direct my first feature.

Q – But what is it about his work that is so transcendent? Why has his work endured the test of time, thematically while some other Masters of Horror have suffered with recent retrospective appraisal?

A – Well, I'm not so sure I accept your premise of a negative reappraisal of the Masters of Horror—that has not been my experience when it comes to the elder statesmen of the genre. But what makes David special is not only his scientific mind, but his deeply real and emotional characters. There is no denying the intelligence and originality of his writing, and his best works—like

The Fly and *Dead Ringers*—plumb deep into human psyches like no other filmmakers. His films are at once literary and visceral... and fearless.

Q – People view him as a cold clinician. Someone who is largely cynical/nihilistic about humanity and the future advances of technology, or at least he communicates a unique horror-filled acceptance of our fates. In your mind, do Cronenberg's films expose his own deterministic view of human nature, or does his work portray the artist as an advocate of human freedom?

A – Interesting question. There is a clinical quality to his stories, but not in the same sense that Kubrick had. David is interested in science and technology, but his stories—particularly from *The Brood* onward—are deeply and heartbreakingly human. I wouldn't necessarily call it acceptance, but one has to surrender to the reality of the world around you. It's neither acceptance nor submission, but a need to cope in a world of increasing demands. The monsters and the villains of Cronenberg's films are not necessarily human, but the humans are infested by them, sometimes voluntarily, and other times as victims. But victims to cancer metaphors, not to so-called evil creatures.

TIM LUCAS

Tim Lucas is probably best known as creator and curator of *Video Watchdog*, a magazine of criticism which specialises in critical discussions of popular and obscure horror, fantasy and science fiction films. We first crossed paths in 2012, when Garrett Cook and I were looking for content for our short-lived anti-*New Yorker* magazine, *Imperial Youth Review*. Tim offered us a wonderful short story, 'Banishton'—his only piece of published short fiction to date. Frankly, he is one of the most underrated writers of his generation. His 1994 erotic horror novel, *Throat Sprockets*, is one of the most visibly Cronenbergian works of art produced in the last thirty years. Yet Lucas also has a direct and enduring connection with David Cronenberg. He first met the man himself while preparing an article on new trends in horror for *Heavy Metal* magazine in January 1981. The two men hit it off straight away and exchanged home numbers. Cronenberg was the first person Lucas had ever met who shared his joint passion for the works of Nabokov and Burroughs—according to Lucas, these two 'literary twains really didn't meet among anyone in the established critical elite, so he was not just an artist I respected but a kindred spirit, someone who I thought could give me renewed direction in my life.'

Tim's most recent novels are *The Secret Life of Love Songs* (PS Publishing) and *The Man with Kaleidoscope Eyes* (Electric Dreamhouse), the latter a fictionalized account of Roger Corman's experimentation with LSD prior to the filming of *The Trip* (1967).

Q – When did your interest in his work start and what finally motivated you to devote so much of your creative energy to covering it?

A – I started out as a writer wanting to be a novelist. I wrote several fiction manuscripts but these were essentially me teaching myself to write by trying on the techniques of my favorite writers at that time. The first was called *The Audience Becomes Flesh*, which I wrote in 1975; that title sounds very Cronenbergian now, but then

I was still a couple of years away from seeing my first Cronenberg film. It was, however, undisguisedly [William S.] Burroughsian. It conflated autobiography and dream and made use of cut-ups and so forth. When I wrote my first real magnum opus, a 500-page novel called *TV Heaven* (again, several years before *Videodrome*), I got a very encouraging response from an editor at St. Martin's Press, so I spent another couple of years finessing it... and when I sent it back to the same editor, I received an almost immediate form letter rejection... and that broke my heart. So I threw my dreams of becoming a novelist in the trash. My work for *Cinefantastique* and also *Heavy Metal* magazine at that time was the only thing paying me any money, and I first interviewed David for a piece I wrote for *Heavy Metal*. This, in turn, led to his inviting me up to Toronto to cover the making of *Videodrome*. For me, who spent most of my time locked in a room in Ohio, the trip to Toronto was a rare opportunity for paid worldly experience. Most of all, I was attracted to Cronenberg's work because we discovered we had the same sources of inspiration—people like Burroughs and Vladimir Nabokov. David was the only other person I'd met who appreciated them both, as I did; in the early 1980s, they were commonly seen as very different kinds of writer, poles apart; the perfect crystallization of thought and word on the one hand, and literally typed pages cut up and reassembled on the other. In my first conversation with David, I remember us also talking at some length about Thomas Pynchon, and I think it was because we connected as writers rather than through film that he gave me his home number and invited me to keep in touch.

Q – You detail your experiences with Cronenberg on the set of *Videodrome*, but would you say it was largely positive? Away from the camera did he remain the obsessive artist we might imagine him to be, or is this merely fan-projection? Were his day-to-day conversations more grounded?

A – Yes, my experiences with David were almost entirely positive. And when I qualify that statement, I suspect he would as well. To list a couple of my own failings... as David ascended in the film business, he sometimes had to accept the decisions of his producer or his studio just to get his films made, and I really had no respect for anyone but the artist. (Probably one of the reasons it took me so long to really achieve anything!) When David told me that his *Twins* movie was going to be called *Dead Ringers*, I could not hide my disdain—I could only think, this was a very serious film—a tragedy, really, as a whole chain of his films from that period are—that would be shipped to theatres with a jokey, ironic title that, worse still, spoiled the ending! (I still hate the title, like a mustache that's been painted on his masterpiece.) So the more years that passed, I found myself feeling disappointed by decisions he was making—because, as I can now see, they weren't mine—and being unable to hide that. I also thought it was ridiculous when he agreed to star in that Clive Barker picture [*Nightbreed*, 1990—ed.]; I didn't understand that side of his nature. That he could be the artist he was and still be—to use his own word—a "ham." And now, if you look him up on the IMDb, that's the first thing you see: David Cronenberg—"Actor." I wasn't seeing the Big Picture, that he was partly acting to promote himself, to learn more about how to direct actors; it didn't occur to me that he might be following an overall career strategy, or a broader life strategy, never mind the overwhelming responsibility he must have felt for keeping a lot of fellow Canadians, people he loved, employed. Not seeing this was my failing completely, but that's how much I came to identify with him. It was really a big warning sign for me that I was investing too much of myself, my own creative energies, elsewhere than I should have done. His wife Carolyn used to chide us (me, really) because I could only talk about his work. It got to be like that because ours became a working relationship; I was always sort of "on the job" around him, but I was also very good about keeping the personal stuff out of the work I filed. I always knew these details were for me, not for general distribution. I even aspired at one point to move past interviewing David to become a kind of press representative for him, and it's a good thing it didn't happen because my singularity of focus on him in the 1980s meant that I wasn't focusing enough on myself, my own evolution, my own work. When I came out the other end of our relationship, I found that I had *finally* become the writer I wanted to be. I had assimilated my influences and inspirations and was able to sublimate them, to write in my own voice. I stopped visiting his sets after *The Fly* in 1986, and it was around that time that my friend Steve Bissette asked me to write a story for *Taboo*, the horror comics anthology he was preparing. Steve told me that I could write anything I wanted as long as it broke some kind of taboo. And what I ended up doing was three chapters of a graphic novel that got enormous critical attention from *The Comics Journal* and the like, and subsequently evolved into my first traditional novel, *Throat Sprockets*.

Q – And *Throat Sprockets* even dresses itself in certain Cronenbergian tropes—obsession, mutation and the venereal. The book focuses on an unnamed advertising executive who trawls porno theatres during his lunch-break only to discover an obscure film called *Throat Sprockets*. An obsession with women's throats soon engulfs his psyche. It sounds like the great unmade Cronenberg movie. Was his influence as overt as I've made it seem? Has Cronenberg ever given you feedback on the novel?

A – David and I haven't actually spoken since I turned down his invitation to write a book about the making of his film of *Naked Lunch*. This would have been in 1990 or '91. There were a few reasons why I turned it down, the most important one being that I had just launched my magazine *Video Watchdog* and was writing most of each issue myself. Had I accepted, the magazine that sustained my wife and me for the next 27 years would have been stillborn. There was simply no time—and, again, I had found my own voice. It was time I started representing and promoting myself... at the belated age of 35.

I did not consciously think of David while writing *Throat Sprockets*. I can see now that one of the reasons why my early writing hadn't caught fire was that I didn't have much in the way of worldly experience; I was young, I had married young, and had read a lot of books! Most of what I knew about life was second hand. But those two weeks I spent respectively on the sets of *Videodrome* (in 1981 and '82) and *The Fly* (in '86), and the two days I spent on the *Dead Zone* set (in '83), were an immense education. I was a more open person than I'd been in school, and I was there to ask questions, so I was exposed to many, many different kinds of people, situations, backstage dramas, little emergencies. A lot of people see *Videodrome* as David's masterpiece, but he was writing it as he was shooting and it was unfinished on the last day of shooting. He didn't have an ending for it. He even asked me if I had an ending for it! He finally had to come back six months later to do some reshoots as he continued to wrestle with it. I didn't have that problem with *Throat Sprockets*, which I suppose owed something to *Videodrome* just because the film and (more so) the experience of being on that set were a tremendous part of myself at the time, but *TV Heaven* was also in there, along with my own fantasies, my love of language, my dreams, and some of my own neuroses. Any resemblance to *Videodrome* is there because it was part of me; the book is ultimately far too personal a novel to just be something I chipped off of Cronenberg.

Q – Why do you think Cronenberg's influence has remained so constant? He seems like one of those rare artists capable of incorporating the flux and mystery of his time into cinema. Do you think some artists, like Cronenberg, are simply lucky enough to live at exactly the right time for their sensibility to be maximally relevant, or does the sensibility also develop as a symptom of the times?

A – Cronenberg writes about the human animal in contrast to the rapidly accelerating technologies and trends of his time. I see what you mean about his influence remaining constant, but I don't think any film he's made since *Dead Ringers*, really, has had the kind of lasting influence you're talking about. This is not an unusual situation; Burroughs was always remembered for *Naked Lunch* though he wrote some wonderful later books. Nabokov was known for *Lolita*, but he wrote dozens of books including several of equal if not greater brilliance. Cronenberg's uniqueness may be that he was the first fantasy filmmaker of his generation to approach films from a well-read literary foundation, as well as an awareness of avantgarde cinema. He wasn't another of those guys who talked all the time about how important *Famous Monsters of Filmland* was to him. He was also Canadian, which made him a more cosmopolitan individual, and Toronto had given the world Marshall McLuhan. As a young man, he had been influenced by McLuhan's philosophy, so we can safely say that Cronenberg started out as an intellectual, and he managed to smuggle that worldly education into the mainstream by revealing those layers of his mind and being in horror films. His contemporaries had very different influences. People like John Carpenter and John Landis really weren't on the same level at all. The one who comes closest is Joe Dante, but Joe's big influence was humorists like Will Elder and Frank Tashlin. His films are jam-packed with nuttiness, and they're also very warm. You can tell he loves people. Cronenberg's films are basically cold—they start out very cold with the early shorts, and then they advance into more commercial terrain (and commercial means they connect with larger groups of people), occasionally experimenting with warmth (as in *The Dead Zone*) but still largely concerned with characters who wander down some very strange avenues in their effort, their struggle to connect with other people. Our world as it is today has everything in common with that aspect of his work, because everything about our world, our communication, our governments, even our sex lives, is now under the knuckle of technology. Wonderful as David's best films are, I don't know that they continue growing with us, as much as we've stopped growing as a people at about the point where they left off in the 1980s. It will be interesting to see what his new movie has to say. I think our world needs what he has to say.

Q – Cronenberg's oeuvre almost seems to serve as a bridge between the mid-century and the late century psychic disturbance: his early films feel like Beckett or Pinter plays. What are your thoughts on his very early work, like *Transfer, Crimes of the Future* and *Stereo*?

In your eyes, how did they set his ascent in motion? Do they have value still?

A – I think their value is much like the value of my early failed novels to me. I'm not saying those films are failures—on the contrary, they have an impressive consistency and a very unique, even droll charisma (I think the 1970 *Crimes of the Future* is especially good)—but they allowed him to learn his craft, to see how far he could advance in that particular guise or persona. Had he remained single, he might have pursued that vein a bit longer, but as he married and started a family, I think more commercial forms of expression needed to evolve from those abstract, collegiate beginnings.

Q – When you discuss his turn toward a more commercial direction, it's interesting to consider how he perhaps began to swim in the same waters of 80s and 90s mass culture that he was also fetishizing and satirizing. What were the opportunities and pitfalls in this double-exposure to commercial culture for a filmmaker like him? Do you think he could have had an even more singular career if he'd remained fully committed to the avant-garde, or is his particular gift that of smuggling avant-garde sensibilities into a commercial format? What might a fully mature Cronenberg who'd remained avant-garde have made instead of *Videodrome* or *Dead Ringers*, or how might those films themselves have been different?

A – You have to remember that, even as he was making *Videodrome* and *Dead Ringers*, his work was being constantly modified to please his producers and the studios involved, or at least he was modifying himself to deliver something recognizably marketable. It's interesting to imagine *Dead Ringers* remade by the Cronenberg of *Stereo* and *Crimes of the Future*; it might have been more documentary-like with more poetical narration, told more like it was a true story (as in fact it was). Likewise, *Videodrome* could have been more Burroughsian, as indeed *Naked Lunch* could have been. I don't feel the *Naked Lunch* movie is particularly successful, due to some of the casting and the special effects emphasis, all of which had to do with making it more attractive to people who knew nothing of Burroughs. At the same time, I happen to know that he turned down some popular musicians like Sting and Patti Smith, who wanted very badly to contribute to that picture. He ended up going with that brilliant Ornette Coleman score—a masterstroke, but hardly a commercial decision. So it would be very wrong of me to suggest that he never got his own voice back from some of the compromises he was compelled to make.

Q – You said earlier that *Dead Ringers* is his masterpiece (I agree!), yet *Videodrome* is overwhelmingly the most discussed and seems like it will almost certainly be the film he's best remembered for. Why do you think this is? What does *Dead Ringers* touch on or get at that might be somehow beneath or beyond critical and cultural discourse?

A – I think *Videodrome* is the most discussed because it IS the least cohesive. People can more easily enter into its space and imagine what they might impose of themselves upon it. This makes it a more personal experience. I would actually love to see David go back to all the different drafts (there were many) and assemble a definitive, cohesive novel using all of its best elements and imagery. The movie doesn't tie up everything. It was not until I did my audio commentary for the Arrow Films release that I realized the viewer can easily impose a circular structure on it; it works that way. As for *Dead Ringers*, the occupation of the two brothers alone was enough to have pushed the film beyond cultural discourse. I remember David had a devil of a time finding a bankable actor who was willing to play not only a gynecologist but TWO gynecologists. Of course, he ultimately got the right actor for those roles, but because the film is not only sexual but so clinically sexual (much in the same way that *Crash* is), people become self-conscious about discussing it because they don't want to reveal (or even find out) on which side of various lines they stand.

Q – Looking in the opposite direction, what about political paranoia, or the possibility of organized forces that go beyond the relationship of the individual to the numinous? You mentioned Pynchon earlier, who's a real touchstone there, and there are numerous times in David's work where various conspiracies are suggested, as in *Secret Weapons,* yet he's never made a film explicitly about this aspect of mass media. Also, as you say, he hasn't necessarily made a film of totalizing impact after the millennium, when the Western world seems to have turned toward a more all-encompassingly paranoid state, and the role of the individual has come ever more into question. Is there any connection here, or anything else to say along these lines? Is there a way that the zeitgeist of the 80s and 90s could more directly speak through him, as compared to the post-9/11 zeitgeist?

A – An argument can be made that every American film made in the wake of 9/11 is a fantasy film. It's not uncommon now, in a television series, for a beloved character to die in Season 3 and continue on as a ghost, a spectral mentor, an imaginary friend, or in flashbacks, through Season 5 or 6. And these are not fantasy series; these are series viewers praise for their "realism." We now commonly accept such formerly "spook show" concepts within our purview of reality. So the entertainment we now receive from everyone—not just Cronenberg—has changed the ways we see ourselves in the mass reflection of our media and made our sense of reality, of the world around us, all the more amorphous and changeable. On a similar point, it's estimated that 0.56% of American adults identify today as transgender; however, I would estimate that the presence of transgender people in films and television is actually of a somewhat higher (read: disproportionate) percentage because films and television have become agenda-based in recent years, committed to portraying a social ideal of equality inclusive of everyone. The goal is to promote acceptance and understanding but it will also likely promote and encourage identification. We all identify with the people we see in films and on television. I'm not saying this is wrong, because some people are unsure of themselves and may need such illustrations to guide them to where they need to be;

I'm saying that this idealized media image of ourselves, as a true melting pot of all kinds of people, will likely encourage mutation in our lives and perceptions—because it's a jolt away from the way films and television have presented the world to us within living memory. And there's no way that all the fallout from this can be good, because no good deed goes unpunished. The inner caveman is always aroused, the pendulum always swings back. This is true amorphousness in action and you could fairly say that Brian O'Blivion predicted all this. Likewise, when he talked about the tumor induced by the Videodrome signal that would lead to mass hallucination, was that really so different to what certain networks have actually done by spreading biased disinformation to millions of viewers, effectively pouring gasoline on a highly flammable audience? I think the vast conspiracies you allude to are also present in *Videodrome* in the person of Barry Convex and the intimated Military Industrial Complex interests behind him. As I mention in my own *Videodrome* reportage, David noted that the quotes attributed by Convex to Lorenzo de' Medici actually came from other people. "Love comes in at the eye" actually comes from William Butler Yeats' "A Drinking Song," and "The Eye is the Window of the Soul" is not-quite-precisely a line from the *Book of Proverbs*. His point was to show how brazen and cynical certain conservative political groups could be about misappropriating and misrepresenting facts for their own purposes. It's a very short step from there to today's "alternative facts."

KATHE KOJA

Kathe Koja has revolutionized the horror novel several times over, perhaps most notably with her 1991 debut *The Cipher*, which introduced the "Funhole" to the world, an entity as ominous, provocative and psychosexually potent as any in Cronenberg's oeuvre. The Funhole acts as a kind of organically-manifesting liminal space, a disintegrator-integrator (or molecular rearranger), mutating input into new and terrifying matter.

Q – Body Horror permeates your work. I'm thinking about your novel *Skin* in particular, which has a character who sculpts her own body as a kind of performance art, reminiscent of an apolitical Petre Pavlensky or Rebecca Horn. You deal with the horror of body-modification and self-mutilation in a very elegant and measured way. What about the political dimensions of body horror, in terms of zombies, infection, reproduction, and other aspects of the biological dimensions of humanity that Cronenberg's films address and call into question?

A – That's an enormous question, and I think the aggregate answer turns on a kind of courage: the courage to look directly, and keep looking, at sights and circumstances that we would normally, as humans, turn away from, be appalled by, or pity, or try to ameliorate. Sight, vision, does none of these things: sight looks. Sight records. Sight is present. The courage to look and keep looking is something Cronenberg's work has always had. *Skin* is the novel of mine that looks most directly at the body (though *The Cipher* is on that same shelf) and the ferocity there would not be out of place in one of his films.

Q – How did Cronenberg's work inform your own in terms of the relation of human desire and psychology to the seemingly inhuman, whether that be environment, technology, or the occult?

A – I can't say there is a direct correlation, but breathing the same cultural air of the same late 20th century, being exposed to the same wrecks and exaltations, means his work, and my work, had the same pool to draw on, the same kind of poisons and nutrients, though filtered through our sensibilities; each person's sensibility who lived through and continues to live in this weirdly perilous era has been shaped and pressured by the increasing demands of tech and the environmental degradation we as humans continue to wreak, in our suicidal fecklessness, on the literal ground upon which we live. It's the same cliff, but different places to stand.

Q – How did it inform your relation to class, marginality, post-industrial America, and the idea of the fringes of cities being sites of particular interest and horror?

A – It's the shared ground, again, and the shared disinclination to look away: and if you spend more than a little time just outside, on the outskirts, of large cities, or—like myself in Detroit—cities that have undergone a beatdown from capitalism, you can see the areas that have been radically marginalized, so much so that the margins have begun to turn on the center. You can see how class is an irritant, an accelerator, to that process, you can see the holes, like rust, eating and eating their way inside. The horror will come from the slant of your viewing. The horror will be particular, but it will begin in that same shared ground.

Q – Your approach to horror is extremely effective at suturing together the cerebral with the visceral. How do these dimensions relate in your process, and how can each bolster the other? What does it mean for your approach to horror that our minds are housed in our bodies but also don't always feel like part of them?

A – We are our bodies, and yet we are passengers, and we are the pains we undergo; if those pains become severe enough, they erode the thinking mind entirely for their duration. Anyone with a hellacious kidney stone can speak to that, anyone post surgery with inadequate pain meds, anyone in the throes of a difficult birth, and so on. The critical mind stands helpless while the body struggles. Great emotion, whether it's fear or something more welcome, can bring us to that threshold too: all we are in that moment is that feeling, and the mind stands, blinking, off to one side, ready to offer rationality or a plan for getting the fuck out of wherever the monster is just as soon as the sweating, staring body can be called to listen, and attend, and act in tandem with that mind again. Cronenberg's work is always so fluid at that boundary, not "comfortable" there but not deterred, either. I hope my own is just as fluid and courageous: Mimicking the mind while it stands to one side, while the senses, and the reader, the viewer, the experiencer, sweats and shivers and stares.

"I Am All the Characters"

An Interview with David Cronenberg

Q – Thinking back to when you first started making films, what was the enzyme that inspired both your distinct aesthetic style and your fascination with what has come to be called "body horror"?

DAVID CRONENBERG – I have no idea. I was not inspired by a particular work or an artist or anything. I was interested in underground filmmaking because it was accessible, and I was attracted to it first just because of the technology. I had always been interested in cameras and imagery and so on. And movies were kind of a mystery in Canada at that time. We had the National Film Board if you were interested in documentaries. And we had some CBC stuff, but we didn't really have a film industry, per se, making movies. Our inspiration and I'm just talking about a group of a few people, including Ivan Reitman, was for me, the New York Underground. This being the 1960s, the ethos was, you don't have to go to film school, you don't have to train on a professional film set, just grab a camera, and go make your own movie. That appealed to me. I looked up "camera" and "lens" in the World Book Encyclopedia. I just tried to figure out how to get the sound to coordinate with the picture, which is different from now. Back then it was very tricky to shoot something with synchronized sound. Then it was a question of, "You want to make a movie, or an underground short film? Well, what is your subject matter?" And then I just wrote some stuff and what came out is what came out.

Q – It wasn't conscious. It wasn't deliberate.

CRONENBERG – No, it was not. As a kid, I saw westerns. Most of the movies you saw were westerns, and I saw some sci-fi. None of that, though, obviously, could you think of as "body horror," which as I'm sure you know, was not my term. Someone else invented that. I've never used that expression myself, so, yeah, it was natural inclination. I was always interested in science. I was always interested in animals. And the strangeness and uniqueness of various creatures from animals and insects. I don't think it was an influence in a usual sense.

Q – Right. It was kind of organic, then. After a career that has spanned more than five decades, has your level of passion to make films increased or waned?

CRONENBERG – I keep thinking I'm finished and then I keep on making another movie. I thought that *Cosmopolis* (2012) was going to be my last movie and then suddenly funding for *Maps to the Stars* (2014) came together and I had been trying to make that for a few years, so I thought, okay, that's my last movie. So, has it waned? I guess it has in that I don't think it's essential that I must make another movie. I feel if my current film, *Crimes of the Future* (2022), is the last film I make, then it's the last film I make. It's okay, it's fine. I've done a lot. I possibly have done enough. However you gauge that, which is always a mystery, anyway. So, yeah, I would say that it waned, and yet when I'm making a movie I'm just as excited and intrigued and obsessive as ever. Certainly, at the beginning of my career when I was wanting to move from underground filmmaking to being a professional filmmaker in the sense of someone who is making his living making movies, yes, there was a real pressure and passion for that to happen, but once that started to happen, then it was just about being a professional filmmaker and navigating those tricky waters because, of course, I was always an independent filmmaker and never an established studio filmmaker.

Q – For those of us who love your films so much, we are very grateful that you keep making them.

(Cronenberg chuckles.)

CRONENBERG – Oh, well, thank you.

Q – Which one of your films do you think most fully captures your vision and which do you think landed furthest from the mark?

CRONENBERG – See, that's an impossible question to answer because I don't have a vision. I suppose I express some kind of a vision, some kind of understanding, in my films, but I'm just telling a story and in it I am putting things that intrigue me, that fascinate me, that bemuse me, that puzzle me. It has nothing to do with a vision, actually. I don't have a list of things that must be in my movies or a philosophical statement of intent. Nothing like that at all.

Q – You actually studied organic chemistry in college and entered an Honors Science program but switched to English and Literature in your first year. Do you find that filmmaking—especially in the genre of speculative or science fiction—has combined and satisfied those two interests?

CRONENBERG – Yes, I think that's definitely true. I really thought of Isaac Asimov, who was a scientist and a science fiction writer, and I thought that maybe that was the model for me. That was well before I ever thought of making films. Then I realized that I wasn't cut out for it, after studying organic chemistry for a year. Just because of the temperaments of my classmates, I really didn't think I was cut out to be a research scientist. And I didn't really want to be a teacher and yet I still did have those interests which were quite passionate, so undoubtedly in creating creatures and physiologies in my movies I am definitely satisfying some of those interests that I had all the way back then. I still have those, in fact.

Q – And exploring them in the most imaginative and exciting ways, honestly.

CRONENBERG – Well, if you're interested in strange creatures, it's certainly fun to invent some of your own. Although I have the greatest respect for the creatures of this planet, which are beyond amazing. It's actually pretty difficult to even match them, but still, I think we will have to remember that being creative is a very childlike thing, not childish, but childlike. It's fun to invent things and creatures and interact with them. Even though you might be now an old serious filmmaker on some level, you're still a child underneath it all, and there is a very playful part of any creative endeavor that I never lose sigh of. I am very much aware of it all the time.

Q – As a filmmaker, illustrator, and fiction writer, I completely agree. You've said in many places that you considered becoming a novelist, and you have of course published a novel, *Consumed*, as well as adapted many "unfilmable" novels, like *Crash* and *Naked Lunch*. How does literature figure into your work, and how have you used this side of your mind to feed into such a visceral and visually singular cinematic output?

CRONENBERG – Certainly, my filmmaking has always involved writing and it's actually how I got to make my first professional films, to write scripts that were desired by producers even though they didn't want me as a director because I only had underground experience, not professional experience. So, it was writing, in each case, though it is true that screenwriting is a very different kind of writing, but the ability to write, I mean there is no necessary connection between being a good director and being a good screenwriter, or any kind of writer. I mean, some wonderful directors absolutely are terrible writers, so it's almost accidental if you're a good director and also a good writer. Writing was definitely for me an integral part of my filmmaking and I guess it satisfied that desire to write for all those many years, though I must say, it was interesting for me to finally write a novel, fifty years later, after I thought I might have done, because I saw how much of novel writing for me anyway was like directing. You're casting it, you're designing the costumes and spaces, you're moving the camera around, and it felt very similar to me to directing but you're using words, of course, in a way that obviously you are not doing when you're making a movie. The dialogue is a critical thing, too. If you could write good dialogue—and not everybody can and certainly a lot of novelists write not great dialogue even though their books might be great, you know—when you try to translate it to screen it doesn't hold up because it's such a different medium, coming out of actors' mouths. Don DeLillo is a wonderful dialogue writer. His dialogue is unique. In *Cosmopolis* [the film], it's all his dialogue. 100%. Not all writers do that, so there's many intricate interlacing between filmmaking and novel writing.

Q – To that point, what do you feel cinema can achieve that literature cannot, and vice versa?

CRONENBERG – They're totally different media. You might say, yes, there is storytelling, and I think it's been well understood, you can get into a head of a character in a novel in a way that you simply cannot in a movie. The information about a character, delivering a character in a movie is very different from the way you do it in a novel. I think when people read a novel, they don't always have a very clear picture of the character, you know, physically. But they have a really great mapping of the interior of their mind. And it's kind of the flip side in a movie, you know, you really have a great idea of what the character looks like, for obvious reasons, but you don't really have a clear mapping of the interior of the mind, at all. They're two media, two different things. Also, for example, I tend to think that whenever I see a movie that is an adaptation of a novel, if the filmmaker resorts to voice over, to monologue, it's usually, not in every case, but usually, it's an admission of failure. Failure to re-imagine the novel as a movie. It doesn't really give you the same feeling that describing the inner life of a character and what that character is thinking.

Q – Do you think, if you'd chosen to be a novelist from the beginning, your novels would have taken on similar themes to your films, or could you see going in a totally different direction?

CRONENBERG – That's kind of impossible to say, honestly. I'm sure that there would be some characteristics that people attribute to my filmmaking. And accurately, probably, that would come out in the novel writing, but I have no way of knowing. Certainly, *Consumed,* is something recognizably from me in terms of connecting with my filmmaking, but different in other ways.

Q – How have ideas of disease and infection changed over the course of your career, both personally and culturally?

CRONENBERG – Let's say, follow the signs. There have been incredible breakthroughs in scientific understanding. When I was born, there was not DNA. Ultimately, there was DNA, and then there was really, seriously DNA and understanding of genetics that go far, far beyond anything that was understood when I was young. Those understandings have undoubtedly influenced *The Fly*, the original short story that the movies are based on. There was, of course, no understanding of DNA, but it was very possible to re-interpret that story as a fusion of fly DNA and human DNA and it just changed the approach significantly. And when it comes to disease and infection, well, of course, once again, understanding of what that is, and how things are transmitted and a much greater understanding of mutation of diseases, but at the bottom of that there was always a metaphor, the political metaphors, underlying disease, fear of infection by foreigners, by the other. That was always there, so I would say anybody who writes about the fear of disease and plague is always talking about human tribalism and fear of cultural encroachment by the other, the foreigners, the strangers. So, on one hand, the scientific part of your storytelling has changed because of the greater understanding of what has evolved from diseases, and look, mRNA is an absolutely brilliant thing, it's really quite fantastic. It couldn't have happened before. So, if you're telling a story now about disease, you might want to involve something like mRNA, but metaphorically what you're talking about with infection would be the same.

Q – For the last two years the big story has been the coronavirus. Seen from today's vantage point, in which a medical emergency has been politicized in extremely perverse and perhaps perversely fascinating ways, how have your interests in the nexus of disease, technology, and human psychology changed? What do you think the David Cronenberg of the 70s or 80s would think about this moment in time?

CRONENBERG – I think I had a pretty good understanding of it back then, frankly. Because this is not the first time. You have to remember that when I was a kid, polio was the pandemic. It primarily attacked children, which made it all the more hideous. And all of the kids in my school, we were all terrified of polio. We were really afraid. And the Salk vaccine was controversial in its time. So, the coronavirus is in some ways really a replay, but with social media and all, you know. But there have been global pandemics before. As I said, I lived through one of them, but what's interesting is how global the response to this pandemic has been, and that is hugely, of course, a result of the internet. There wasn't that then, so the fear of polio felt very localized. It felt like you and your community and your family and maybe even Canada, but mostly the city of Toronto, that's how it felt, whereas now, in terms of travel, the coronavirus pandemic is instantly global and as is the response, for good or ill, so that's quite a different thing, but the actual disease and how to combat it, they're the same. They're the same as Daniel Defoe wrote in *A Journal of the Plague Year*, talking about the Black Plague in London, in the 1600s. Depending on your education in terms of disease history, this is either unique and unprecedented, which it is in some ways, or it's sort of disease business as usual.

Q – As you look back on your early work now, knowing where it led, how does this knowledge compare with where you imagined it would lead when you were making it?

CRONENBERG – I never imagined. I really didn't. I guess people think you must anticipate walking up the red carpet at Cannes or something like that. I was very much a "be here now" kind of person. It was a 1960s thing.

Q – Sure, be present.

CRONENBERG – Live in the present and you know, my anticipations about what I might do were simply, I would have some interesting cinematic adventures. Things would happen. Something would happen, but it was only sort of when *Stereo* or *Crimes of the Future* were made, but the idea that they could be in a film festival was certainly nothing I ever imagined. But then it started to happen, and the films were in the Adelaide and Auckland film festivals. It's not like a career mapped out in any way any more than I had a vision.

Q – At the time of this interview in November 2021, you've only recently completed production on *Crimes of the Future*, which is also the title of your second film released in 1970 and your first original screenplay since 1999's *eXistenZ*. Is there a difference in feeling for you when you direct a script that you conceived versus a script that was a collaboration or based on a novel?

CRONENBERG – No, there's no difference. In fact, I wrote *Crimes of the Future* twenty years ago. It's as if it's a film written by somebody else. I often said to the crew, when they said, "How are we going to do this?" I said, "I don't know what the crazy screenwriter was thinking when he wrote this." I'm being funny, but I'm also being serious. Once you have committed yourself to it, it's the same, and there is no sacredness. It's not like each line of dialogue is Shakespeare and must not be messed with by an actor or whatever. It's completely in the present, deal with it. For example, I wrote *Crimes of the Future* for Toronto and I ended up shooting it in Athens. I completely embraced Athens as a world of the movie rather than try to fight it and make it feel more like I originally thought. It's a very organic, ongoing process for me.

Q – With which of your many characters do you most deeply identify? And why?

CRONENBERG – I identify with all of them. As a director, you are an actor. Any time a character speaks as you are watching that character on your monitor with your headphones you are being that character and that's how you test the veracity of the performance for me, as a director of actors. Am I that character at that moment? I feel like I am all the characters. Male. Female. Whatever they are. And so, I don't really identify per se more with one than the other. Flaubert can say, "I am Emma Bovary." Well, I completely understand it and I feel that he is telling the truth.

Last Transmissions

We Can Remake It For You Wholesale

Andrew Farkas

I awoke—and wanted Mars. Not Kurt Neumann's *Rocketship X-M* Mars (where the astronauts plan to go to the moon and, uh, right, sure, I guess, take a wrong turn?), not Brian De Palma's *Mission to Mars* (De Palma having become a parody of himself by the time he made this flick, which showed he could become a parody of a parody), not John Carpenter's *Ghosts of Mars* (so much a remake of *Assault on Precinct 13* that I think of it still as *Assault on Precinct Mars*), not Ridley Scott's *The Martian* (Scott having been, in my opinion, replaced by an extraterrestrial or cyborg after *Alien* and *Blade Runner*, since the rest of his films are dreck), nor Antony Hoffman's *Red Planet* (unless maybe we can get the good stuff, the backstage fights between Val Kilmer and Tom Sizemore, and none of the godawful "script"), nor Yakov Protazanov's *Aelita—Queen of Mars* (though the Red Menace on the Red Planet does have a nice ring to it), nor Ib Melchior's *The Angry Red Planet* (except I do think Mars would be even scarier if it and its denizens looked like they were constructed via a bargain basement technique with a snazzy name: CineMagic), nor Byron Haskin's *Robinson Crusoe on Mars* (but only because the title should've been *Robinson Crusoe innnnnnn Spaaaaaaaace*), and definitely not the Flaming Lips' *Christmas on Mars* (a flick I watched at the Music Box in Chicago all by myself, thinking the entire time, "I could just go. At any time, I could just get up and leave. The door to the rest of my life is right there. There it is. No one would stop me. And, honestly, if I stay for the whole thing, well, I'll only have myself to blame..."). No, none of these. Not even Paul Verhoeven's *Total Recall* Mars (though it's full of so much campy goodness). No. No, no, no, no, no.

I wanted David Cronenberg's Mars.

In my mind, I created a wife for myself who said: "I made coffee." My simulated spouse looked like Sharon Stone from *Total Recall* with some teenage boy-style modifications (thanks to the fact that she doesn't exist anyway).

But with my coffee, I wasn't focusing on Sharon.

I will see it, I said to myself. *After all these years, now that they're remaking the Philip K. Dick story, since everything gets remade and remade again, I will* finally *see David Cronenberg's Mars.*

There was a time when that seemed impossible. After Verhoeven made *Total Recall* (a movie I enjoy, by the way), I assumed I would never get the perfection of Cronenberg directing a film based on PKD's work. And set in Chicago! I lived in Chicago! If the film were made, maybe they'd use the intersection of Diversey and Halsted for the Rekal, Incorporated office. The innocuous environs (a Walgreens on the northeast corner, an old shop that sold fur coats called The Furry Godmother on the southeast corner, a Dunkin' Donuts on the southwest corner, and then there it'd be: Rekal on the northwest corner), well, it'd be perfect. And, you know, any problems could be cleaned up in post. Daily, I could walk down the street and watch one of my favorite directors work...

Instead, the darkness of my kitchen, the unreality of my beautiful wife, my mounting student loans, my suspicion that I'd never get an adult job—everything conspired to remind me of what I was. *A miserable little graduate student headed for the adjunct farm*, I said to myself with bitterness. Unlike Kirsten, Douglas Quail's wife in "We Can Remember It For You Wholesale," Sharon didn't have to bring me back down to Earth. I was already below it. I lived in a garden apartment—real estate code for a basement.

"What are you laughing about?" Sharon asked, her impossible glamor model looks apparently projected by a machine from the defunct Museum of Holography that used to exist in the West Loop on Washington. "A dream, I bet. You're always full of them."

She should know...

"Listen," Sharon wrapped her ethereal arms around me, pressing her impossibly large, though flickering breasts against my chest, "you already have *Videodrome* and *eXistenZ*, two of your favorite movies. You already have *Scanners* and *The Fly* and *The Brood* and *The Dead Zone* and *Dead Ringers* and *Naked Lunch*. You even have *Eastern Promises*, though it makes you think Martin Scorsese called in sick one day and so, as if auteuring were like pizza delivery, Cronenberg took over. The fact that someone else is going to—" She broke off. "You're not listening. You should be. This obsession you have with seeing him remake 'We Can Remember It For You Wholesale…' You're doomed, Andy. You're… What's going to become of you?"

"I'm going to campus," I said, finishing my coffee, readying myself for the long bus ride down Halsted to UIC.

Sharon vanished, but I could still hear her voice. "You're getting worse. More obsessed every day. Where's it all going to lead?"

To where I've always wanted to go, I replied in my mind.

—

Standing at the corner of Diversey and Halsted outside the mysterious empty storefront on the northwest corner (mysterious because who in their right mind would allow such prime real estate to lie fallow?—and it remained that way for four years!), I saw the building transformed into Rekal, Incorporated. Not a science fiction-looking structure, but an unimposing brick three story with an awkward awning over the door bearing the name of the business. There I imagined two meetings.

The first was the scene between Quail (the protagonist) and McClane (the boss at Rekal). At the time, I saw Philip Seymour Hoffman in the Quail role, while McClane would be played by Jon Polito. Here, McClane describes what Rekal does. They don't book a vacation to Mars for you, they implant a memory of a trip to the Red Planet into your mind. When Quail asks what good that is, McClane says it's actually better than the reality could ever be. Reality, after all, is messy, unpredictable, and often disappointing. After *Videodrome* and *eXistenZ*, this idea that the simulation is superior would be perfect in Cronenberg's hands.

The second meeting, this one between David Cronenberg and Ronald Shusett (a producer and screenwriter on *Total Recall*), requires a bit of an explanation. As a teenager in the 1990s, I often heard the term "sellout." It was one of the most insulting labels for any artist, used with the greatest derision. I don't feel like that happens at all anymore. The first time I heard this term was in relation to the band Metallica. I was told, by quite a few people, that *Kill 'em All* (1983) was a great album, but by the time of *… And Justice for All* (1988), the group had sold out. The idea was that a band, or any artist, really, could cave in to market forces, ditch their old principles, and give the masses what they want (which normally meant becoming bland) in order to make a lot of money. A high profile version of this insult came when Tom Waits said Michael Jackson should just get an office at Pepsi headquarters already since he (Jackson) obviously wanted to work there so much.

David Cronenberg isn't the kind of artist who would sell out (seeing as how he turned down the chance to direct *Return of the Jedi*). And so I saw him entering my Rekal office, played, of course, by himself, having worked on the "We Can Remember It For You Wholesale" script for a year, to meet Ronald Shusett, the producer who owned the rights to PKD's story, played by a man with a bag over his head, since I don't know what Shusett looks like or anything about him.

"You know what you've done?" said Ronald Shusett in a voice quite clear for someone with a bag over his head. "You've done the Philip K. Dick version."

"Isn't that what I was supposed to do," said David Cronenberg.

"No, no, we want to do *Raiders of the Lost Ark Go to Mars*," said bagman.

Cronenberg declined, went on to make *The Fly*, and, if they ever heard about it, scored points with just about everyone I knew in the '90s.

Crossing Diversey to catch the #8 bus, I wondered, if Rekal actually existed, what memory would I have implanted. On my way to campus, I figured it'd be one with no student loans.

—

"Why are you home so soon?" said Sharon, her holographic projection stronger for now.

"Who's going to direct the remake of *Total Recall* ?!" I asked, sweating, flustered.

Beat.

"You already know. You keep pretending you don't know, but you do."

"I think I know. And simultaneously I think I don't."

"Make up your mind."

"It's..."

Earlier, as I went past the Chicago Loop, the crawling of the #8 bus didn't bother me. What bothered me was David Cronenberg's more recent movies at the time. *Spider*, although a difficult film to enjoy, is admirable and fits with the director's work; *A History of Violence* and *Eastern Promises*, although good, don't really fit with his work at all. And *A Dangerous Method* seems like someone else entirely made it (though *M. Butterfly* feels that way too).

But then I began to think that not only was David Cronenberg going to direct the remake of *Total Recall*, he already had. And I'd seen it. Watching the flying cars soar over the skyscrapers, I wasn't imagining what *would* be in his movie, I was remembering what *was* in his movie. It's in a cab (one I've always seen up in the air) that Quail, in the PKD short story *and* in the Cronenberg picture, begins to realize his simulated vacation to Mars wasn't simulated at all. And it wasn't a vacation. His wish to do black ops on the Red Planet, which he thought of as a themed adventure holiday, was instead his actual reality in the past. The reason he hadn't remembered that he'd already been to Mars, that he'd been a secret agent is because Interplan, the shady security corporation he worked for, used science fiction technology to alter his memory so he wouldn't know what he did or who he was.

"You're drunk," said Sharon. "Or worse."

"I don't know."

"You don't know if you're drunk? Then you probably are."

Having read "We Can Remember It For You Wholesale" many, many times, I can say this is the moment when it becomes obvious what PKD is doing—he's critiquing the pulpy branch of the science fiction genre. Through McClane, we learn that Rekal implants twenty of these "Secret Agent on Another Planet" fantasies a month because that's the sort of thing 1966 SF did. Back at the Rekal office, the secretary is topless. Why? Because for a very long time, sci-fi readership was predominantly male (who, thanks to the time period again, were assumed to be heterosexual). And then, when Rekal's technicians go in to give Quail his ersatz experience, they learn *he actually was a secret agent on Mars*. So he's not some loser who has to pretend a life of adventure, he really and truly had one. In other words, as the story progresses, Quail becomes a superhero of sorts, which is exactly what happens over and over in the genre (think of Neo's evolution in the original *Matrix* trilogy). However, in this case, PKD doesn't want you to cheer for Quail, he wants you to think about this predictable, beat-to-death transformation.

"Look, I have both memory-tracks inside my mind; one is real and one isn't. And whereas I feel like I know which is which, I don't understand how the wrong one can seem so right."

"Andy, if you don't pull yourself together, we're through. I'm going to leave you."

I would say Cronenberg does something like this in many of his movies. Max Renn in *Videodrome*, Seth Brundle in *The Fly*, Cameron Vale in *Scanners*, Allegra Geller and Ted Pikul in *eXistenZ*, Johnny Smith in *The Dead Zone*, Cronenberg either shows us the impossibility and therefore absurdity of such characters (Vale, Geller, Pikul), or how horrific it'd be to actually become one of them (Renn, Brundle, Smith). And then, finally, with *We Can Remake It For You Wholesale* (Cronenberg deciding to use a tongue-in-cheek version of the original title), he fused his critiques of the super-character and updated Dick's commentary on science fiction (for instance, by including a hologram that matches each client's type, instead of a topless secretary).

"I'm in trouble. Probably I'm heading into a psychotic episode. I hope I don't end up like Max Renn in *Videodrome*," I said.

"This is goodbye, Andy," said Sharon. "Len Wiseman, a hack, sure, directed the remake. I hope you realize that someday. When you do, call me." She vanished again. But I wasn't worried. I knew she'd come back. She always came back.

It's interesting to note that Cronenberg was wrong about one thing: he was unimpressed with the original *Total Recall* because he thought Arnold Schwarzenegger shouldn't have portrayed the main character, who is supposed to be an everyman of sorts. But Verhoeven is known for sneaking in commentary that isn't always immediately apparent (give *RoboCop* and *Starship Troopers* another watch and you'll see). So much as PKD's short story critiques science fiction of the 1960s, *Total Recall* critiques action movies of the 1980s. In other words, Schwarzenegger wasn't supposed to be an everyman, he was supposed to be how the American male saw himself in his dreams. An interesting tidbit, then, is that the main character in Verhoeven's movie doesn't learn that he's a superhero, he learns that he used to be a villain. He has to choose to become good.

—

Alone, my hologram wife gone, I sat in front of the BAT-V (short for Big Ass Television 5, a name given to it by its previous owner and my friend). On the screen, there was static, until it was replaced by a first person image of a man walking away from my garden apartment on Burling Street. It was only a short stroll down to Diversey, then over to the intersection with Halsted, where I could make out the Rekal sign on the awning, reminding me that PKD's Rekal is only a business, while Verhoeven's is much more sinister (we hear about people having been lobotomized, after all). Near the entrance to the modest building was a newspaper vending machine sporting the headline: "Ridley Scott Exposed as Extraterrestrial Imposter by Creative Writing Graduate Student."

Inside, we get a quick montage showing the hologram behind the desk changing for a series of customers to meet each client's sexual proclivities. And then the still faceless first person walked into an office and shook the hand of a man with a bag on his head. Watching this on the BAT-V, I thought about the fact that another way to sell out was to continue to be who you always were as an artist. To never change. To give people exactly what they wanted, which is what you've been doing since the very beginning.

Bagman said: "Mr. Cronenberg, you could be an artist, you could have principles, or," really dragging out that *or*, "you could be a simulation of an artist. You know, the simulation is *always* so much better."

Mr. Cronenberg reached over and pulled the bag off the man's head and it was me. But then the camera turned and, yes, it was also me.

Quail, in "We Can Remember It For You Wholesale," learns that he's a kind of superhero.

"So," the version of me who was formerly wearing a bag said, "do we have a deal? The version you would've made in 1990? The Philip K. Dick version?"

Arnold Schwarzenegger's character in *Total Recall* learns he'd been a villain. He has to choose to be good.

There was a pause as I thought about my own offer.

"We do," I said to myself, the two of us guffawing, shaking hands, until the screen is taken over by static once again.

"Was... was that what you wanted, Mr. Farkas, sir?" said David Cronenberg.

"It'll do, Dave. It'll do."

Who chooses to be good all the time?

On *Videodrome* and the Paradox of Unmediated Revelation

Joseph Vogl

(Translated from the German by David Leo Rice)

1

As a way into the paradoxes of David Cronenberg's 1982 film *Videodrome*, I want to begin with three questions: 1: How does the film relate to the intellectual and cultural climate of the 1980s? 2: Which physical and psychological processes are depicted in the film? 3: Which general structures in the relationship between humanity and spirituality, mediated by various technologies, emerge when considering these questions in depth?

If we understand this film as a representation of media phantasms, centering on television, video and hallucination, then how should we best approach it? What concrete object is at the center of these ideas? To begin with, I believe that the true theme of Cronenberg's film is not the emergence of a video and television phantasm that leads to hallucination (i.e., the indistinguishability of perceptions and ideas). Rather, the true theme is video and television *discourse*.

In order to thematize this discourse as such, *Videodrome* deals with many of the concepts, narratives, arguments and images that were used to address the role and impact of new media at the beginning of the 1980s. In this way, the film is saturated with argumentative topoi, which make it clear that it is not simply telling a story, but rather dealing with real-world discourses in a narrative mode. So let me first gather and address a few elements (or signals) with which Cronenberg's film engages these discourses, and is thus historically situated in the early 80s.

First, *Videodrome* satirizes the rumors that were circulating at that time about the introduction and spread of new media—first television, and then video. In terms of television, the most salient rumor had to do with the supposed effects of unnoticed, hidden signals, which could not only manipulate the viewer's thoughts and personality, but actually change their physiological makeup. Rumors of this kind have accompanied television since its earliest mass dissemination, and here Cronenberg parodies them with the motif of brain tumors, a hyperbolic, grotesque intensification of the dangers of so-called "influence machines." This harkens back to the earlier history of media controversies, such as the "reading addiction" panic at the end of the 18th century, where lonely readers were thought to be in danger of turning into nymphomaniacs and masturbators.

A more contemporary rumor involves the video market and the proliferation of so-called snuff films. This began with the American B-movie *Snuff*, directed by Michael and Roberta Findlay (1974), which spawned a rumor that still hasn't been dispelled, namely that one scene depicts the actual murder of a prostitute, filmed in Mexico.

These rumors are naturally bound up with history of censorship, which took another turn after the emergence of the video market in the early-to-mid 1980s. In response to an unregulatable market for horror and hardcore videos (as we see today with the Internet and video games), the topic of censorship took on new urgency, raising questions such as: are depictions of violence frightening, or do they cause a kind of habituation and emotional blunting? If so, does this encourage imitation?

A third aspect is the way in which the film deals with media-theoretical discourses themselves. It is natural that Cronenberg quotes his fellow Canadian Marshall McLuhan through the mouthpiece of his "media prophet" Brian O'Blivian—entire passages of the film can be understood as variations on the theme, "the medium is the message." When Max Renn, the producer and video freak, fuses with the recorder, when he dives into the cathode ray tube, and when a gun grows into or out of his flesh, one cannot fail to see an illustration of the concept of media as prosthesis or organ augmentation.

This is media theory taken not only seriously but literally, exemplified by O'Blivian's thesis that, "the television screen has become something like a second retina... The screen has become the second retina of the mind's eye. It is part of the physical structure of the brain."

A number of other cultural-critical and media-theoretical topoi are also relevant here, such as the idea that television is a medium of forgetting (already suggested by the name "O'Blivian"), or the much-discussed involution of TV-man to caveman: think here of Renn's apartment, which resembles a cave, and then think of the ending, where the television in the belly of the wrecked ship is set up within what looks like a caveman's dwelling, complete with an artificial fireplace reminiscent of a scene from ancient times.

—

The film goes even further, outlining a whole history of optical media—think of the glasses from Spectacular Optics, then the Medici of the Florentine Renaissance who are mentioned in the Spectacular Optics show at the end, bringing in a reference to the patrons of Galileo and his telescope experiments; think of the various pictures, tapestries and window and door frames that are conspicuously carried in certain scenes; or the movie posters and the poster of the moon landing: all of these fit into a patchwork of media discourses that expands into a conversation about the whole occidental history of seeing.

Finally, Cronenberg's film deals with a series of infrastructural and technical changes associated with the standardization and commercialization of video. In the USA in the 1950s in particular, developments in video recording were driven by the need to maintain the social economy of time on televisions across time zones, recording and then shifting programming in a standardized way to accommodate the rhythm of viewers' daily routines. Since the 1970s, however, the opposite process has taken over: the privatization and atomization of the economy of time, as the video recorder finally detached the TV program from any standardized broadcast timetable, and thus pulled domestic television viewing out of the rhythm of public, social time. This process became even more radical with digital media and the total dissolution of any coherent, dominant and socially-coded time economy, which also led to hyper-specialization in programming (MTV, for example, emerged around 1981, at first focusing solely on music videos).

—

This process informs the character of Max Renn: from the beginning, we see that he has fallen out of social time; he is thoroughly flexible, open to anything, bound by nothing. Speaking from this position, he explains the rules of the new TV market, defined now by niche programming, pay-per-view, and narrow-casting. The market is no longer a mass of unified viewers, he explains, but rather a fragmented multitude of private spectators who behave in a disparate manner toward the television they consume.

Situated at this moment of cultural shift, *Videodrome* uses the technology of television and video in two key regards. First, in terms of real-time transmission: the indistinct Videodrome signal seems to have been transmitted from Malaysia, then from Pittsburg, and then finally it turns out to have been simulated by a videotape. And second, in terms of the conversion of images into signals. Here, the video camera is not a recording device, but a *transmission* device. Between the image that's broadcast and the image that's received there is always a transmission process, a process of decoding and recoding, which in many ways consumes the message it was engaged to transmit.

This process therefore stands between the image and the viewer as a kind of wall, which means that there is no longer an *outside*, even when the lens is fleetingly opened. Indeed, Cronenberg's film mostly takes place in windowless rooms, or in rooms where the external light is heavily filtered, such as through church windows, just as what is shown on video is not an image of a real place, but a modulation of electromagnetic waves, in which the difference between foreground and background, inside and outside, is theoretical at best.

Taking all this together, we can see that a paradoxical demystification of media discourse is underway, precisely insofar as the film mystifies these media processes to such a consistent and even hyperbolic degree.

2

Let us now take a closer look at the story of *Videodrome*, which is not just the story of Max Renn, the TV producer, and Videodrome, the ominous broadcast signal, nor is it just the story of how this producer and the strange thing hiding within Videodrome ultimately merge. Rather, the narrative has a more classic character, using a model that has been developed over the centuries: it follows the logic of a quest. More precisely, it follows the logic of a quest to transgress boundaries.

According to narrative theory, every narrative event is the transgression of a limit—this applies to the ancient epic as well as to the fairy tale, to the chivalric romance as well as to the Bildungsroman, and it still applies to narrative styles today. No matter how problematized the narrative structure of a given work may be (e.g. in the nouveau roman), these problems are always connected with the problem of drawing and crossing borders. *Videodrome* is likewise about borders and transgressions. In this film, the transgressions are themselves called "Videodrome," and, in the last sequence, they come together in a striking image, where Max Renn crosses the border of an ominous zone marked with a "Keep Out" sign. This is the epitome of demarcation, a literal border-crossing that leads to a wrecked ship, which since antiquity has been a vessel for fantasies of leaving rule-bound society behind.

In this light, transgression is the essence of the narrative, shaping both the events and the ideas in the film. Some key transgressive gestures here include:

1. The crossing of spatial borders. What is initially linked to an exotic fantasy of Malaysia is then reduced to Pittsburg, an all-too-American locale, which nevertheless remains a mythic abstraction, as the radio presenter Nicki Brand (played by Debbie Harry, lead singer of "Blondie") disappears there.

2. Aesthetic transgression, which emerges through the search for the *authentic,* that which is no longer television or video, but rather somehow *more than* television and video. In other words, the Videodrome signal is televisual but isn't television, as Max Renn puts it several times. It functions without staging, without actors, without representation, without design, and without aesthetic embellishment. The show's attraction stems from a *genuine televisual desire*: the search for something in the picture that is no longer a picture; the search for that which the picture hides, rather than what it reveals, which can only be accessed through the dismantling of the picture itself.

3. This longed-for manifestation of the *real* from within the image has several characteristics. First, it involves an excess of violence, with uncontrollable orgies of torture. This plays on a cultural code that always endows violence with extra authenticity, as if it were the surest means of getting closer to nature. Here, too, an occidental pictorial tradition is at work, in which realism takes refuge in violence, as if violence were a guarantee against deception.

4. Another related aspect is that of sexual excess, tending toward uninhibited, overwhelming enjoyment. This is not the usual intercourse, nor even any standard pornographic scenario. It is, rather, an excess on the edge of the imaginable. Max Renn and Nicki Brand take tentative steps in this direction with the erotic games they

play together, but ultimately these only point toward something that is occurring in another, inaccessible place—in Videodrome itself, always visible yet always beyond reach, as Nicki's disappearance proves.

5. This idea recalls how distant, unobtainable enjoyment is defined by psychoanalysis, especially that of Lacan: such enjoyment is not pleasure, nor gratification or wish-fulfilment. It is, rather, a *beyond the pleasure principle* kind of enjoyment, which is always that which you do not have yourself, so you can only imagine that someone else does. In Freud's mythology, it was the primal father who owned everything, including all women, and was allowed to do anything and everything with them. The father's inaccessible enjoyment was therefore also guarded by a primal prohibition (the child must not seek what belongs only to the father), and where primal prohibitions are effective at creating a rigid boundary, there is always the perception of extraordinary enjoyment beyond them. This means that, from any given person's point of view, the object of enjoyment has always already been snatched away by another—it's always precisely what that person lacks on a structural level.

6. This question of enjoyment leads to a *beyond the law* fantasy, a longed-for licentiousness that appears sovereign, and is thus taboo. The closest image for this kind of enjoyment is in de Sade's texts, with the excesses of his libertines and how their enjoyment transcends even their own pleasure, strength and self-preservation. It is therefore no coincidence that Cronenberg demarcates this place of enjoyment with the strange father figure of Brian O'Blivian, who becomes the guiding light and lure in Max Renn's search for transgression, as only he seems to know what this enjoyment really is.

7. Another aspect of this transgression is the penetration of bodily boundaries. The integral body is still too much of an image, its shape still too familiar and pictorial, so the search for the *real* through transgression continues beyond this point, finally digging into the bodies themselves, until they disintegrate into unrecognizable pieces. This violation of the body's boundaries is more than a breach of its surface, and thus more than a mere penetration, becoming a full disorganization of organic law and a derangement of the bodily form itself (think of the exploding screens and the shattering of Videodrome producer Barry Convex).

8. Ultimately, therefore, the site of the *real* is death, but not any kind of episodic death that can be discussed as such, for example when you realize that none of the actors on Videodrome (as in a so-called snuff film) can be seen a second time. Rather, the film suggests a *death beyond death*, a kind of death that shows itself through Nicki: murdered and yet still present, not in anything resembling an afterlife, but as an avatar of a death that never ends, an endless deadly process that cannot be stopped, ongoing without going anywhere.

3

Taken all together, the above attempts at transgression define the quest narrative that gives *Videodrome* its form. As Max Renn pursues them, however, he initiates a process that has a dual effect, and perhaps also a dual lack of effect. On the one hand, his transgressive actions do not lead to the outside or the transcendent *place of beyond* where the longed-for licentiousness, excess, authenticity and superhuman enjoyment reign. Rather, his transgressive actions lead into a zone of indistinguishability, where hallucination reigns—a hallucination that is no more than the indistinguishability of perception and imagination. In this zone of thwarted transgression, the perceived is indistinguishable from the imagined, and everything becomes de-realized through the very process that was intended to finally establish it as real. The other result concerns Max Renn himself as he enters a series of transformations, which amounts to a psychotic process.

But what happens in this process? To begin answering that question, we can track this character through a series of physical spaces. Just as the Videodrome signal is shifted from Malaysia to Pittsburg and then ultimately revealed to be a fake, a simulation of a transmission, so too in the course of the film are interior spaces always pushed open only to lead to deeper interiors. Before the film ultimately arrives in the cave landscape discussed earlier, it moves through other subdivided spaces that have no openings. These include Max Renn's apartment, where instead of windows there are only screens and glass blocks that serve as filters to diffuse the light from outside, as well as Brian and Bianca O'Blivian's headquarters, where the video archive is lined with stained glass windows and the only exterior view is of the "cathode ray mission," itself an interior.

This becomes particularly clear when Harlan, the video pirate who turns out to be a member of the Videodrome conspiracy, pulls his hand out of Max Renn's stomach, only to find it transformed into a grenade. He's blown up and tears a hole in the wall—a hole that only leads to another wall. Even if Max Renn were to go through this hole, we now know that it would only lead to another interior. Thus, we are dealing with an environment of endless confinement, as in Kafka's *The Trial*, where all addresses, rooms, offices, and attics belong to the same court, so that there can be nothing outside of it. Each opening only marks the closure of the previous space.

—

There is a generalized endogeneity at work here, which emerges from an even more fundamental operation within the film's structure. The film opens with an image of a screen—a screen on a screen—which displays the word "Videodrome" in a distorted video font, immediately calling into question whether this title belongs to Cronenberg's film or to its subject. In other words, from the very beginning, we are made to wonder whether we are watching a film *about* the media entity known as "Videodrome," or confronting that entity itself. Expanding from here, the film consistently presents screens framed in other screens: a television program, for example, that itself features characters on television, etc, just as all the central characters first appear on video or television screens: the secretary with her wake-up call at the beginning; Nicki Brand on the talk show; Barry Convex on screen in the car; and, of course, Brian O'Blivian, who only appears "on TV, on TV."

If there is an ontology of things and characters in this film, their being-in-the-world is determined by the image, by video and by television. This is the source of the grotesque comedy when the image inside a whipped TV set begins to howl in pain. People come into reality through the image, and vice versa. Here, the film has the advantage of being unambiguous: there shall be no doubt that video, television, and reality are being systematically confused to reveal a deeper truth.

—

In this same way, the narrative is arranged as a Möbius strip where the narrated world merges seamlessly with the world of the narration, the intra-diegetic intertwined with the extra-diegetic, which sets up a narrative structure that is always both inside and outside at once. Cronenberg establishes this with a few effective techniques: not only at the beginning, where "Videodrome" starts at the same time as *Videodrome*, but also with Max Renn, who is always both in the world and in his head at the same time, and with the ending, where the world of the film ends exactly as the main character takes his own life.

This concept also comes through in the sound direction, for example when Brian O'Blivian speaks as if over a loudspeaker from the video on the screen in Max Renn's apartment, but then suddenly the sound level changes and it becomes a voice from offscreen: the voice *in* the film narrative becomes the voice *of* the film narrative. Here too, the Möbius strip works like a membrane that renders inside and outside interchangeable, and thus relates to the importance of membranes in the film overall: the surface of the screen that curves and moves; the clay wall of living torture scenes; the skin that leads to the inside of the body, etc. The narrative structure can thus be found in this membrane, in the thinness of this border, which always allows the inside to recur on the outside—and vice versa.

—

This entanglement (or indistinguishability) of inside and outside, of images and world, of narration and what is narrated, contains a further dimension through which the horror of Cronenberg's film manifests most clearly. This dimension involves the literalization of metaphors, which leads back to what I have called *the psychotic process*. When the video pirate and conspirator Harlan says to Max Renn, "Open up!" Renn's stomach literally opens into a gaping wound. Here, Renn (in his video dependency) does not function metaphorically *like* a video recorder; he literally *becomes* a video recorder. In the same way, the video images do not function like people; they fully become people. The material on the videocassettes begins to live accordingly: as life itself.

This corresponds to the structure of dreams, which, according to Freud, are psychotically organized in that they swap ideas about words and ideas about things. In a dream, a hurtful sentence can cause a physical injury. In terms of Cronenberg's preoccupation with media phantasms, this too is taken literally: Max Renn's metamorphosis (like many of Kafka's) demonstrates the physical realization of a metaphor. This also partakes of the logic of the Eucharist. In contrast to Protestantism, the transformation in the liturgy of the Catholic Church represents a literalization of the metaphor of the body. What one sees in the eating communion is actually Christ's body, not a stand-in for it. In Cronenberg's work, it is not the word that becomes flesh, but the image.

This also leads to a final branch in the psychotic process, which grows from the fact that the film never leaves the perceptual space of its main character. Anyone who enters or exits any scene, anyone who appears in or disappears from the field of view, does so at the same time and only for Max Renn himself. As Manfred Riepe noted in his 2003 study of the body in Cronenberg's cinema, we are obviously dealing with a film in the first person, or even a film that does not recognize the difference between a first person and other people. For this reason, there is no such thing as a subjective camera in *Videodrome*, for there is only one possible perspective.

The various aspects that I have described so far—an expanding inside without an outside, an endogeneity that erases the difference between image and world, the Möbius strip of the narrative and finally the literalization of metaphor, in short, everything bound up in the psychotic process—all recur in this extreme singularity of perspective. As Cronenberg said in an interview, "It's the first first-person film I've ever done. And Jimmy Woods is that first person. He is in every scene and everything is seen from his point of view. He's a relentless first person, and because of that, it creates a lot of confusion among people watching the film. Because when I say that reality is changing for this character, the reality of the film is also changing, and it also bends the physical laws of the universe as we know it. For Max, as Brian O'Blivian explains, his perception of reality becomes what is real to him. His whole self changes. I established this rule in *Videodrome* and followed it consistently."

Along with the fact that this is an apt description of the hallucinatory, this rule leads to dire consequences for the construction of the character and his world. The first is a process of doubling, such as in scenes where Max Renn is cut together with the mutated Max Renn, or where a character in "real space" mirrors the character on a screen, such as in the final suicide sequence. This also inheres in the way that the supporting characters are confused for and swapped out with one another, as in the torture scene where the faces switch between Nicki Brand and the elderly video agent, pointing to an overall instability of people and situations.

—

Just as Max Renn's hallucinations consist in erasing the difference between perception and idea, and between one person and another, so too does the film erase all difference between its own and its main character's perceptions. The ego of this main character spreads across all the characters in the film, creating a situation in which it communicates with itself in other guises—and in the guises of others. This can be seen as a failure of the metaphorical dimension, or, again, as a literalization of metaphor.

The meaning of the word "I" works linguistically only under the condition that the expression is a so-called *shifter*, a linguistic tool which, like others (e.g. you, here, there, etc.) does not have a specific content, but is instead determined situationally. You can't find an entry in the dictionary for "I" that lists definite characteristics and properties, the way you can for most nouns. This "I" has no specific scope. It is only because of this vagueness that sentences such as, "When I think about the fact that I was a child once too," or, "When I think about what I did back then..." are possible to say and comprehend.

Furthermore, the vagueness of this shifting "I" also determines its metaphorical dimension and makes it possible for it to appear as subject and object at the same time, as well as for another person to use the same word, while meaning something else by it. In the most varied of positions and circumstances, I am I, but at the same time I concede that others—you, for example—are an I too, and can call yourself "I" just as sanely as I can. Therefore, the loss of this metaphorical dimension (or the psychosis of taking it literally) has a double effect: on the one hand, the ego becomes a proper name, which designates a special person with certain characteristics, and this "I" becomes that person's sole property and extinguishes the possibility of other "I's" being equally legitimate; on the other hand, it multiplies and comes back in different forms. For example, one can meet a strange child in a dream, but this strange child might perhaps be nothing but the literalization of the sentence, "When I think back to the fact that I too was once a child…"

In short, the elimination of the ability to see metaphors as metaphors simultaneously leads to the totalization and to the breakdown of the ego. The ego is transformed from a shifter into a name that embodies distinct properties. This is Max Renn's condition: he encounters himself in various forms and transformations, but at the same time encounters no one whom he can recognize as an Other, and thus ought never gain access to a "real" outside world or even an outside perspective that he can accept as such, thereby rendering his selfhood unreal through its suffocating totality.

The various elements of the film (the insurmountable interior spaces, the indistinguishability of image and world, the Möbius strip of the narrative and the literalized metaphors) all coincide at this point, which has two consequences for the film's narrative. First, the sought-after Videodrome signal becomes the crystallized core of a paranoid fixation, which Cronenberg pushes to the point of comic exaggeration: there is repeated talk of a "secret connection," of "encryption," of a conspiracy, or of the fact that all of Videodrome is "much more political" than it first appears. At the same time, however, the existence of the film perfectly coincides with the existence of Max Renn: the doubled suicide scene at the very end, which occurs once in the video that Renn is watching and then once in the film itself, also ends Cronenberg's film, proving that this film and Max Renn were one and the same being—the very opposite of a situation with far-reaching sociopolitical implications.

4

I have tried here to understand Cronenberg's film not simply as a piece of video delirium, but as a representation of the media discourses that revolve around video delirium. The film isn't a work of media criticism (e.g. about media contagion, erasing the world and making it psychotic), but rather a film about those paranoid fantasies that are inherent in certain varieties of media criticism. This is how Cronenberg's film deals with paranoid fantasies about media and its effects. The video signal, which is encrypted, triggers cancerous growths as well as psychotic processes: this is an almost satirical take on the evil that supposedly emanates from our screens. To put it more bluntly, Cronenberg's film does not deal with the evil of the media, but with many discourses and fantasies about the evil of the media. This leads me to my final questions: what is the structure of these discourses? How does this variety of media criticism work? Which discourses has Cronenberg demystified through his own process of mystification?

The media discourse in *Videodrome* is of an apocalyptic nature. I mean 'apocalyptic' in the literal sense, as configured first by the apocalyptic prophecies of the Old Testament, and then especially by the Apocalypse of John, appended to the New Testament. In Greek, 'apocalypse' means revelation, unveiling. In the New Testament, the apocalypse reveals the end of the sinful world and the victory of eternal, heavenly Jerusalem, the kingdom of the blessed and elect. Since this apocalypse is now so canonical, revelation and destruction have become somewhat synonymous.

I do not need to go further into the famous Apocalypse or Revelation of John, except to state the following: this Apocalypse involves a text in which the narrator reports how he is suddenly seized by the Spirit, how he then hears a powerful voice, how the radiant image of Christ then appears to him, and how he is finally commissioned by Christ to describe what has been seen and revealed—namely, the meting out of plagues upon the world, the fight against the capital of sin, and the "great whore of Babylon" and her horrible downfall and the victory of the heavenly ones—and to write all this down, so as to pass it on to the larger Christian community.

In Cronenberg's film, a number of apocalyptic motifs are interspersed, such as:

1. The "media prophet," who predicts the end of the (real) world.

2. The doomsday scenario, wherein the world of Videodrome is not only entropic, riddled with mountains of garbage and populated by lepers, but is also a sinful world, ruled by vice, debauchery and excess.

3. The quasi-theological discourse on the old vs. the new flesh, and the downfall of the one, which engenders the eternal survival of the other.

4. A kind of final battle where one party is represented by the extravagant Nicki Brand, who appears in a red dress, the color of sin (the allegory of sin in the Apocalypse of St. John also wears red), while the other party is represented by Bianca, who already bears the white color of innocence in her name, and who stands in for the Father on earth (the departed but ever-present O'Blivion), fighting for the salvation of this strange world inside the "cathode ray mission."

Intriguing as they are, these apocalyptic motifs are only the tip of the iceberg. More saliently, at one point in the Apocalypse of John it becomes clear how the Apocalypse functions as a media network. The text says, "And I saw a [...] strong angel coming down from heaven; he was enveloped by a cloud [...]. In his hand he held an open book. [...] And the voice that I heard from heaven spoke to me again and said: Go, take the little book that is open from the hand of the angel that stands on the sea and on the earth. And I went to the angel and said to him, Give me the little book! And he said to me: Take it and eat it! It will be bitter in your stomach, but in your mouth it will be sweet as honey. And I took the little book out of the angel's hand and devoured it. It was sweet as honey in my mouth, but when I ate it, it was bitter in my stomach. And

I was told: you must prophesy again of many peoples, nations, tongues and kings."

Here, the problem of apocalyptic discourse is explicitly addressed as a media problem. On the one hand, this revelation has to be transmitted—it has to go through channels, messengers, and stations, so that it can reach earth from heaven. On the other hand, it only arrives unadulterated if all these transmissions are removed, if all the intermediate carriers are switched off—in short, if the messengers disappear in favor of the message itself. Hence the incorporation of the book into the body, and the transformation of Scripture into a living witness. The message is therefore not read and communicated, but incorporated (eaten): this literalization of the metaphor is at the same time the creation of immediacy. As Derrida would say, the broadcast of the apocalypse is nothing other than the end of the apocalypse as a broadcast. So the truth of the apocalypse or revelation only appears at the moment when the process of transmission interrupts itself. The paradox of the apocalyptic message is that it is transmitted only when it jams its own transmission. This is what makes it divine.

—

And this, after all, is the crux of Cronenberg's *Videodrome*: here the word is not devoured, made flesh only to lie heavy in the stomach. Instead, it is the video that is incorporated, inserted gruesomely into the stomach. At one point we learn very clearly that Max Renn is the "video word made flesh." This is the apocalyptic structure of the film, and perhaps of all reality: all revelation that is sought after is shot through with longing for the disappearance of the very channels and transmissions we must use in order to seek it. In our fantasy of the *real*, the "encrypted signal" works directly in the brain and the videotape directly in the body.

In this way, Cronenberg's film presents a media discourse that is heavily marked by its theological ancestry, and as such follows an ancient apocalyptic pattern. Within this discourse, the effectiveness of the media is bound up with the end of the world: that is, in the effectiveness of a message that—if it gets through all the intervening channels—entails the end of the *real* world. Therefore, salvific history is not yet over. Here, it is concentrated in a media phantasm which, with every transmission, awaits the advent of a horrible or redemptive revelation.

Farewell from the Children of the New Flesh

David Leo Rice & Chris Kelso

With this invocation of media as self-defeating Revelation, we arrive at one of the central theses of Cronenberg's entire body of work. As Joseph Vogl argues, the theme and purpose of *Videodrome* is discourse. That *Videodrome* might be a vehicle for demystifying discourses regarding media—or a means of discussing the processes by which these discourses eventually calcify into a reality of their own—brings the film's relevance right into our present day of post-truth conspiracy theory and omnidirectional distrust, our lunatic fixation on finding the *real* within the media, the one place that can never offer it to us.

In Cronenberg's world, lies become truth through the power of the channels they traverse. Astonishingly, this is the world we now inhabit, so that rather than science-fictional or profilmic, the discussion of his work has become ontological and empirical. In no uncertain terms, his prophecy has come true.

For most of us, the waves of new media flooding into our sensory fields are overwhelming. The sheer degree of incoming data leaves us feeling like we're already past the saturation point. Superficially, we want for nothing in 2022, yet the basic joys allude us, vaporised by a new dependence on inter-connectivity and gratification in the global village of the damned. We are trapped in an amnesiac prison. Exhausted vectors addicted to forgetting. Yet while these themes are central to Cronenberg's *Videodrome*, and to his filmography overall, his work remains entirely non-judgmental. We are not being presented with a worst-case scenario or a warning to reform before it's too late—Cronenberg is simply tracing the arc of Max Renn's journey to its natural conclusion, albeit in a parodic manner. He has no placard or message to leave us with. His stories are simply human.

As in *Videodrome*, the subliminality of media transmissions in our time appear to have altered and manipulated our consciousness, warping what they claim only to reveal. But we embrace this manipulation because we are lonely. We already *are* the outside, the 'other,' trying to look in through the screen to catch a glimpse of where life is happening. This feeling exists within our fragile armour of bone and intellect, as we seek comfort in the hope that there may be peace in the oblivion of information; maybe among the relentless screeds of data we might find something that explains why and who we are. In Mark Fisher's 2017 essay collection, *The Weird and the Eerie*, he says:

> "We could go so far as to say that it is the human condition to be grotesque, since the human animal is the one that does not fit in, the freak of nature who has no place in the natural order and is capable of combining nature's products into hideous new forms."

To claim that the human animal is the ultimate outsider that needs to adopt hideous new forms in order to belong is nothing new. And when considering our affliction, there are clearly benefits to the raft of hyper-specialised programming at our disposal—YouTube and TikTok content is of course tailored to the most specific recesses of taste. No one need *feel* like an outsider when it comes to consumption of content. The problem arises when the media entity is itself forced into sentience by pleasure-addicted human vectors with out-of-control egos.

By allowing this to happen, we serve ourselves up as protoplasmic entrees to the starving suicide machine we helped manufacture. *We* are the media phantasms doomed to live a third-person life in the relentless first-person. We trust this entity to deliver entertainment and validation, but also to fulfil an epistemic purpose. Our dependence is such that the entity becomes our primary means of keeping up to date with the world and engaging with societal matters, conflating the serious and the frivolous, the personal and the political, in increasingly deranged ways. This has enabled a dangerous rise in far-right conspiracy theory, congealing into a worldview where all opposition leaders are paedophilic, cannibalistic cabal members. Soon this becomes consensus truth, revealing the insidious urges that the entity has harboured all along.

As this entity reveals its true nature, it summons another insidious entity out of the murk—that of renewed calls for censorship. In the age of cancel culture, when many imagine that the solution to a fraying consensus reality and the proliferation of paranoid and even delusional speech is simply to shut it down and pretend it doesn't exist, Cronenberg still refuses to offer criticism or warning. He remains steadfast in his commitment to observing what is, rather than what he or anyone else believes *should be.* Spiritually attuned but never pious or dogmatic, his work offers us dark truths we have to accept. Because he offers no judgement, he is uncancellable. No ideology is ever stated. There is no agenda, only an idiosyncratic method of ontological discourse—that of always seeking flesh inside the signal. Things haven't changed since he was growing up as an inexperienced filmmaker trying to get his country to love him back.

Freud's notion of the pleasure principle is illuminating to consider here, alongside Cronenberg's commitment to the flesh. Freud believed the unconscious was capable of operating on a transcendental plateau, beyond the governing facets of the perceptual-conscious system, as Joseph Vogl also mentions in his discussion of the Videodrome broadcast as a realm of impossibly over-the-top enjoyment and disinhibition. Today, as both sides close in, limiting the horizon of human consciousness via a grotesque overabundance of feverish discourse or a grotesque attempt to throttle that discourse with the cudgel of censorship, we need to break out into a new awareness. Onto a new plateau, where pleasure has not yet been sorted, for commercial purposes, into licit and illicit categories. And what better jolt than trauma? That which kicks a transcendental shock into motion.

Cronenberg, like Lovecraft, utilised modernist imagery to invoke the traumatic emergence of the 'other'—or what Mark Fisher defines as the 'Weird,' which lurks always within us, yearning to be born. Rather than allowing it to emerge in the degraded, deracinated forms that contemporary media encourages, or attempting to halt its emergence now that it's already in progress, why not, with Cronenberg as midwife, allow it to be born in all its weird glory, even if the shock destroys us in the process?

Many artists throughout history have proven influential on subsequent generations, but very few have offered to serve as midwives in this way. More than anything, this book has been our attempt to elucidate the terms of the offer, and the reasons why we should accept it while we still can.

The theme of reproduction recurs throughout Cronenberg's body of work, but there are never direct lines from parent to child (for him, this would be redundant, as it never entails transformation). Rather, in a literal sense in *Crimes of the Future, The Brood, The Fly* and *Dead Ringers*, and in a more metaphysical sense in almost every film, reproduction occurs through vast cerebral and technical networks, botcheries, doublings and triplings, biological anomalies and secret experiments gone wrong or abandoned halfway through, all fecund processes that understand whatever life we're currently living as a byproduct or preparatory phase of something else. By this logic, one way of framing the spiritual yearning that courses throughout Cronenberg's explicitly atheistic project is as an attempt to answer the dual questions of, "what accidental process is our existence the byproduct of, and what monstrous offspring are we preparing to release?"

Cronenberg's influence also serves as a guide for relating to the century we all emerged from, while remaining committed to the daunting task of navigating the one we've emerged into. Bridging the two eras may in fact be his career's supreme act of mediation. Our engagement with his work therefore partakes of a certain nostalgia, a certain profound desire to retreat to the video basements of our youth and young adulthood, while continuing to imagine that a safe (and thus safely ignored) world exists just outside the shaded windows. And yet our motivation for undertaking this project was never only that, just as the motivation to have children can never (or ought never) to simply be the desire to relive one's own childhood. As a collective endeavour, this book is, rather, our response to a galvanizing signal, a beacon that showed a way *through* the postmodernism of our early lives and toward whatever comes after, something still too strange to be named, rather than an invitation to huddle in the warm darkness of a bygone age, gestating forever without being born.

Umberto Eco famously described postmodernism as a condition that all eras eventually reach, not only the modern era of the early-to-mid 20th century, which birthed Cronenberg in 1943. The postmodern condition, Eco argued, occurs when too much history piles up in the living memory of a given population, making it impossible to express sincere emotions without recourse to an overwhelming number of associations with prior instances when the same emotions have been felt—since our emotions endlessly recur—so that any attempt at direct self-expression seems naively confident that a certain emotion hasn't been felt before, or that a certain idea hasn't yet been considered.

The solution, according to Eco, is not to suppress or deny these emotions and ideas, but to express them through explicit reference to that overfull past—to say, for example, "That guy has a real Patrick Bateman vibe" (the version of *American Psycho* that Cronenberg considered directing, from a script that Bret Easton Ellis wrote for him, is one of cinema's great tantalizing unknowns), rather than to describe a vain, sinister Wall Street trader without acknowledging that he's been described before. In this way, we work with rather than against the conundrums of a time when the world seems over-described and yet the urge to go on describing it never abates.

Cronenberg worked through postmodernism in his own perverse manner, deploying many of its tactics, such as combining high and low culture into a devious pastiche—remaking a 50s monster classic like *The Fly* as a piece of philosophical high art about the inner life of an insect that "dreamt he was a man," mashing up Heidegger and *Final Fantasy* for the sake of *eXistenZ*—and exploring the postmodern suspicion that all present-tense activity is a reenactment of a more heroic time (the cutting-edge eroticism of *Crash* is predicated on the desperate re-staging of "real accidents" that occurred long before, in the glamorous 50s, when the modern had not yet become *post*, while Max Renn's suicide at the end of *Videodrome* is a reenactment of the same event that he's just seen on TV).

Still, he never got lost in the arch and overly knowing excesses of the postmodern movement, which is why his work feels so vital today. He remained, as ever, rooted in the flesh, determined to rummage around in the necrotic tissue of the past in search of new life in the present. By honoring this concern so assiduously for so long, he accessed something that's ever-present in the world, a force that exists outside of time or flows through all times, manifesting as disease or obsession or monstrosity, in the visions of saints as well as the fever swamps of online message boards, a signal that can travel through blood and semen just as it can through wires and waves.

Today, our cultural memory has grown so overstuffed that its seams have burst and, at long last, the world is new again. Or, if not new, at least no longer defined by its being too old. The clock may not have reset at the turn of the millennium, but the postmodern condition of excess memory that Eco describes is clearly no longer our biggest problem. On the Internet, and in the world that the Internet has wrought, the past is dead but not gone. Instead of rotting away, it just sits there, turning funny and sad and scary all at once, rendering the entire space we occupy into a land where nothing quite lives or dies, nor is anything quite remembered or forgotten. In this third state, an endless present of hazy association and constant reconfiguration, where public and private life bleed together while both are revised and refuted in real-time—where we can watch dozens of livestreams of the same event, all claiming diametrically opposed interpretations—and the distant past can breach the surface just as suddenly as the present or even the future can vanish without a trace, the logic of postmodernism is itself only one inert worldview among millions of others.

Had Cronenberg staked his claim on this approach to the late twentieth century, his work would likewise be submerged in the streaming ocean, cracked out of the plastic video shells that once protected it and moldering like a dead mussel in the surf. Instead, he weathered the rise and fall of postmodernism and has emerged now with redoubled relevance because he didn't enact a narrative mode of reference or critique, but rather got a head start on seeking the undead, heretical lifeforms that were already squirming when he set out from the University of Toronto to take his place in history.

Like Dr. Frankenstein suturing together pieces of dead and forgotten paupers to create a new being that, in short order, takes on an unpredictable interiority of its own, Cronenberg found a means of suturing together science and fantasy, matter and spirit, trash and art, brain and genitals, and, ultimately, past and future, so as to conjure a corpus of video-life that has helped lead us to the point we find ourselves at now. As we look back on our New Flesh Childhoods to pay tribute to this video-life and to the ways in which it has bonded with our own organisms, reproducing inside us while also having played a role in our own conception, we must also look forward, toward whatever lies in store as we move beyond the end of the end of history, into an age of hyperobjects that dash all hope of comprehension or even encapsulation by any known form.

Therefore, the way forward requires engaging in the dangerous process of cherishing the past without succumbing to it, of giving nostalgia its due without becoming its acolytes—here, Cronenberg's intellectual promiscuity is the only principle we should remain loyal to. With this in mind, our goal must be that of summoning enough courage from these volatile past materials to allow the gestation process to complete itself and birth our own new forms, leaving our old ones behind. Now more than ever, the heroic pervert is ready to emerge.

At the end of this trip through the Skin House of our spiritual father's auspicious beginnings—his own *self-fathering childhood*—let us say, all together one last time: "Long Live the Children of the New Flesh!" The road ahead is sure to be strange and much about the journey along it will be heavy, but, once we give birth to our new selves, we will have at our disposal all the sense-making organs that our bodies can house. And perhaps a few extra to boot.

END CREDITS

David Leo Rice is the author of the novels *Angel House*, *The New House*, and the *Dodge City* trilogy. His story collection, *Drifter*, was named one of the best books of 2021 in the *Southwest Review* and *Locus Magazine*, and his next collection, *The Squimbop Condition*, will be out in 2023. He lives in NYC and is online at www.raviddice.com.

Chris Kelso is an award-winning, multi-translated writer. His short fiction, essays and art have appeared in numerous magazines, while his longer-form prose/poetry has been published by an array of international presses.

Tremendous thanks to **Brian Alessandro** for organising and conducting the interview with Mr. Cronenberg. Brian is a writer, illustrator, and filmmaker whose work has appeared in *Newsday, Interview Magazine, PANK,* and *Huffington Post*. He also moderates interviews for Culture Connection, founded the journal, *The New Engagement*, and co-edited the anthology, *Fever Spores: The Queer Reclamation of William S. Burroughs*, as well as co-adapted Edmund White's 1982 classic, *"A Boy's Own Story"* into a graphic novel for Top Shelf Productions.

Matthew Mark Bartlett is the author of *Gateways to Abomination, Creeping Waves,* and other books of supernatural horror. His monthly chapbook subscription service, *The WXXT Program Guide*, is now in its second year of publication. His stories have appeared in a variety of anthologies and journals, including *Forbidden Futures, Year's Best Weird Fiction Vol. 3, Ashes & Entropy,* and *Vastarien*. He has recorded two albums for Cadabra Records, *Mr. White Noise* and *Call Me Corey*, both with backing music by Black Mountain Transmitter. He lives in Western Massachusetts with his wife Katie Saulnier and their cats Peachpie and Larry.

Stephen R. Bissette, a pioneer graduate of the Joe Kubert School, taught at the Center for Cartoon Studies (2005-2020) & remains best known for his work on *Swamp Thing*, *Taboo* (launching *From Hell* and *Lost Girls*), *'1963,'* and *S.R. Bissette's Tyrant®*. A comics creator, illustrator, and author (*Teen Angels & New Mutants*, short fiction for *Hellboy: Odd Jobs*, *The New Dead*, co-author *Comic Book Rebels, Prince of Stories: The Many Worlds of Neil Gaiman, The Monster Book: Buffy the Vampire Slayer*), he co-created John Constantine and created the world's second '24-Hour Comic' (invented by Scott McCloud). Bissette's newest work: *Cryptid Cinema*™, 'Midnight Movie Monograph' David Cronenberg's *The Brood*, sketchbooks *Thoughtful Creatures* and *Brooding Creatures*, and co-authoring *Studio of Screams*; currently collaborating on a new graphic novel with Nalo Hopkinson and John Jennings.

Blake Butler is the author of seven book-length works of fiction and nonfiction, most recently *Alice Knott* (Riverhead).

Tobias Carroll is the author of four books: the novels *Reel* and *Ex-Members*; *Transitory*, a short story collection; and *Political Sign*, a work of nonfiction.

Michael Cisco is an American writer, Deleuzian academic, and teacher currently living in New York City. He is best known for his first novel, *The Divinity Student*, winner of the International Horror Guild Award for Best First Novel of 1999.

Charlene Elsby is a philosophy doctor and former professor, the Vice President of the North American Society for Early Phenomenology and the General Editor of Phenomenological Investigations. She is the author of *Musos* (Merigold Independent), *Affect* (The Porcupine's Quill), *Hexis*, *Psychros* and *Menis* (CLASH Books).

Brian Evenson is the author of over a dozen books of fiction, most recently *The Glassy, Burning Floor of Hell* and *Song for the Unraveling of the World*. He has received the World Fantasy Award, the Shirley Jackson Award, and a Guggenheim Fellowship. He teaches at CalArts and lives in Los Angeles.

Andrew Farkas is the author of *The Great Indoorsman: Essays, The Big Red Herring, Sunsphere*, and *Self-Titled Debut*. He is an Assistant Professor of Creative Writing at Washburn University and the fiction editor for *The Rupture*.

Mick Garris is a director, producer, and novelist. He has written or co-authored several feature films (*Riding the Bullet, Batteries Not Included, The Fly II, Hocus Pocus, Critters 2*) and teleplays (*Amazing Stories, Quicksilver Highway, Virtual Obsession, The Others, Desperation, Nightmares & Dreamscapes, Masters of Horror, Fear Itself*), as well as directing and producing in many media—cable (*Psycho IV: The Beginning, Tales from the Crypt, Masters of Horror, Pretty Little Liars*, its spinoff, *Ravenswood, Witches of East End* and *Shadowhunters*), features (*Critters 2, Sleepwalkers, Riding the Bullet*), television films (*Quicksilver Highway, Virtual Obsession, Desperation*), series pilots (*The Others, Lost in Oz*), network miniseries (*The Stand, The Shining, Steve Martini's* The Judge, *Bag of Bones*), and series (*She-Wolf of London, Masters of Horror, Fear Itself*).

Jonathan Greenaway is a writer and academic from the North of England. He is an expert in horror studies and his work has appeared in *The Guardian, The New York Times* and many other online platforms. He is the co-host of the leftist horror podcast *Horror Vanguard* and is the author of the forthcoming book, *Capitalism: A Horror Story*. He can be found @thelitcritguy on Twitter.

Matt Neil Hill lives in the UK, where he was a psych nurse for many years. What he is now is largely open to interpretation, although he is *definitely* a husband and a dad. His weird/crime/horror fiction has appeared or is forthcoming in various venues including Vastarien, Weirdpunk Books, Mysterium Tremendum, Splonk, Shotgun Honey, Weirdbook, and the Dark Peninsula Press anthology, *Violent Vixens: An Homage to Grindhouse Horror*, with non-fiction at *3:AM Magazine* and *Invert/Extant*. He is working, glacially, on at least one novel. You can find him on Twitter @mattneilhill.

Evan Isoline is a writer and artist living on the Oregon coast. He is the author of *Philosophy of the Sky* (11:11 Press) and the founder/editor of a literary project called SELFFUCK. Find him @evan_isoline.

Joe Koch writes literary horror and surrealist trash. Joe (he/they) is a Shirley Jackson Award finalist and the author of *The Wingspan of Severed Hands*, *The Couvade*, and *Convulsive*. They've had over fifty short stories published in books and journals like *Year's Best Hardcore Horror*, *The Big Book of Blasphemy*, and *Not All Monsters*. Find Joe online at http://horrorsong.blog and on Twitter @horrorsong.

Kathe Koja writes award-winning novels and short fiction, and creates live and virtual immersive events. *Dark Factory* is her newest project: https://darkfactory.club/. She's based in Detroit and thinks globally.

Tim Lucas is a film critic, biographer, novelist, screenwriter, blogger, and publisher and editor of the video review magazine *Video Watchdog*.

Patrick McGrath is the author of ten novels, including *Spider*, *Asylum* and *Trauma*, and three story collections. He is a Fellow of the Royal Society of Literature in the UK, and has a doctorate in Literature from the University of Stirling. He lived in New York for many years, and taught graduate courses at The New School, Princeton and elsewhere. Currently he lives in London and Spain. Three of his novels have been filmed, including *Spider*, which starred Ralph Fiennes and was directed by David Cronenberg. It had its premiere at the Cannes Film Festival.

Callum McSorely is an author based in Glasgow. His short stories have appeared in *New Writing Scotland, Gutter Magazine, Monstrous Regiment,* and *Shoreline of Infinity* among others.

Elle Nash is the author of *Animals Eat Each Other* (2018), *Nudes* (2021), and *Gag Reflex* (forthcoming 2022). Her work appears in *Guernica, BOMB, LitHub, The Nervous Breakdown, New York Tyrant,* and elsewhere. She is a founding editor of *Witch Craft Magazine*. She can be found on Twitter @saderotica.

Tom Over is a reptilian limbic system currently manipulating a hominid cortex somewhere in Manchester, UK. *The Comfort Zone and Other Safe Spaces* is his first book. He is not on Twitter.

Graham Rae first got published as a teenager in the late 80s in cult American horror zine *Deep Red*, and has not looked back ever since. He has written for venues like *American Cinematographer, Realitystudio.org, 3ammagazine.com, Dangerousminds.net,* and a whole lot of other places he can't even remember now. Graham also provided invaluable historical context, line editing and archival research throughout this book's development process.

John Reed is a writer who lives in New York City. He can be found on Instagram & Twitter @easyreeder / easyreeder.com.

David Roden is a philosopher and writer interested in dubious alternatives to our existence. His monograph *Posthuman Life: Philosophy at the Edge of the Human* was published by Routledge in 2014. His experimental prose work has been published by *Zeno press*, *Gobbet*, *Dis Magazine*, *Spontaneous Poetics*, *Plutonics*, *Neko Girl Magazine*, and *Sunk Island Review*. His novella *Snuff Memories* is published by Schism[2].

Filip Jan Rymsza's directorial debut, *Mosquito State,* premiered at the 77th Venice International Film Festival, where it was awarded the Bisato d'Oro for Best Cinematography. *The New York Times'* Jeannette Catsoulis called it "a disquieting merger of body horror and social commentary... pierced by moments of disturbing beauty" and made it the NYT Critic's Pick. His next film is *Object Permanence.*

Gary J. Shipley is the author of numerous books, including *Bright Stupid Confetti* (11:11 Press), *Terminal Park* (Apocalypse Party), *30 Fake Beheadings* (Spork), *You With Your Memory Are Dead* (Inside the Castle) and *Warewolff!* (Hexus). His monograph on Baudrillard, *Stratagem of the Corpse*, is available from Anthem Press and Cambridge Core. He has been published in many literary magazines, anthologies and academic journals, and is the founding and managing editor of Schism Press. More information can be found at Thek Prosthetics.

Joseph Vogl is Professor of German Literature, Cultural and Media Studies at the Humboldt University in Berlin and Regular Visiting Professor at Princeton University. Recent monographs include: *On Tarrying* (2011), *The Specter of Capital* (2014), *The Ascendancy of Finance* (2017) and *Capital and Ressentiment* (2022).

Bruce Wagner is a novelist and screenwriter. He wrote the 2014 film *Maps to the Stars*, which Cronenberg directed.

Art

Matthew Revert is a writer, musician and designer from Melbourne, Australia.

Bruce McIntosh is an illustrator from North Ayrshire.

3 Extra Organs

An Interview with Vincenzo Natali

Chris Kelso

As the world continues to mindlessly writhe around like a splat of hysterical maggots on a coin-operated mattress, the arrival of David Cronenberg's newest transgressive impact event, *Crimes of the Future,* feels like a vital instrument in the quest for psychic clarity. His new film is a parabolic mirror reflecting our corporeal future across its curve - a body-vision long overdue. Cronenberg shows us what we could become if we advanced our minds beyond the technology-saturated mediaswamp and into the realms of true physical and spiritual transcendence. All the while the Canadian maestro's artistic progeny seek to inflict their own aftershocks upon the weary consciousness of the celluloid city. Vincenzo Natali is one of Cronenberg's most devoted partisan, a true child of the new flesh and burgeoning 'heroic pervert' in his own right. Natali also happens to be an immensely talented filmmaker with five feature films behind him and a litany of award-winning television propping up his curriculum vitae. Natali is a totemic presence in today's disposable culturedump - an auteur with a cinematic philosophy. I caught up with Vincenzo to discuss his childhood, the literary influences that shaped him - as well as adapting the work of J.G. Ballard and William Gibson, plus his thoughts on Cronenberg's latest landmark, *Crimes of the Future.*

CK - You were born in Detroit but grew up in Toronto – if you have any sense of national identity would you be happy to consider yourself a Canadian director?

VN - I mean, I have no living memory of Detroit. I was born there, but my parents divorced each other shortly after and my mom took me to Toronto. So, I grew up here, which is where I'm right now.

So, yeah, I definitely identify as Canadian and with Toronto and in particular, which is part of the reason the Cronenberg films, I think, resonate with me. I kind of recognize where they're from. And then he, I think, makes an attempt to set his films in Canada quite often. So yeah, there's some kind of personal resonance.

CK - You cut your teeth at North York's Canadian Film Centre (CFC), founded by Norman Jewison (Fiddler on the Roof and The Thomas Crown Affair) and where Cronenberg is on the board of directors.

VN - I would be the least bit surprised yeah. Jewison came in a couple of times while I was there.

CK - We'll talk about Cronenberg soon but I'm curious what your path was to where you are now? Was it always on the cards that you'd go into filmmaking?

VN - I mean, in my early childhood, I wanted to be a comic book artist, and I still at the ripe age of 53. I'm still aspiring. I'm sorry.

CK - There's plenty of time. You could still do it.

VN – Well, actually, over the course of the pandemic, I finished a graphic novel, so they'll hopefully get out there this year. But I really love that art form and consider it probably to be the most closely related art form to movies. But subsequent to seeing Star Wars at the tender age of eight, I did fall in love with movies in a way that eclipsed my love of comic books. And from that point onward, that's sort of what I wanted to do in one form or another. And I'm very typical of my generation. I grew up making super eight films with my friends, and just like the J. J. Abrams movie, we just made these crazy science fiction films in our backyard growing up, and that was my past. It was like from the age of eleven onward, really. I got into it and then I've matured very little since then.

CK - No, not at all. You're a very mature filmmaker. That was something that I feel was part of your kind of your design as an artist - you're dealing with fantastical themes and stories, but you treat your subjects very seriously. I think that's to your benefit.

VN - Oh, thank you. Yeah, I've suffered for that a little bit, too. I think I care so much about those movies, those kinds of movies, that I just can't do the, you know, the rote version. Also, it's just such an investment making a film, you know, kind of in it all or nothing.

CK - What do you think it is about horror and science fiction genres that draw into its kind of magnetic field? Do you think there's kind of restorative, therapeutic value in genre cinema for a viewer as well as a creator?

VN - I think you hit it on the head. Yes, that is exactly what it is. I think that when it's in its best form it's always metaphorical. I'm thinking of all of the cinema fantastic core science fiction fantasy. It's always dealing indirectly with something that exists in the real world, but by not approaching it in a direct way, it actually allows people to confront those things and simulate them in a way that they couldn't if you were just doing a docu-drama or straight, realistic contemporary story.

CK - Absolutely. So did you have Canadian filmmaker heroes growing up, apart from David Cronenberg?

VN - I hate to say that really was just David Cronenberg. I mean, Norman Jewilson is intensely important to me because his film school changed my life. He's a lovely man and a great filmmaker, but his films for me are actually kind of the opposite of what I do. I like them and I enjoy watching them, but they're not influential to me personally, just because that's not my interest or what I do. But obviously he'd be seminal. I think Norman McLaren, who is very famous for working with the National Film Board and did a movie called *Neighbors*. It was an animated film. He was very eclectic as an influence, I have to say. Not to get too much into the weeds, but you see, growing up in the late 70s we had a thing called the tax shelter system. And essentially what it did was offer a way to jump start the English Canadian film industry by allowing pretty much anybody who wanted to invest in movies and get a tax break. So you suddenly had dentists and lawyers and all these people with no understanding whatsoever in the film industry becoming producers. And it was sort of a Wild West time. And that's, I think, partly why David Cronenberg has the career he has and the start that he had, because there was just a lot of money coming into the system and looking for commercial movies to make. So not necessarily art house films, which is more the trend that Canadian cinema took post the tax shelter years. And at that time, as these films were being made, they were largely seen as trash and they were actually quite widely distributed and a lot of Canadian products sort of slipped into the studio distribution stream without anyone even really knowing they were Canadian movies. And that's part of why there was a backlash later on, because there was a lot of, you could say, government investment in these films, but what was perceived of as very little cultural return on the investment. But I think in hindsight, you can look at that period and go, oh no. Even though the movies weren't wearing the Canadian flag on their sleeve, actually you can kind of feel their Canadianness in a way that's perhaps even more authentic and subtle than some of the films that came afterwards that were more overtly declaring their national personality.

CK - And David Cronenberg's films would fall right into that category?

VN - Certainly on the edge of sort of exploitation horror movies that on their face seemed like they would sit comfortably in the Drive-in double bill. But when you actually took a closer look, you realize they're highly subversive works of art, very Canadian and very culturally specific. So, there are a lot of other movies like of that period like *Black Christmas* by Bob Clark.

CK - Oh, yeah.

VN - It would be a very famous example. A lot of horror films. *My Bloody Valentine* was a very famous one. And other ones like – oh, there's a really cool movie no one talked about but I've always liked a lot called *The Amateur*, which is a CIA thriller in that period. Those films, I guess, would have been influential to me but I think the only filmmaker that I would have recognized at that time was Cronenberg.

CK - There seems to be quite an interesting phenomenon that Scotland and Canada share, I think, and it's that we're quite self-facing, I think for the book we focused on seven of Cronenberg's short films but we actually couldn't get a hold of quite a lot of them. I mean, there were three early documentaries, another episode of *Peep Show* called *The Victim*, a few TV films, *Scarborough Bluffs, Winter Garden, In the Dirt* and a few others. Scripts and kinescopes were consigned to the warehouses of the CBC complex in Toronto. I always thought he'd be a celebrated artist in his home country, given retrospectives, etc.

VN - Oh, wow.

CK – So, how is he regarded in Canada today?

VN - Oh, highly regarded. Highly. I don't think there's any lack of interest here. Quite the opposite. I think he's sort of enshrined as a very important cultural figure. Who knows? Maybe he doesn't want you to see those movies.

CK - Possibly.

VN - Hey, I don't know. Or maybe they were just so small and obscure that they didn't survive long enough to be discovered when he was venerated. As a great filmmaker here, Canada has an odd sort of (I'm sure maybe Scotland is like this, sort of in line with what you're saying) an odd process of at first attacking its artists and belittling them and in a kind of self-loathing way perceiving them as less than the kind of artists that come from other places like the United States, for instance, our big brother to the south. But then when they find acceptance in the international realm, they come back as heroes and then they're venerated. And that's actually what happened with David Cronenberg, famously, when he made his first feature film that *Shivers*. There was a cultural critic here named I think his name was Robert Fulford who wrote an article saying 'do you know where your tax money is going?' That's paraphrasing. So he wasn't appreciated here immediately, but as his career evolved and he became an icon absolutely.

CK - I think it's funny as well that you're talking about Scotland and Canada again. We've both got the Big Brothers that we can we live in the shadow because Canada has got America, Scotland has England.

VN - Yeah, exactly.

CK – Maybe we've been bullied into this odd temperament, an intrinsic artistic self-consciousness. You once said, "I'm afraid for Cronenberg to see *Splice*. I'm scared to find out what he might think of it," - did you ever find out what he thought?

VN - Very indirectly. I shouldn't even say because I'm not sure. No, I never had that conversation with him. But he has always been very nice to me. When I made my first film, *Cube*, I invited him and Norman Jewison to see it right after it was finished. And he very kindly gave me a quote that ended up on posters all over the world that was very flattering. And as a gift to him, I sent him Alderson's severed head - the guy who's cubed at the beginning. And then he just has consistently invited me to screenings of his films and so on. And then my second film, I screened for him personally once, and he gave me great feedback on. So, I don't know him well, but he is a very nice man who's very supportive of local talent. And I've always felt like I didn't want to impose myself, frankly. And I always when I really admire somebody, it's hard for me to relate to them in a kind of relaxed social situation.

CK - Cronenberg's work almost seems to serve as a bridge between the mid-century and the late century psychic disturbance: his early films feel like Beckett or Pinter plays (there's an element of that in films like Cube and Nothing which are very self-contained, almost elaborate chamber pieces). What are your thoughts on his very early work, like *Transfer*, *Crimes of the Future* and *Stereo*?

VN - I have. Yeah. Well, I think it's funny because it's hard to know how to attribute these things. But I do think that there's just a cultural thing that comes from growing up in the same city. And Canadians tend to be very inward looking in contrast to Americans. If you look at Canadian cinema, it tends to be quite dark and quite introspective. Actually. It feels more akin to Scandinavian cinema than it does to American cinema. Even though we're right across the border from the United States. There's actually quite a stark contrast. And I think the other aspect that comes into play is just we don't have a lot of money to make our movies with. So making a chamber piece is as much a practical solution as it is kind of an artistic imperative. And so I think I found myself in the same boat somewhat for all those reasons. But I'm sure he's influenced me, too, in that regard. I have to say *The Fly* was definitely an influence on Splice because I really loved how that film, which is unquestionably a creature movie, is so heavily focused on the relationship and it just makes it intensely interesting because, of course, most creature movies tend to be much more about spectacle, and the human beings very often are not that well rendered. But in his version of *The Fly*, they're intensely the human component of it is about as emotional as any movie I've ever seen.

CK - Absolutely.

VN - And then it just sort of reaches new heights because it has this creature element pasted onto it, which is, I should say, an essential part of its DNA. But that was inspirational for Splice, for me, for sure. I wanted to do a Frankenstein contemporary genetic version of the classic Mary Shelley Frankenstein story, but really not let the creature escape into the world, which is invariably where those stories always go, even the Mary Shelley version. And I wanted the scientists to imprison their creation and develop this kind of perverse psychosexual relationship with it. That to me was very exciting and I feel, frankly, that's very Cronenbergian, so I unquestionably took that from him.

CK - I think there's another kind of piece of connective tissue here. I think something that separates Cronenberg from other auteurs is that he considers himself a writer first, like Truffaut and Goddard. It's obvious from your films that there's a depth and complexity there, and I was wondering what your literary influences are specifically? I can see elements of cosmic horror, like Lovecraft and Ligotti but also Stephen King and the like. Anything surprising or left of centre that people might not think of?

VN – I was lucky that I had a very special early childhood. Because, not to get too autobiographical, but my parents were divorced, but I would spend my summers with my dad, who lived in a little log cabin in upper New York State wilderness. And there was no TV, there was no town close by. Like it was very isolated. And so he read to me and that was my entertainment. And he probably read virtually all of the classics, plus the entirety of *The Hobbit* and *The Lord of the Rings, the Chronicles of Narnia*, the Cascada books. I think a lot of my literary influence, whatever they might be, came from that time. And then I remember a very significant moment for me was when I read *The Shining* when I was eleven years old, the Stephen King book. And that was the first adult book, quote unquote, that I read on my own. And it really affected me. I think the Stephen King influence is absolutely there and then later, William Gibson and JG Ballard are very important to me.

CK – Oh, William Gibson! I love Ballard as well. But William Gibson is interesting because the Neuromancer film has been in development hell for so many years. Do you feel that's too lofty a project to take on yourself or...

VN - I was supposed to do it!

CK - Oh, seriously? Oh, sorry.

VN – No, no! I spent years working on it. Yeah, I feel like it was one of the best to be honest, one of the best scripts I ever wrote. I hope I'm not deluding myself, but I felt I had cracked the book and Gibson really liked it. Everyone liked the script, and it was just a very hard film to finance. I just couldn't raise the $100 million or $60 to $100 million that I needed to make that movie. So, yes, I don't know if this is official. Anyway, I happen to know that it is being made somewhere. I don't know if it's been announced yet, so I probably shouldn't say, but it is out there. But I have since done my own TV series based on William Gibson's book, The Peripheral, that will be coming up fairly soon through Amazon.

CK - That's exciting.

VN - Yeah. I definitely stayed in the orbit of his work and him, and he remains very important to me.

CK - Cool. Is there any Ballard work you would love to translate or adapt?

VN - Yeah, well, again, you're touching on the two big failures of my career! I love talking about them. The two ambitious projects that, I won't call them failures, that were never made. They were very successful to me in so much as I felt like the scripts were great and everything was great, I just couldn't raise money for them. I couldn't raise enough. But I was going to do Ballard's *High Rise* and worked on that for a long time. But there are other Ballard works that I remain interested in and continue to pursue, which I probably shouldn't even talk about. So, yeah, I think he's a genius. I feel like Gibson and Ballard are kind of related, very different from each other. One is so consummately British and the other is very American, even though he lives in Canada. I don't know what Ballard thought of Gibson, but I know Gibson was greatly influenced by Ballard, and you can feel it. And I feel like there are two guys who really understand where we are headed. They understand the relationship between humans and technology in a way that I don't think many others have.

CK - I was going to ask about Boroughs again just to link it back to Cronenberg. Whenever I read William Gibson, I was reading *Burning Chrome* last month, and I was like, these stories are, like, super Burroughsian. And I don't know if you ever felt this?

VN - I'm sure Burroughs is equally influential. Yes, absolutely.

CK - How is your perspective of Hollywood as an insider? What do you think would have become of artists like David Cronenberg had he gone to Hollywood earlier in his career?

VN - I think he would have just come back. I think probably knew that. He probably thought, I'm better off where I am. I think he's wise enough to know that going down that road would not suit him. That would be my guess. Famously, he was offered all these crazy movies like *Top Gun* or *Return to Jedi*. But, yeah, he's one of those filmmakers who has to have creative control in a way that Hollywood doesn't permit. Like there are other filmmakers I have met that fall into that category, like Terry Gilliam. You just can't tame these wild beasts. It doesn't work. You either work with them or you work against them, and there's no middle ground. And that's what makes them so intensely exciting as artists, because they're utterly single minded in their purpose and they really don't know how to compromise themselves on that level. And I mean that, of course, in the best possible way. And I think he probably didn't need to go to Hollywood. That's the thing. He somehow managed to be relatively commercially viable over the years. And certainly, some of the huge hits, I think the early ones, all returned on their investment and then much more. And then as he drifted more into, for lack of a better word, arthouse cinema he probably found himself a little more outside the commercial mainstream, but still viable. And I was so excited when The new *Crimes of the Future* was made.

CK – Which leads me to my last question. I was going to ask if you'd seen it and what you thought of it.

VN - I did see it. I saw it in Toronto. We have a cinema tech here called the Bell Lightbox, and I saw it with Cronenberg and the cast were in attendance. So it was a very exciting environment to watch it in. And I thought it was amazing. That was great. That was very inspiring. To see somebody at that stage in their career doing something that is so intensely relevant and kind of more in tune with this moment than probably a lot of films made by people half his age. And that it was so, as he always is, bold and transgressive and yet emotional at the same time. I think there's a lot to unpack in that movie. I need to see it more times. But it feels like the work of a master. It just feels like every stroke, every shot in it is done with such ease and confidence that only comes from that kind of maturity as a filmmaker in its simplicity. Not to say that it's simplistic, but that it's just done with elegance. It's just very spare, to be honest. If I have a complaint about it, it's just I wish it was longer. I usually have the opposite complaint about most contemporary films. But it was outstanding. I was really looking for another 15 or 20 minutes, which is why I really need to revisit it to kind of see how I feel about that. But my first view, I was like, oh, wait, that's it. There are a few more narrative threads that were going to be tied up.

CK - It does end very abruptly. Ends with Saul Tenser accepting that his body digests plastic. Then it kind of ends.

VN - Exactly. Yeah. Maybe that is the best way to end it. I just felt at that time I was really involved in the story. That's why I was intensely interested in how this is all going to play out. Aside from that and a few quibbles, I really thought it was just a magnificent and utterly original film made by one person. He also had the very unique and appealing trait of not presenting any kind of clear moral perspective. I think it's interesting how much like JG. Ballard he is here – which actually makes sense when you read *Crash*. He looks at human behavior from a dispassionate, almost scientific lens.

CK - Yes. He doesn't make sort of ethical statements. He's very non-judgmental.

VN - Exactly. Which I think is really unusual in movies partly because I think there's a pressure on the filmmaker to make those statements to satisfy an audience. But by remaining in that kind of ambiguous realm is quite courageous of him because I think audiences are often made uncomfortable by that and in this particular case. Because it's looking at the human relationship with nature and how we're effectively destroying our own habitat and environment. Considering that this phenomenon might be a natural extension of our evolution and therefore not necessarily a bad thing is just refreshing and very interesting and most importantly, thought provoking. I have no idea where he stands on it and I think that's kind of great. That's sort of a question that certainly weighs heavily on me at this particular moment. So it really touched a nerve. And then I just thought this story about this man trying to kind of explain his child's death was really profound, too. Yeah. Just went in interesting directions. And the funny structure that started quite aggressively grabbed you by the lapels and dragged you into that world and then it became kind of languid and was served to me on the verge of losing direction. But he saved it, the way he always does. A master.

Art is the New Puberty: On 2022's *Crimes of the Future* and David Cronenberg's Portraits in Flesh

David Leo Rice

At the root of David Cronenberg's lifelong project is, of course, the flesh. And at the root of his engagement with the flesh is an apparent parting of the ways between evolution and reproduction. On the one hand, his most iconic characters—Seth Brundle in The Fly, Max Renn in Videodrome, the twin gynecologists in Dead Ringers, and, now, Saul Tenser in Crimes of the Future—turn away from the "normal" path of biological reproduction and toward a shadow realm where flesh and spirit combine. They are driven to explore the twisting tributaries and back alleys of the human bodily experience rather than passing their genes on to the next generation (with the possible exception of Seth Brundle). Having refused to become fathers, these men become artists, seekers compelled to abandon the human community, with its seemingly redundant circle of life, in favor of lonely but essential contact with the taboo forces that swim through our DNA just as powerfully as the urge to reproduce and care for our young.

The grotesque ways in which these body artists (to borrow a phrase from Don DeLillo, one of Cronenberg's literary inspirations and spirit colleagues) offer themselves up as vessels for the new flesh are immensely stylish and alluring, but, in every one of Cronenberg's "body horror" films before *Crimes of the Future*, they've also been biologically doomed, usually culminating in early death. I think of this archetype as the "heroic pervert," a kind of warped hero who redeems those who witness his dissolution not by conquering evil or sacrificing himself for the greater good, but by following his own compulsions beyond the furthest limits of self-regard, unraveling his organism in thrall to the unholy forces of media, madness, and disease.

Saul Tenser, a performance artist blessed or cursed with the ability to grow new organs of unknown function, played in Cronenberg's new *Crimes of the Future* by his latter-day muse Viggo Mortensen, shares much in common with his forebears—his inability to look away as his body confounds his understanding of it; his sexuality becoming bound up with dysfunction and disfigurement and closed off from what he calls "the old sex"—but he is also something else: an older man who knows the value of life and who decides, in the end, to embrace rather than throw it away. In this regard, he's a new kind of hero for Cronenberg, proof of an evolutionary process within a filmography that has tried to reconcile the often violently opposed dictates of body and mind, and to seek a place in the future where any distinction between them vanishes into the past.

Being, like all of us, appreciably closer to death than he was forty years ago (when he made his defining masterpieces), Cronenberg has now made a film that bears witness to the value of life as only an older artist can, after a season in the wilderness. *Crimes of the Future* is his first new feature since 2014's *Maps to the Stars*, and the first "full Cronenberg" film since 1999's *eXistenZ*, in the sense that he wrote as well as directed it, based on his own script and original story, also penned in the late '90s. I don't want to consign this towering figure to a premature grave—especially as he's already cuddled his own corpse in last year's short *The Death of David Cronenberg*, and now has an even more death-obsessed-sounding film, *The Shrouds*, in preproduction—but there's no way to watch *Crimes of the Future* and not perceive a strain of valedictory wisdom animating its tissue. Where once it was cathartic to see the heroic pervert burn down his life in its absolute prime, catharsis now comes from seeing an artist well past that prime grasp the deeper wisdom of acceptance. No longer does he court death as a rebuke to a sickening excess of life; now he does what it takes to live, in the only body he has, in the only world there is. If the earlier archetype defined Cronenberg's punk phase, this one marks the onset of his monk phase.

The slogan "Long live the new flesh," which has become a rallying cry for all that goes with Cronenberg fandom, was first uttered with bitter irony at the end of *Videodrome,* just before Max Renn, driven mad by the pirate signal (or else long-since coopted into its snuff extravaganza) blows his brains out. Striking a very different tone, *Crimes of the Future* ends with the stark, affecting image of a man who's made a career out of publicly killing the new flesh—offering his body as the canvas upon which his partner, Caprice, played by Léa Seydoux, "paints" by removing each new organ in order to preserve the sanctity of the old flesh—at last accepting that his body has changed for good, and perhaps also for the better. He gives in to the growths that have coalesced into a new digestive system and, with a grimace that conveys both trepidation and relief, bites into a purple candy bar made of industrial waste, the fruition of an evolutionary process that cannot be stopped and, if allowed to take hold, might save us all from extinction.

To call such an ending "hopeful" or "humanistic" might sound glib, but I don't think it is. Cronenberg has shepherded his heroic pervert into a new realm here, safely beyond irony and suicide. Insofar as the years weigh on *Crimes's* star and its director, this weight makes the final image of candy-bar-as-Communion-wafer genuinely enlightening, a sacrament imbued with spiritual uplift. It's a cliché to point out that almost all atheistic artists turn mystical as they age, but rarely has this turn come across more sincerely.

The politics of this monk phase are commensurately different from those of Cronenberg's heyday in the postmodern Reagan '80s and the nihilistic Clinton '90s: in those films, yuppie scientists, surgeons, and media moguls, trapped by a sterile excess of bourgeois stability and consumer chic, torch their own lives out of morbid curiosity and a need to re-engender the funk and filth that allows a *culture* to grow, in both the social and the biological sense of the word. As in *American Psycho*, the adaptation of which Cronenberg nearly directed, the heroic perverts of the late twentieth century were malcontents within a system of too much Western stability, a post-political hegemony that must've seemed eternal and immovable, a *what now?* epoch animated by the lack of any external crisis, which led to the fear that the call was coming from inside the house.

Now, in the 2020s, as in *Crimes of the Future*, the world has grown appreciably less stable, while the characters' commitment to staying alive within it has grown more so. There's less countercultural glory in throwing your life away when the world is trying to take it from you. Operating under these new conditions, *Crimes* presents a near-future not of gleaming chrome and glass clinics, or shabby broadcast stations staffed by bored pornographers and their snarky assistants, but rather one of shadowy bureaus, underground factions, infiltrators, assassins, secret police, unverifiable rumors, basement rituals, and conspiracies within conspiracies. It's a paradigm that feels more like that of Cronenberg's earliest films, from the '60s and '70s. All in all, the world of John Le Carré has returned, while that of Bret Easton Ellis has receded.

The 2020s have come to resemble the '60s and '70s in all of these ways and many more. A shortlist would include wild inflation, racial and sexual unrest, bitterness at the prospect of any collective values, escalating conflict with Russia and China, a weak and out-of-touch government, mounting street violence and militia activity, and a massive growth in doomsday cults, psychotropic drugs, and alternative realities. Given such a post-millennium redux, it's no surprise that the film's central conceit, that of humanity evolving to meet its moment by metabolizing that moment's poisoned atmosphere, is so resonant right now. It speaks directly to an era where we, too, must wonder whether we're evolving. And, if so, into what?

Like the underground factions in many of Cronenberg's early films—from the 1972 short *Secret Weapons*, about a biker gang opposing a pharmaceutical corporation that has merged with the Canadian government after a "Second Civil War," to the "scanner underground" opposing another corporate-government merger in 1981's *Scanners*—*Crimes of the Future* abounds with agents and counter-agents. These range from the cultish secret surgery enthusiasts among whom Saul and Caprice are stars, to the "New Organ Registration" employees whose motivations are ambivalent to say the least, to, most crucially, the dissident surgeons (reminiscent of the gearheads and garage-dwellers in *The Italian Machine*, a short from 1976, as well as Willem Defoe's body-mod mechanic in *eXistenZ*) working in secret to redesign the human digestive system through the mind-body alchemy that Cronenberg has never stopped trying to conjure. This fusion of man and machine defines a threshold where clinical secularism takes on the power to produce a "miracle child"—a young boy born with a new digestive system already in place.

This miracle riffs on the Christ story after the young boy is martyred and then publicly autopsied to show all those who can see it the way forward, out of the decadence of the old flesh and into a new age (the cloistered autopsy reminded me of the early Christians meeting in caves outside of Rome—another story of humanity evolving to begin a new chapter of its history). Strange as it sounds to say that a Jewish skeptic like Cronenberg has told a Christian savior story, the times are strange enough to warrant it. "Chop off your little finger, and your kids are born without little fingers?" Tenser asks, as the enormity of this shift begins to dawn on him. Here, for the first time in Cronenberg's filmography, evolution and reproduction sync up. The imperative to seed the new generation and the imperative to think in such a way that said new generation is actually *new*, achieves a harmony that makes *Crimes of the Future* Cronenberg's most hopeful and life-affirming film, truly open to the future, as its title implies, for the first time.

The question of how such humanistic affirmation has found its way into the work of an artist more commonly associated with exploding heads and gibbering insects has been on my mind a great deal over the past year, as Chris and I worked on the book you've just read. The more we worked on it, the clearer it became that Cronenberg had indeed generated new life, seeding something real—a new organ in its own right—within many of the writers we admired most, and that this organ had both a timeless and a contemporary function. Here, too, the tension and possible harmony between evolution and reproduction, between intellectual fecundity and sexual deviancy, was of critical importance, as we grappled with the challenge of synthesizing Cronenberg's influence—the way in which he's come to serve as a father figure for a certain strain of art and writing today—in our own guts and gestating it into something new and worthy of being called the *children* of the New Flesh, not merely its avatars or adherents.

—

His early and mid-career films exert an overwhelming nostalgic pull on many of us who came of age in the video era, but, in today's moment, gorged on a streaming infinitude of denatured and re-packaged nostalgia by and for millennials beginning to approach middle age, it also, crucially, does something else, something far more volatile and generative. Cronenberg would balk at being called a savior figure, but the new film wouldn't be such a welcome return if it didn't posit the possibility of salvation from within. At root, his films espouse a belief in evolution, in all the fraught beauty of that phase. As our culture fragments into manifold and incompatible strains of extreme dogma, abandoning the supposedly anti-dogmatic (or purely commercial) ethos of the late twentieth century, his work serves as a testament to how the human being can find grace in the flux, not so much finding something to hold onto as finding a way to thrive while holding onto nothing—a way to embrace the disease in order to rediscover or reinvent what it means to be healthy. Beyond the particulars of its plot, *Crimes* embodies this idea in its very being, birthing a new lifeform from and into the Cronenberg corpus, a new means of persevering beyond the dead ends of regression and extinction.

When Kristen Stewart's twitchy, horny bureaucrat Timlin utters what's become the film's tagline, "Surgery is the new sex," she means it on an erotic level, that of the new arousal stemming not from genital interpenetration but from the penetration of metal and belly, the deliciously contradictory notion of the violation of the willing flesh. It's a theme that runs all the way through Cronenberg, back through his two great inspirations, J. G. Ballard and William S. Burroughs, and into the Middle Ages. Indeed, *Crimes of the Future* partakes of an appealing neo-medievalism—Tenser's black robe (culled from the same dank closet as the red Inquisitor gown from the surgical theater of *Dead Ringers*), the solemnly observed mutilation ceremonies that form the film's major set pieces, the hermetic dwelling where Tenser and Caprice cohabitate, and the devices, like iron lungs made of bone and sinew, that Tenser sleeps and eats within—building to the implication that we are now in a "middle age" of our own. Just as the last Middle Ages led to the Renaissance and the Enlightenment, perhaps, now, the twilight of the world that those epochal shifts brought about will lead to the dawn of a new one.

The other meaning of "surgery is the new sex" also emerges from this medievalism, recalling the idea of the "Word made flesh," another key Cronenbergian theme, and another throughline between Jewish and Christian thought, with Christ himself as the hinge between them. In this reading, surgery is literally sexual in that it leads to the conception of a new body we can all hope to live within. Reproduction and evolution fuse here, so that art—surgeons are always artists in Cronenberg films—becomes a means of genuine innovation, not only of repairing or revising what's already the case. The Second Coming may not be imminent outside the sanctum of cinema, but a major shift in who and what we are clearly is.

Art, therefore, becomes a form of puberty, a dangerous and exhilarating process of growing into our next form. When I think back to my own teenage obsession with Cronenberg's classics, which dovetailed with (and probably expedited) my own early artistic stirrings—my own sense of what it might mean to evolve into an adult form I could be proud to live within, rather than committing suicide or seeing adulthood as a living death where I'd have to smother the perversity I could feel coming alive as I watched *Videodrome* and *Dead Ringers* in my room in the middle of the night—I think exactly of this cusp. I think of how I hoped that filling my head with certain signals might lead to certain ideas that might in turn lead to my bodily transformation into *an artist* who, like Saul Tenser, processes reality as it comes, painfully growing organs in the deep interior of the body and then offering them up to the public in exchange for the right to occupy a bearable space in adult society.

—

It is often said that teenagers take huge risks because they believe they're immortal, but I think the opposite is truer: they take huge risks because they can't imagine living beyond their twenties. To pass through this phase and enter true adulthood is at once to accept the limitedness of life and also its potential length, the weight of supporting yourself year after year after year, a burden that, if you're lucky, art can ease, but one that it can never alleviate in the way that your teenage self imagined it could. Having meditated on Cronenberg's own artistic development, from his early twenties to his late seventies, this transformation couldn't be clearer, as the weight of fully accepting life implies the weight of fully accepting death, in a way that the punk ideal of the early films, a rarefied version of the "live fast and die young" ethos of the postwar moment he came of age within, never could.

On the planetary scale, apocalypticism, yet another strain of '60s and '70s thinking back in the zeitgeist today, works according to the same logic, that of renouncing the entirety of this world out of a bifurcated belief that, on the one hand, it isn't worth salvaging and, on the other, there *must be* another world awaiting us. The mature Cronenberg resists both delusions and argues for the power of art as a means of finding a third path, that of remaining in a world that seems to be ending.

Beyond its role in the life of an artist, art is thus also a form of puberty in the life of a culture. It succeeds by rendering itself obsolete. When Saul finally eats the plastic bar, his life's work is a failure in that the organs he's tried to remove have instead coalesced and changed him from within. Matter has conquered mind. On the other hand, his life's work is a success in that it's made him ready—just as the film has made us ready—to appreciate the necessity of this transformation, beyond which life itself, in all its fullness and finitude, awaits. Early in any artist's life, refusing to join the human race is the most radical act you can imagine. You imagine that art can save you from the dullness of culture. Later on, if your early work has succeeded in bridging the gap between adolescence and adulthood—if the child has succeeded in becoming the father of the man, and the art has entered rather than ignored the culture—agreeing to join humanity anyway is more radical by far.

Crimes of the Future does not end with any wild messianism, but it vests this humble revelation with tremendous import, and serves as proof of its own concept by initiating a third phase in

Cronenberg's career, one that resembles the first—following the logic by which older artists so often return to the fixations of their youth, here by resurrecting the title of one of his earliest films—but imbued now with the gravity of having worked through the second, of the '80s and '90s, and thereby finding a way to see beyond the death of the twentieth century and the whirlpool, here in the 2020s, of its endless, maddening repetition and relitigation. Maybe, Cronenberg has returned to tell us, in the language that only he can access, the human story isn't over yet. Maybe we're still undergoing puberty on a radical scale—to even suggest that we have a future seems radical today—and maybe the adulthood on the other side will be a kind of death that is also a kind of life after death, an afterlife in this world, which, for Cronenberg, is the only world there ever was and need ever be, provided we find the courage to inhabit it.

The Inner technology of Crimes of the Future

Chris Kelso

Silent Mutations

"I don't like what's happening with the body. In particular, what's happening with my body, which is why I keep cutting it up."

— Saul Tenser, *Crimes of the Future*

In 2018, a study published in the journal *Scientific Reports* revealed that researchers from New York University's School of Medicine have identified a new component of our biological structure. Dubbed the *interstitium*, the new organ is a long-hidden system of fluid-filled cavities found everywhere in the human body – thriving between membranes, buried within organs, and extant in our entire circulatory system. Far from vestigial, interstitium fulfil several integral functions, from transporting nutrients and solutes to playing an important communication role in our immune regulation. More recently there have been reports of a new pair of salivary glands located in the posterior nasopharynx of the human throat. So, this begs the question: are humans summoning dormant organs for some imminent hominin event, silently re-adapting on the precipice of unknowable futurological opportunity?

Establishing what this next phase will be, as well as the nature of the event, is more complicated. It has long been established that environmental factors are no longer the motivating forces for evolutionary change. In fact, the dominant stimulus for physiological change is sexual selection. This process is predicated on mutations that improve special reproductive competitiveness, seductiveness, and mating resistance. It is physical desirability that propels the rate of evolution in areas of the genome encoding for these functional characteristics. In the wild, female peacocks prefer to mate with males with more ornate trains. Male redback spiders deliver sperm to the female using evolved mouthparts – the male is completely subservient, driven by the desire for sexual acceptance, so much so that he will offer himself as food for the female during the mating process. It's a powerful evolutionary process, and therefore the central preoccupation of our waking reality.

If human beings have stopped evolving in visible ways then perhaps it's time to let outside technologies intervene. Take ExistenZ, for example. Cronenberg explores the much-fêted realm of cyberspace for the first time and connects our bodies to the mainframe network via parasitic conduits called 'Umby-chords'. Jennifer Jason Leigh plays Allegra Gellar, a mercurial video game designer presenting her latest game, ExistenZ, to a focus group of frothing admirers. After a botched assassination attempt Geller is forced to go on the run with a naïve PR pen-pusher called Ted Pikul (Jude Law). Along the way, Geller encourages Pikul to relinquish his virginity by having a port inserted at the base of his spine (via brutal penetrative stud-gun procedure) so they can finally share the game space together. But prior to the surgery Pikul has clear reservations about his own body fragmentation: "I've been dying to play your games, but I have this phobia about having my body penetrated…surgically". He eventually gives in to this symbolic invagination and in doing so becomes a viable sex object in Allegra Geller's eyes. When the spine-port becomes infected Geller sees fit to lube up the cracked entry-point, massage the outer edges, twist organic umbilicus in and out of it, and ultimately reassure Pikul that this new orifice will provide a gateway into a more exciting reality. She certainly comes good on her promise. When the gamepods are later dissected we see a nervous-system of bio-tech. The Umby-chord lives and breathes, occurs organically, and when it is inserted into a port the conduit has reality-deforming sex with its human partner. As David Cronenberg's new film Crimes of the Future reminds us, the body is still reality. For now, at least. Surgery might even be the new sex.

—

The Wizard Behind the Curtain

To most, the sight of our own intestinal tract would elicit an understandable abodyemigphobiac (the irrational fear of human internal anatomy and physiology) response. As recently as last week my friend visited the doctor for a routine colonoscopy and described the sight of her intestines as resembling a 'palpitating nest of worms' – we are simply not meant to see the wizard behind the curtain. It reminds us of the frailness of our innermost meat, and the dualist illusion of eternal consciousness (or a soul) starts to break down. We already have a distant dysmorphic relationship with our innards – the surface dream we are locked into, and value, does not permit a meaningful connection with the functional processes of the lonely pink islands fluttering quietly inside us. In a sense this is similar to an individual's common phobia of mirrors, spectrophobia, where any refraction of an ugly reality is likely to be avoided/rejected for the sake of maintaining our own daydream. These organs are a reminder that we are machinic. And how can a machine achieve transcendence with nature and spirituality? A machine is cold, not just atheistic but aspiritual. A famous critique of the mind, body relationship occurs in Ryle's *Concept of Mind*. Ryle determined that the logical fallacy of Cartesian rationalism was its attempts to evaluate the relation between mind and body, as if they were two notions existing in the same logical category. But they are not comparable, they are unrelated to each other. Just the way we like it. The body is frail and fallible. The mind could go on. Two separate realities and never the twain shall meet.

It's a strange notion, that we might not know or understand our own bodies. That they might even be so alien to us that we require an enforced denial of sorts to maintain our mental well-being. But wouldn't it be healthier for my friend to view this same intestinal system with admiration more for its aesthetic than its digestive function? The parasites in Cronenberg's *Shivers* (1975) and *Rabid* (1977) can seize control of human organs, dulling the mind to favour cannibalistic impulses but ascending the host organ to new evolutionary plateaus of survival. In the new parasite-driven society we would reappraise what we once deemed meaningful and beautiful. In a new reality the common aesthetic would transform and we would start to view entry wounds as sexually stimulating, look upon the peeking armpit parasites within us with familial fondness. For the first time in his filmography, Cronenberg rejects the notion of a creeping singularity or oneness with the technological. It's time to embrace the innermost meat.

The new film's protagonist, Saul Tenser, suffers from "accelerated evolution syndrome", a disorder that leads his body to continually develop new vestigial organs. Cronenberg enjoys making mutants out of his characters and is clearly inspired by real-life performance artists. The unfortunate 'casualties' in the aforementioned Shivers and Rabid are forced to step into the next phase of genetic mutation by their infection, but some of his characters make the conscious choice to evolve. Take the basic mortar of Seth Brundle, deteriorating to neonatal art for the sake of science when he enters the telepod in The Fly (1986) – shedding great swathes of his own flesh, bone, and viscera until all that's left is the new chitinous insect membrane underneath. It is the final Lazarus performance – life transitioning to death then back to life (then back to death). In 1964, Orlan, the French performance artist who was a source of inspiration for Cronenberg's Crimes of the Future, produced a controversial and ground-breaking photograph of herself giving birth to a mannequin, entitled Orlan S'Accouche d'Elle M'Aime. She would take it one step further in 1978 by filming her own ectopic pregnancy in 1978, the non-viable foetus almost killing her mid-recording. Orlan did not want to die, which is why she had the procedure and why she has pursued a career in the ego-sphere of art. Brundle had the commitment to go all the way. He is largely unconcerned with his own fate if a scientific breakthrough can be achieved. He put his body on the line, took the risk of destroying what he once was, so he could emerge anew. Both Orlan and Brundle are essentially destroying their own tissue, but only one of these performances results in the death of the mother.

(Max Renn makes a similar journey in Videodrome, consciously obliterating his old flesh so it can be replaced by something new; a media/human crossbreed. Suicide being the quickest way to achieve the new reality for his body.)

Even Klinke, or ear man in the film, seems like a riff on performance art, in this case the work of the Australian Stelios Arcadiou. In 2006 Arcadiou, also known as Stelarc, had a third ear cultivated from cells in a lab and surgically inserted on his inner arm. The ear, described by Stelarc as a prosthetic augmentation, was constructed from soft tissue and flexible cartilage harvested from his ribcage instead of any hard materials. Ear on Arm is Stelarc's longest performance and took him over a decade to find surgeons willing to perform the procedure. People consider Stelarc an evolutionary revolutionary, albeit his transformation required the unnatural intervention of surgery. And, of course, to Cronenberg, surgeons are priest-like figures. Honourable, shamanic in bib and doff. These surgeons helped Stelarc become a celebrated mutant and respected artist. They give meaning to the machine as well as the agency of the ghost within.

Both Tenser and Klinke are essentially celebrated mutants in Crimes. If one were to consider fossil records of the moment the film is set, Tenser might represent a transitional entity who links current homosapiens back to homoerectus and then forward to the next hominin event. Whether we transcend the physical parameters naturally or colonise space in our current bodies first before later adapting to a new cosmological environment, changes are coming and they're as inevitable as death and taxes. This next stage could take on a functionary configuration. There are vocal factions of scientists who argue that, with the help of chromatophore transplants, human beings could eventually acquire an ability to consciously alter the colour of their skin, a mechanism that would help us camouflage against predators the way chameleons do. There is a biologist working at Sheffield University who makes serious assertions that we could one day grow beaks! More resilient than teeth, a rostrum would make our oral functions 'more robust and practical'. Cartilaginous skeletons would allow us to become more flexible and would make evolutionary sense, eliminating that inherent physical fragility that inhibits our daily consciousness. Then there's natural regression. With the increasing need to engage with technical interfaces, there are some who believe we will spout tentacles during the next stage. After all, our ancestors were organisms who lived in the Vendian sea and were likely radially symmetrical instead of bilateral. A return to the Vitruvian man. Regression as a means of evolution.

Tenser may be a living link of sorts, a preamble to the big transformation – or maybe he is a vague future-dream of what we are about to become. Maybe he is the final stage before complete corporeal reconfiguration.

—

The Transcendent Image

"The creation of inner beauty cannot be an accident…"

— Adrienne Berceau, *Crimes of the Future*

Crimes has a distinctly scenic, if prosaic, Mediterranean setting. We land in an Athens we can all recognise – a place of littoral caves, sandstone, and marble pantheons, all of which rest in distinctly banal realism beneath the familiar Greek acropolis. This setting of Greece feels deliberate on Cronenberg's part, especially when one considers the themes inherent to the film - Hippocrates contribution to the 'natural' treatment of disease and Anaximander theory on fossil records and the origin and evolution of life feels particularly relevant to the genetic makeup of *Crimes of the Future*.

The interior sets are ones of rusty spigots, corroded metal spice racks, brassbound spiral stairwells, grates, and factory buildings. There is age and rust and material deterioration everywhere. This real-world backdrop roots in a 'near-future' and proposes a reliance on natural methods - granted there is use of an acoustic medical device, reminiscent of a stethoscope, but it's made evident that while technology can record and manipulate, it cannot incite change. A union of the organic and technological on the other hand will get us much closer to that spiritual transcendence we seek.

Crimes of the Future posits a world where a new bio-technology reigns supreme, but interestingly for a contemporary film on this topic, there is no social media facsimile here. No obsession with surface or the theatrics of an elevated ego. There are no circuit boards spilling insulated entrails of cable-trail to be found. There is no cyber-talk and there are no futuristic transpecial accoutrements to speak of. The only technology present, or the prevailing form of it at least, is the SARK autopsy bed, which looks like a dentist chair composed of weaved bone and beetle shell. The SARK module has an exoskeleton, honeycombed and armoured. It is a natural-looking, physical object which manipulates the physical structures of the interior human domain. Cronenberg's new vision extends to us a world governed by uncaring Darwinism, not by the interventions and advancements of any industrial folly. Nothing feels man-made or unnatural. It is conceivable that the SARK was never designed and distributed by a human engineer, but rather simply came into being the way the rest of early sentient life came into being. The technology was born of its own, existing, evolving, and functioning in the world the way any creature might.

Still, while the modern apparition of cybernetic technology appears absent from Cronenberg's latest film, there remains an element of self-design or morphological freedom at its core – something that devoted carnal artists like Orlan, Neil Harbisson and

Manuel De Aguas would recognise as part of their own central creative philosophy. These are artists driven by functional imperative. In Spain, the Transpecies Society is going strong. Founded by Harbisson, an Irishman who became the first self-identified cyborg, the society has many artists as members. One member, Manel de Aguas, developed an artificial organ called Weather Sense which allows him to connect to peripheral meteorological conditions. De Aguas states that "my life as 'propioespecie' will be my performance art — a piece with an indefinite duration in which I will perform my life as a non-human species, who is sensorially hyper-connected to the atmosphere." These artists are dedicated to personal nonconformity, rallying against what they define as the radical 'anthropocentrism' of today's society. He goes on to say that 'the desire to add a new artificial organ or not may be something in our nature. We should all have the freedom to do whatever we want with our bodies and our minds.'

And like the confrontational showmanship of these artists (which involves self-mutilation and the implantation of osseointegrated devices), the visual element of Saul Tenser's art remains and elicits similarly strong polemic, only we need an autopsy bed to witness the new developments as they happen. As a result, Tenser's work actually becomes *more* confrontational, *more* theatrical. Tenser offers an audience, not just his heart and soul, but literally his blood and guts. Interestingly, Klinke's ears are non-functioning and so his aberrant appearance is deemed pretentious and escapist propaganda by the intelligentsia. He is a poser. Had they been fully functioning he may have achieved credible art, like the beforementioned Stelarc. Tenser's mutations, however, are admired, even lusted after by Timlin (played by Kristin Stewart). He is a rockstar to those who appreciate his *functioning* uniqueness. Timlin is proud to archive the artists organography.

—

In Defence of Ugliness

"Artists are like insects, with more sensitive antennas than most people to pick up things around."

— David Cronenberg

The ultimate goal of all transhumanists, as is the case with all artists, is to achieve immortality. The act of creating art, an artistic body of work, is itself transhuman, a shot at the immortal. Art is in our image, it become us, and also surpasses us. In Cronenberg's world, artists have retreated completely inwards in their efforts to achieve this, away from the direction of any technological subsumption. To many of us living in this version of reality, where our personalities are sanitised and our fleshliness filtered, the world of the film seems positively utopian. Every artist in *Crimes of the Future* is a committed analogue and seem wholly fulfilled by their work. Nothing is ethereal or transient. Even the gyrating ear man, Klinke, engages in semi-purposeful mutilation – unalterable scarification that will never and should never heal. This art, human art, cannot be lost to the hungry coded abyss of cyberspace. These artists are willing to sacrifice their very organic carapace in order to achieve a kind of transcendent imagery. With the exception of those few performance artists mentioned earlier, can you imagine any creative figure in our culture willing to part with their physical avatar with such a profound finality? And I include myself among those who'd refuse. True art is the antithesis of beauty. Beauty is only what we think we want in this current evolutionary cul-de-sac. Limiting and superficial.

—

The Death of David Cronenberg: Surviving Death as an organic posthuman

"Technology is an extension of our bodies. For me, it has always been an expression of human will and creativity – and the body is in its centre."

— David Cronenberg

Just before *Crimes* dropped, Cronenberg starred in a one-minute-long NFT entitled *The Death of David Cronenberg*. This short depicts Cronenberg entering his childhood bedroom before tearfully embracing his own supine corpse. It seems like a relatively straightforward materialists' metaphor for mortality salience – a fear of body-death - but perhaps it is also a veiled comment on potential evolutionary advancement. The fundamental paradox of the short is that Cronenberg's corpse lies before him, yet he is still there to oversee it. He can hold his own physical image the way a hologram might covet its user-of-origin. Now, undoubtedly, Cronenberg's career and legacy are enough to immortalise him in the minds of those who admire his art, but maybe the director is illustrating to us the second life. If you consider the way planaria (flatworms) can regenerate lost tissue, is it so outrageous to imagine that the next phase of human evolution could see us manifest consciousness to an infinite number of organic shells? One body dies but the consciousness' will to power manifests and imbues a mirror body as a means of surviving after death.

This is a common theoretical discussion among futurologists and usually centres around the concept of whole brain emulation (WBE). Here the brain is essentially copied and uploaded to a computer. The hope is that by copying the brain to computational substrate the memories therein will also be transferred - it would be a machine intelligence, a facsimile for consciousness, but it's about as close as we can get to extracting the fragile phantom of authentic awareness from the host vessel.

WBE requires brain mapping and simulation: basically, you need billions of pounds of investment in technology in order to achieve the digital facsimile of a human personality. Cronenberg has organic means. The creative organ, stronger than any computerised alternative. Driven by the Artist in the Machine. In the same way that all cosmological systems, like our universe, can creatively muster atoms and molecules from nothing, our latent Darwinian processes (variation and selection) put the creation of new species of organisms in motion.

—

Potential for enlightenment

"It is time to stop seeing. It is time to stop speaking. It is time to listen."

— *Crimes of the Future*

In the 1990s there was something of a body art renaissance. People were starting to acknowledge their bodies in a different way. In Dan Brooks's *New York Times* article, 'The Existential Anguish of the Tattoo', he explains that "Like many important signifiers of the 1990s, tattoos began as a gesture of rebellion and became so ubiquitous as to carry no stigma at all." The 90s was a time of freedom and self-experimentation without fear of ridicule. Brooks continues:

> I know a dozen people with full sleeves, and all but one of them have children. Their sleeves now read as an indictment of nonconformism rather than an assertion of it – which is weird, because the tattoos themselves haven't changed.

Standard blackwork tattoos were on the rise but so were more unusual practices, like keloiding, subdermal implants and stretching. Soon the performative side of body modification had been appropriated by the art community. The potential of transformation felt endless, and it seemed the human mind had finally made peace with the body, seeing it as more of a personal canvas than a decaying vessel for consciousness to tour the planes of our physical environment.

And so Tenser's neo-organs become a simple metaphor for creativity. Those with vestigial organs become artists while the bureaucratic registry doctors and sentinels of the New Vice Unit are simply cold, logical sceptics and afficionados of the creative performance. Artists are determined to inculcate their public with a sense of transcendental worth. *Crimes* is a film preoccupied with what human beings can achieve naturally – what we can achieve without the phantom broadcast of *Videodrome* present to encourage our tumours or the jolting trauma of *Existenz*'s reality-altering bio-port surgery. And it's important to make the distinction that while these films all share a common grammar, *Crimes of the Future* is not *Videodrome* or *ExistenZ*. In *Crimes of the Future* there are no victims because none of its characters can feel pain. In a sense this is Cronenberg's most humane film.

Then there is 8-year-old Brecken, who is smothered by his mother in a brutal act of filicide during the film's opening set-piece. She feels he is an abomination because he consumes and digests plastic. This is not such a science-fictional concept. It was discovered recently that microbes in oceans and soils are evolving to do exactly this. There are over 30,000 different enzymes able to degrade different types of plastic, with the human body already able to deal with 50,000 particles of microplastic. Some scientists believe that consumption might be a feasible way to counter plastic pollution. But when we think about these changes in terms of futurological opportunity we may not be ready to shed the body just yet – maybe we're preparing to completely recalibrate our internal digestive tract first. Perhaps a body that can digest synthetic polymers can develop stronger respiratory and cardiovascular systems to counter the effects of heavy metal pollution and our own biotoxicity. We would see a reduction in the progression of diseases like Alzheimer's, asthma, Parkinson's and other risk factors of environmental contamination, if only our bodies were completely unlocked of their full potential. So, it's established that we have a built-in reverse-vending machine ready to recycle our worries away. Yet Brecken's mother is disgusted by this ability and expunges him. It is the non-artist who fears the evolution of the body. The anti-technology of *Crimes of the Future* reveals itself in its mutants. The characters who are fearless in the face of their physical decay because underneath, beneath the creases of subcutaneous tissue, wonderous new technology is waiting to bloom forth from within. The artists in *Crimes of the Future* engage in self-autopsy, which is really a new way of looking inwards, towards the soul. It is the non-artist who will cease to evolve and survive, while the artist takes the body, even that of a child, and without reservation seeks to turn autopsy into art. The artist transgresses physical boundaries.

11:11 Press is an American independent literary publisher based in Minneapolis, MN. Founded in 2018, 11:11 publishes innovative literature of all forms and varieties. We believe in the freedom of artistic expression, the realization of creative potential, and the transcendental power of stories.

Made in the USA
Monee, IL
21 September 2023